GET
BETWEEN

Leave a Legacy by Writing a Book

THE
COVERS

Neil Shulman, M.D.
& Eric Spencer

MORGAN JAMES PUBLISHING • NEW YORK

GET BETWEEN THE COVERS

ISBN: 978-1-60037-314-5 (Hardcover)
ISBN: 978-1-60037-315-2 (Paperback)

Published by:

MORGAN · JAMES
THE ENTREPRENEURIAL PUBLISHER™
www.morganjamespublishing.com

Morgan James Publishing, LLC
1225 Franklin Ave Ste 32
Garden City, NY 11530-1693
Toll Free 800-485-4943
www.MorganJamesPublishing.com

Cover/Interior Design by:
Rachel Campbell
rachel@r2cdesign.com

Habitat for Humanity®
Peninsula
Building Partner

What readers have to say

Better own this book for assisting in your journey."

—**Gene Landrum, originator of Chuck E. Cheese concept of family entertainment and author of 11 books.**

"Writing lore has it that Flannery O'Connor was asked whether writing courses discouraged people from writing novels. Her response was 'Not nearly enough.' Although witty, her response lacked compassion for would-be novelists.

Your book goes in the other direction. Let people write away and put their stories down. The process of writing, though painful, is also liberating. Like launching yourself into the air—exhilarating but scary."

— **Henrietta S. Muñoz, J.D.**

"I've read every page...what a great book. As a librarian I know the amount of research time involved as well as the personal time. What an awesome task you and Eric have done. You are so right--there's a book in every one of us.

So many thank you's for sharing this masterpiece of insight and how-to's. It will be very helpful to me and many others."

—Jane, medical librarian

"Let me say this will be a best seller, I am completely awed! And the advice contained within is amazing; touching the raw nerves where it matters and yet providing soothing advice to novices like me who know nothing beyond typing things on MS Word. Thank you for everything Dr Shulman…you are one in a billion."

—Edwin, reader

ACKNOWLEDGEMENTS

THE AUTHORS WOULD LIKE TO EXPRESS SINCERE THANKS TO Anna Zoe Haugo for her generosity with the editing of this book. She spent lots of time. She went beyond the call of duty............her insightful contributions made the text very reader friendly. Also, we would like to thank all of our readers, especially Peter Fiskio, for your brilliant suggestions and positive feedback.

With the 2nd edition, we would like to thank David Hancock and his team of experts at Morgan James Publishing for helping us to keep this dream of motivating thousands to write books a reality.

NEIL

As one ages, it's a joy to have a young brain around....with lots of energy, a passion to inspire new authors and innovative approaches to help them. I want to salute the work of my co-author, Eric Spencer. One could not ask for a better collaborator.

ERIC

I would like to thank my family and friends for always believing in me and in this project over the course of the five years that it took to create *Get Between the Covers*. Thanks also to the many individuals who contributed their stories of success and the lessons that they learned from temporary failure in the publishing industry. The book would be just a raw skeleton without the depth, body, and entertainment that you added to it. And, of course, thanks to Neil for your knowledge, insight, coaching sessions, and brilliant writing.

DEDICATION

NEIL

THE BIRTH OF THIS BOOK coincides with the birth of Myles Shulman, my first child. I wish Myles a wonderful journey through life. I hope that this book acts as a catalyst to improve the literary world which Myles will grow up in. Ideally, if we communicate better with each other, we will create a friendlier world.

ERIC

THIS BOOK IS DEDICATED TO YOU, the reader, for picking up a copy of *Get Between the Covers*. You have the knowledge, creativity, and skills to write your own book on something of importance to you…without the millions of people like you, who share the same desire to write a book in their lifetimes, we would never have had the drive to complete this book.

"The worth of a book is to be measured
by what you can carry away from it."
—JAMES BRYCE

"We do not write because we want to;
we write because we have to."
—W. SOMERSET MAUGHAM

"Writing is easy.
All you do is stare at a blank sheet of paper
until drops of blood form on your forehead."
—GENE FOWLER

CHAPTER LIST

PREFACE

SINCE THE PUBLICATION OF THE FIRST EDITION of *Get Between the Covers: Leave a Legacy by Writing a Book* in late December 2006, there have been many fortuitous occurrences. We originally published the title with AuthorHouse, a leading web-based publisher, in order to get the material out in the marketplace as quickly as possible and test some of our assertions and methods for giving advice and helping you to take action.

Early in the five-year process that writing this book entailed, we had interest from large New York publishers, but rather than take the traditional publishing route, we wanted to prove our belief that the newer paths to print can work and net positive results when combined with other efforts (marketing, forming partnerships, etc.). When you publish using any method, anything truly can happen…you never know who will read your book that might be able to take it to the next level. Conversely, if your writing never leaves your house, nothing will happen.

After the book became a bestseller and received a reasonable amount of attention, we were put in touch, through Rick Frishman—publishing connector extraordinaire—with Morgan James Publishing, one of the industry leaders in working with authors/entrepreneurs, two categories which blend nicely for us. Their leadership shared our vision for opening the doors of the publishing industry to thousands of new people and to the many programs that we would like implement with schools, associations, and corporations. It is through the talented staff at Morgan James that you now hold the 2nd edition of our book.

If you've read the previous version of *Get Between the Covers*, you will notice some subtle differences in the 2nd edition—new author and publishing insider anecdotes, updated information on publishing options, and the reformatting of one or two chapters. However, the core message remains the same.

As authors, it is exciting to bring you this 2nd edition and to further motivate and encourage *any* person to write a book in their lifetime.

Neil Shulman M.D. AND *Eric Spencer*

JUNE 2007

INTRODUCTION

ON SEPTEMBER 28TH OF 2002, the *New York Times* published an article in which it was stated, "According to a recent survey, 81% of people feel that they have a book in them…and should write it." If you do the math, that's over 200 *million* just in the United States alone who have a desire to write a book in their lifetime! What a *staggering* number! Yet only a little over 75,000 books are published by publishing companies each year, with only another 100,000 self-published books entering the market—meaning that tens of millions of us aren't following through on this most worthwhile of projects, especially when you consider that many authors account for multiple books in those totals. Through *Get Between the Covers*, it's time to reverse that trend…

If you are one of the millions who have a desire to write a book and publish it, then you likely reside in one of two camps. The first consists of novice writers, those who have never taken on the challenge of writing a book, but are intrigued by the idea. This group does have some often overlooked writing experience, albeit in other aspects of life, such as in everyday emails or correspondence, school papers for high school or college, proposals for work, or maybe just a few stories or articles for their amusement and for the entertainment of their friends and family—some of whom may have encouraged this individual to write an entire book.

Tens of millions of people around the world in this first group comprise the bulk of the 81% from the *New York Times* survey listed above. Hopefully our approach in the following pages will be what finally opens the door for them to try their hand at this endeavor, even if it is just once in their lifetime.

The second group consists of those who are struggling to write a book or to have their manuscript published. They may have some general knowledge of the publishing industry, but are unfamiliar with the specifics that could help them to succeed and enable their literary project to see the light of day. There are hundreds of thousands of individuals who find themselves in this position, and they are the ones who would be likely to write several books in their lifetime, once they could get all the way through the process successfully and start reaping the benefits.

Regardless of your starting point, you may be motivated to write a book for many reasons. It could be that you just want to write something that entertains your friends and family, in addition to you, of course. Your book may even end up being a sort of family heirloom that is passed down through the generations. Writing a book can be a cathartic process which brings you and your family closer together—it's cheaper than therapy and may help you work through your problems even if you are writing fiction.

If you are in the academic or research world, perhaps your goal is educate others around the globe and you would like to write a textbook for classes of eager (or at least willing) minds. Or, your book could be an extension of your business or the company that you work for, and you hope that its success will increase your customer base or boost your career. You may want to be an entertaining, commercially-successful novelist read by sunbathers on beaches everywhere or you may have aspirations to write prose that stands the test of time and is read by secondary school students for years to come. No matter what your psychological reasoning is, at the end of the day, you may also have a very economic motive for wanting to write your book, seeking to add a second source of income and getting to do it in an enjoyable way.

In spite of your possible incentives to write a book, perhaps you need convincing that you have the necessary know-how and skill set to go about it. This book is organized to help you—wherever you are coming from and wherever you plan to go—in your literary endeavor. It includes a wide spectrum of easily referenced chapters covering everything from unblocking writer's block to approaching publishers after completing your manuscript.

The setup of this book allows you to come back and reread sections quickly, even though we recommend that you go all the way through the first time in order to gain a more complete picture of the process and your options, as you work through the representation of your personal goal fulfillment—your book.

The introductory chapters deal with the process of starting a book, from acknowledging the skills you already possess, to finding the time, to deciding on your subject and genre, and, more importantly, figuring out how you might approach the writing of the book. These chapters are primarily meant to motivate new writers and get them excited about the process to follow, but a more experienced writer may also want to read this section, as it offers suggestions on how to come up with new ideas, find that surge of energy to sit down and write, or to attempt to write in a new genre.

The rest of the book is broken down into all of the various considerations on the "path to print." For further inspiration, we have included anecdotes and advice from authors at all levels, from relatively-unknown self-published writers, to perennial best sellers whose names you see every time you walk into a bookstore. Various publishing insiders also contributed their know-how and uplifting words to those considering writing a book.

The authors were chosen from different ranks to demonstrate that incredible success is possible, in the case of best sellers, and to help you relate to the many non-professional writers who produce books every year. Hopefully their perspectives will enhance your experience with this book and maybe even allow you to—a la self-help guru Anthony Robbins—model some of your thought processes after their mindsets in order to help you to achieve your goals. Robbins has worked with world leaders, *Fortune 500* executives, and other notable individuals for years in order to help them unlock their potential, often by having them retool their thoughts to believe that they can accomplish anything and to restore their confidence in their abilities. Learning more about the psyche and strategies of those authors who have come before you may be just the boost of adrenaline that you need to chart your own course and will make you a believer in your own ability in completing this endeavor.

We've attempted to make this book concise and manageable, so that you can get started on *your* book. Our aim is not to go in-depth into each specific element of the writing or publishing process, but instead to give you an overview. We also refer you to many experts and other useful resources which address particular publishing needs. You may want to read other books or enlist the services of these publishing insiders or publishing-related companies to further develop writing skills, learn to market, or find publishers. However, this book gives you the big picture, and it provides a "one-stop" approach to get started and see the task to completion.

Get Between the Covers, as you will find, is about more than just educating you or teaching you how to fish, to borrow from the famous metaphor. We hope to excite you about the prospect of going to the pond with your fishing rod and tackle box in the first place. We want to stir up your creative juices so you're eager to sit down to write and get that first book published. The reasoning behind this approach is simple. There have been many information-based books published in this market for the past 30 years, and while they are well written and researched, they haven't motivated people, at least not in great numbers, to take action and actually sit down and write their book, even though there are potential authors, from all walks of life, around the globe.

To see the value of this approach, look to the world of instructional/motivational books about sales. The authors of the best books for salespeople (e.g. Zig Ziglar) realize that the key to getting the intended result (helping people sell more) is to educate them a little—but to motivate them even more. That way they will be confident enough to give it a try. It is through action that we truly get better and learn the ropes. There is no substitute for experience. But, without the confidence and the motivational push to begin, you may never sit down at your computer and gain that experience.

One question that may be on your mind at this point is why should Neil Shulman and Eric Spencer be the ones to write this book? Or, rather, who are Neil Shulman and Eric Spencer? We have spent five years writing this book because we respect the literary world, but feel that there is a huge creative hole in our society, and we'd like to fill it up with your books.

Neil has authored and co-authored over 20 books—from novels which were made into feature films to consumer medical books which have improved the quality of life for thousands of readers to children's books which have kids everywhere rolling in "stitches" and learning valuable lessons. He has published these books using a variety of different means, from going through the largest publishers in the United States to using his own publishing company, Rx Humor, to self-publish several critically and commercially successful books. Eric, who hadn't written a book until now, has a 5 book humorous nonfiction series in development, 2 innovative self-help books, and a novel currently underway. In addition to writing and contributing innovative ideas he piloted this project like a startup company—a startup company with the desire to change the literary world. Neil draws on his creative background and on his publishing experience, while Eric leans on his extensive entrepreneurial, business, and communication success, even though he is only 27 years of age (now 28 at the time of 2nd Edition).

Both authors have spent the past five years studying every aspect of the publishing industry (and we continue today), in order to best be in a position to present you with *Get Between the Covers*. Using our existing knowledge and our research into the vast publishing industry, we collaborated to produce the book that will hopefully launch millions of books and new authors, even those writing in their spare time, and will boost literacy worldwide to a level that's never been seen in history.

We truly believe that everybody has the ability to write at least one book in their lifetime—perhaps many more. Of course not everyone agrees. In fact, in the *New York Times* article mentioned, the author even recommended that the majority of people *shouldn't* even try to write a book because they aren't good enough writers. The author is, of course, entitled to his opinion, but we will spend the rest of this book convincing you to believe in yourself and in the incredible benefits writing a book can bring to your life, no matter how experienced or talented you are as a writer. And if you have great ideas, but still need someone to help you with the actual writing, there are always plenty of collaborators around the corner to help you get those ideas into print.

Hopefully this book will be more than just a useful guide, and an enjoyable read…ideally it will help launch you into the world of authorship. We look forward to seeing your name on the cover of your own book in the near future!

Neil Shulman, M.D. AND *Eric Spencer*
OCTOBER 2006

PART 1

YOUR LEGACY
CAN BEGIN TODAY

ido Qubein, a successful businessman, author, and one of the best public speakers in America, likes to ask his audiences, "What is the one thing you would regret not having done if you died tomorrow?" After letting them digest this thought for a moment, he continues, "Since most of us are not going to die tomorrow, what's stopping you from getting started today?" For the millions who have expressed interest in writing a book, perhaps spending several months or even years researching, writing, editing, and publishing an original work of their choosing would become their regret if they didn't undertake the endeavor. Why put off getting between the covers any longer?

In Part 1, we will provide the basic framework for the writing process, from finding time to write, to selecting a topic, to approaching the writing in a particular genre, to eventually editing your written material. The chapters are ordered in a manner that tracks how the process flows for most writers. We've presented solutions to some of the mental roadblocks that you are likely to experience along the way. The ordering of the process may be different for you if you already have a publishing deal in place and have a timeframe established, but for most readers, the order presented should be the most logical.

The next eight chapters serve to not only briefly walk you through the writing process from day one, but more importantly to inspire you to sit down and get started, so you can cross "write a book" off of your life's "to-do" list. Later, you will learn more of the business aspects, including the considerations that go into your publication options—perhaps the best part of the writing process for you.

Even if you are a more experienced writer, you will likely gain insight into your craft by reading through this section. You may improve your existing skills, in the same way that successful musicians continue to take music lessons and well-known actors practice with their acting coaches because they constantly learn and re-learn. As you will see, this section is less about telling you exactly what do, and more about helping you to brainstorm and to channel the ideas and style that you already possess onto a piece of paper.

CHAPTER 1

You Have What it Takes

I*mmortality.* The mere notion of it has tantalized humanity for centuries. At some point in our schooling, we have all read stories of the immortal Greek gods, sitting high atop Mount Olympus surveying the passing ages of humankind. Wouldn't it be ideal to be immortal—to be able to see rulers rise and fall, to watch countries spring up and disappear, and to determine if the 80's really are the most unfashionable decade of every century? Unfortunately, your chances of attaining immortality are slim.

But just because you will not live forever, it doesn't have to mean that a little piece of you can't remain for posterity—allowing those in the future to see what you've left behind. The piece of you that remains may not be stored in a cryogenic laboratory; rather it will be found, printed in ink or saved in cyberspace, in the book you wrote.

Incomprehensible perhaps: *You* as an author. You are certainly no Grisham, Crichton, Updike, or Rowling, right? And you don't count yourself among their non-fiction counterparts, Dr. Laura, Richard Carlson, or Joel Osteen, do you? Their books have sold tens of millions and they have been the basis for an impressive list of successful films and television shows. You, on the other hand, may have never written anything except school papers, emails, personal diaries, or business proposals at work. Perhaps, if you are a little more experienced, you may have written some short stories or even attempted to write an entire book and get it published. Regardless of your writing prowess to this point, it may take some convincing on our part, but you might not be as different from the authors listed above as you may think. Everyone, including you, has a bit of "the famous author" in them.

To borrow some medical knowledge from Neil, all of us have one trillion brain cells between our ears. Even though some of us may have habits that either kill off these cells or condemn them to a lifetime of disuse, there probably are still enough functional ones "upstairs" to write a book. But it is not the simple presence of this collection of cells that will enable you to construct your opus. Your masterpiece will be crafted from the information that these cells contain. More specifically, it is the memories of your unique collection of experiences that are the real gems in your personal library. When you combine your experiences with your untapped, vivid imagination and broad knowledge base of everything from the Boston Red Sox to Dutch flowers, you have the ability to harness a powerful creative force. The recipe of memories, the capacity to imagine, and your knowledge base are what make it possible for each and every person to offer the literary community a fresh new view of the world.

Even if you believe that you possess these basic ingredients for writing a book, you may be struggling with the idea of taking on the challenge. Yes, it is a challenge and a considerable time commitment, but then again, so is high school, yet hardly anyone gives that a second thought.

Part of the mental struggle could stem from comparing writing a book to other endeavors or occupations in life, where we are often discounted or presented with a barrier to entry if we don't have the necessary educational background or level of expertise. There aren't any doctors or lawyers, at least there shouldn't be, practicing in their specialty without having gone to a graduate school and obtained an advanced degree. In the business world, rarely does someone become a CEO, without years of industry experience or without developing a certain level of proficiency. Fortunately for you, you won't need to meet any qualifications or hold any kind of degree or certificate to write a book.

Another incentive for seniors to write books: there's no such thing as "forced retirement due to age" in the world of writing. Bestselling author P.D. James is 85 and still going strong, and there are thousands of others from her generation who churn out the pages each year because they are enthralled with the process. It's never too late to get started; James Michener, who wrote so many successful (and quite lengthy) novels over the course of his life, didn't even write the first one until after he reached the age of 40. When it comes to writing a book, all you need to begin is an idea and the willingness to learn new skills along the way. Above all, the most important things that you can bring to your book are a passion for your project and a belief in your ability to see it through.

So let's just say that you are capable of writing an entire book (and later we will show you that there are far fewer barriers to publishing in one way or another than you may realize), but why *should* you even consider writing a book in the first place? For starters, this is your chance to express yourself creatively, which in many of our occupations and daily routines isn't always possible. All of us have something to say, a voice that needs to be heard. If you want more than just the close circle of people around you to hear it, you simply must write and publish a book.

Beyond just the present, creating and ultimately publishing your book is your opportunity, as time passes and generations change, to share knowledge that might be lost if you don't put pen to paper. People years from now will need and want the ability to look back and search through the thousands of books from before their time. If you doubt this, consider that people still reference historical and religious texts from centuries B.C. and continue to read the first novel in the world, *The Tale of the Genji* by Lady Murasaki, just over a thousand years after it was published. Not to mention that hundreds of classics from the last several hundred years find their way into classrooms all over the world year after year. In other words, good writing never "goes out of style."

Looking at the bigger picture, as part of writing your book you will also develop writing and communication skills that you can apply to other aspects of your life, which could be very useful if you are not as strong as a vocal communicator. Additionally, it's certainly possible that you will generate an extra source of income and perhaps gain more of a business or entrepreneurial sense as you work to market your book to readers. When you publish, anything can happen; you could end up selling a significant number of copies, or you may end up speaking around the country, designing animated characters from your children's book, improving your academic standing if you are on the faculty of a university, or hosting your own radio or TV show.

Even if you do none of those things as a result of your book, your efforts will never be in vain, as you are also increasing literacy in society; with more books published on a variety of subjects, readers are more likely to find what interests them—beyond the fact that *you* will likely start reading more often. And perhaps the best part of writing a book, other than feeling a great sense of accomplishment: *it's one of the few opportunities in life where you have almost total control over the outcome.* If you don't like a character in your novel, you can simply kill them off, which is generally not recommended with any of your "ex's" in real life.

When you sit down to write that first page of your book, you might be both ecstatic and a little scared, even though there are so many great reasons to get started today. Hopefully, in a few months you will have written your own book—an exciting possibility. Getting the wheels in motion is sometimes difficult because you might have received discouragement from the people you know or may be intimidated by the thought of not living up to the works of the masterful authors who have come before you. Perhaps you have shared the beliefs of Charles de Montesquieu, who summed up his view of the writers of the world, "An author is a fool who, not content with having bored those who have lived with him, insists on tormenting generations to come." The message you may have received from the environment around you is that achieving the goal of writing a book is simply out of your reach—that the publishing industry is only for a few, and that it will take you *forever* to complete this endeavor.

Enter *Get Between the Covers*. We truly believe that you have the raw talent to complete this endeavor and that you will be able to smooth out the rough edges and become a more skillful writer with enough time and effort. Even though there are a number of books, classes, and online forums that can help you to develop your skills, just like with most things in life, the only real way to get better is to dive in and get the hands-on experience. As Ayn Rand writes in *We the Living*, "No one is born with any kind of talent, and therefore, every skill has to be acquired. Writers are made, not born. To be exact, writers are self-made."

This is not a "how-to" book, at least not in the traditional sense. We *will* give you information about how to get a book published from start to finish, in a user-friendly format, with plenty of suggestions for helping you to develop the necessary skills. But this is about much more than just imparting what knowledge we may possess. Instead of telling you how exactly to write your book, which is difficult, if not impossible, for anyone to do, this project is about showing you how you can own a piece of the publishing industry and ultimately leave your legacy—big or small.

The bottom line is: there are now many innovative, inexpensive, and accessible ways to publish, and it's time for more people to explore them and to try their hand at writing a book, since they no longer have to worry about their finished product never seeing the light of day. We want you to be aware of every aspect of the publishing industry, but more importantly, we want to help you overcome any and all obstacles on your path to completing your very own book.

CHAPTER 2

Anyone Can Find the Time

"Don't let the fear of the time it will take to accomplish something stand in the way of your doing it. The time will pass anyway; we might just as well put that passing time to the best possible use."

—**EARL NIGHTINGALE**

I f you are someone who would like to write a book, but have been reluctant to begin, it could be due to the numerous responsibilities that you already have in your life: work, school, family, or even hobbies, in addition to some of the psychological stumbling blocks, such as fear of rejection, not feeling skilled enough, or simply feeling overwhelmed by trying to understand all of the elements that go into writing and publishing. From a time management standpoint, it often seems that you simply cannot add another activity to your life, especially one that takes several months or more to bring to fruition; so you put off sitting down and getting started. Once you know you have the basics necessary to write a book, the next step is finding time to research, plan, and write it.

We will offer suggestions on the actual researching and planning in the next few chapters, but first let's focus on time management as it relates to writing. As you write and consider the process ahead, keep in mind the words of Susan Driscoll and Diane Gedymin, who in their book *Get Published!* write, "Remember, you're not in a rat race against time to see how fast you can write a book. Your objective is to write the best book you can, no matter how much or how little effort and time it may take."

For starters, let's discuss making it past writing the first ten pages, then quitting and giving up for any number of reasons. Don Aslett and Carol Cartaino, authors of the book, *Get Organized, Get Published!*, believe that the reason that more people don't see the process of writing a book to completion, even though they have an idea that they feel passionate about, is due to "the world's most highly developed art—procrastination!" Because writing is something that we largely do in private and the amount of work and our progress through a project is tough to chart on a daily basis, it's easy for us to convince ourselves that we are moving along just fine, even if no words are finding their way to the page. Bestselling author, Steven Pressfield, points out how we rationalize our procrastination in his book, *The War of Art*. "We don't tell ourselves, 'I'm never going to write my symphony.' Instead we say, "I am going to write my symphony; I'm just going to start tomorrow.'"

For starters, when thinking of adding a new time-consuming activity to your life, consider just how many successful authors have other primary occupations and perhaps even more time constraints than you do. Jimmy Buffet, best known as a popular singer and composer of music appreciated by Hawaiian shirt-clad fans, found time to write several books and become one of only six people to have *New York Times # 1 Bestsellers* in both fiction and nonfiction. Ashley Power, the creator of Goosehead.com, an Internet site for teenage girls, wrote the *Goosehead Guide to Life* while attending high school. Even basketball great Shaquille O'Neal managed to write a children's book when he wasn't dunking over helpless opponents.

Similarly, finding the time to research, write, and revise this book was an issue for us. Neil is a medical doctor, associate professor at Emory University, and a frequent lecturer around the country. Additionally, he has to wheel and deal in Hollywood and other places to keep his many entrepreneurial efforts alive. Needless to say, he keeps himself very busy. At the same time, Eric, during the writing of the book, was a representative with a national business firm that specializes in designing executive benefit plans for companies around the country and was often on the road, in addition to working other literary projects. *Get Between the Covers* took longer than expected to create as a result of these obligations, conflicting schedules, and different working styles, but the important time management lesson that we took from this was to stay the course and to try to do a little bit each week because then the project never stalls and it stays fresh in the minds of the authors.

The problem that most people have with beginning any project and keeping it going, especially writing a book, is that they don't think of completing the process in small terms. It may be a cliché, but the journey of 1000 miles truly does begin with the first step and continues one step at a time. If you get too caught up in looking at the entire process then you will get trapped in what's been termed "paralysis by analysis." To ease your mind, do some simple math. For example, if you can write only 1 page a day, you could have a 180 page book completed in six months. Most of us probably write at least one page in emails or instant messages to friends daily. If you really think about it, averaging one page a day is not too much to ask of yourself.

Even some of the most successful writers use a daily page tally to keep them on track—although it is typically on a larger scale. Stephen King, in his book, *On Writing*, describes how he completes ten pages each and every day when writing a novel. Regardless of how long it takes, he will continue working each day until he finishes this set number of pages. This method allows him to finish a book of considerable length in around three months, which is how he has produced such a volume of novels over the years. This can be a useful method once you have done some trial runs and know what your "baseline" is for an average number of pages per day, since you can then budget approximately how long the process will take for you to complete your work.

Some days you might be extremely busy, while others may leave you with a great deal of spare time. Setting a fixed number of pages to write every day works for many people, so it can sometimes be a source of discouragement for those who fail to meet the daily goal on a particularly busy day. Also, you wouldn't want to have to punish yourself in the style of Victor Hugo, who gave all of his clothes to his servant every day and could only have them returned if he finished the day's writing quota. Though it is wise to avoid setting unattainable daily goals considering your daily schedule, it is a good idea to have a plan for your writing process. Otherwise, it may gradually slide if you wait until moments of inspiration to begin working each time. As Leonard Bernstein notes, "Inspiration is wonderful when it happens, but the writer must develop an approach for the rest of the time…The wait is simply too long." Just be willing to be accepting of your time limitations when there are occasional spikes in the weight of your responsibilities during certain days or weeks.

Fortunately, there are a variety of strategies that authors use to pace their writing and maintain their discipline, thus keeping their output fairly consistent. Different forms of pacing allow you to stay on track without burning out from overdoing it. This sometimes happens to the most successful authors who have the public demanding their next book as soon as possible. The key is to find a compromise between producing enough pages to move your book forward and avoiding being shackled to your computer; after all, this is supposed to be an enjoyable experience for you. The following are three possible approaches, and you might want to try each of them on for size until you find the one that harnesses the most efficient use of your talents. For any method that you ultimately use, be sure to set specific goals so that you can track your progress.

Obviously, your approach will be completely different if you've already signed a publishing contract and have a timeline that you must adhere to, but these will provide a good starting point for most people.

Writing Within a Block of Time

Phil W. is a business consultant at a large firm. He is 27 and single. He doesn't have family obligations, but he typically works 12 hour days, Monday through Friday. He enjoys his job, but the long hours can be burdensome. He has always wanted to write a book about how to get your first job out of college. Unfortunately he doesn't have the spare time during the work-week to write a set number of pages each day. Instead, he decides to set aside a four hour block to write on both Saturday and Sunday. Some days he is able to write eight pages in those four hours—other days it is only a paragraph. It doesn't matter to him how much he writes, as long as he is working on the book for the entire four hours. After those four hours, he always leaves feeling a sense of accomplishment. He views any amount of writing as successful. Trying to write a set number of pages in a certain amount of time seems too much like a deadline and he has enough of those during the week. The four hour approach allows him to feel relaxed and he enjoys the quiet time alone. As long as he continues working in these four hour blocks, he will finish his book in several months, without having to stress out about a bunch of "mini-deadlines" along the way.

Phil's strategy is perhaps the most common one applied by notable authors. Richard Carlson, author of the highly-successful, *Don't Sweat the Small Stuff…and it's all small stuff,* describes in the introduction to his book how he found time to complete his work early in the mornings before he had to leave for his day job and see patients for the rest of the day. Working early, well before sunrise, allowed him to focus, without the distractions of the phone ringing, taking care of his children, or having to worry about his 9-5 soon to come.

Don Aslett and Carol Cartaino, whom we've already mentioned in this chapter, recommend blocking off a few days or even a week or more and taking a "writing vacation." If you are writing about that which you are truly passionate about, the entire process will feel like time spent enjoying a hobby, even if you are writing with the hopes of generating some income.

You don't even have to spend the money to go on vacation somewhere exotic—just take a few days to yourself in the comfort of your home and let your literary journey be your source of adventure and relaxation.

PAGES PER WEEK

Marsha B. is a 42 year old mother of three. Her husband, Bill, is a doctor, and she does not work outside the home; however, taking care of their three children is more than a full-time job. She wakes up early, makes the children their brown bag lunches, drives them to school, then returns home for several hours, before having to head back to school to pick them up. Then she has to shuttle them to the soccer and cheerleading practices and the music rehearsals. Most days are hectic, but there are typically pockets of free time here and there. Marsha has always wanted to write a biography about her mother, who was a famous adventurer, but with the daily fluctuations in her schedule it's difficult for her to set aside a predetermined block of free time each day. Therefore, her tactic is to establish a goal of completing a set number of pages each week, and ten is the number that she decides is reasonable. Her weekly quota allows her to write more on the days when she is not so busy, while not writing at all on a busy day, but always having a goal to work towards. Marsha's method suits her daily schedule, and she feels a sense of accomplishment when the ten page weekly tally is reached.

RIDING THE WAVE OF INSPIRATION

Barbara C. is 74 and is a retired newspaper advice columnist. She has always wanted to write a humorous novel dealing with the newspaper industry, but is struggling to find the method that works best for her. She has enough time to set a daily quota of pages, a weekly quota of pages, or to set aside time blocks during the week. However, none of these approaches have proven to be effective. Most of her humor comes off the top of her head, and she needs a moment of inspiration to create her best work. This inspiration comes and goes, and she finds that forcing herself to write when she doesn't have it results in material that isn't funny. Therefore, she doesn't even try to schedule writing sessions; she writes only when ideas pop into her head. They might come to her while she is watching a basketball game on TV, while she is reading a book, or even when she is in the shower. In order to ensure that her ideas aren't lost, she keeps a notebook with her at all times to capture her thoughts.

Whenever her creative juices start to flow, she immediately heads to her computer and writes. Sometimes she only writes for thirty minutes and other times it may be for hours. Barbara has found this method of writing best suited to the way her brain is wired—by capitalizing on the moment when the next good thought comes. Writing is exciting for her because she never knows when the moment will come. It will be possible for her to finish a book in several months, provided, of course, that she diligently follows her inspirations when they occur.

Even with proper planning and efficient time management, it may take longer than you anticipated to complete the book. You shouldn't despair though, because you are learning new skills as you move from the first page to the last. In fact, Jay Leno, when interviewed on *Inside the Actors Studio* with James Lipton, described the creative process as similar to creating a chair out of a block of wood. You don't look at the block of wood and simply say that it will be a chair tomorrow. You need to put in the time designing, carving, shaping, and refining it, much like you need to with your writing skills in order to reach the finished product.

Usually the more you write, the faster and better you write. Also, once you've been through the entire process of writing a book, you better understand all of the elements involved in the effort...whether it is outlines, punch lines, character development, plot structure, research, or editing. You will most likely proceed with greater ease and efficiency when you write your *second* book. Who knows, you may even end up like Ray Bradbury, who wrote *Fahrenheit 451* in nine days on a typewriter that he borrowed from a library.

Part of the beauty of writing a book is that, unlike many other diversions in life, the main investment in the process is time, rather than money. This means that every time you sit down to write, no matter how much you produce, you never lose a thing and always gain material. If you start on your own with no obligation to a publisher, you can start, stop, and restart when time permits. It can provide a restful, productive time slot during the week for an adventure of the imagination. Not to mention that it's cheaper than bar hopping or eating in a posh restaurant, and more convenient than fighting traffic to get to a movie theater.

Even with all of these perks, you will most likely experience the full spectrum of emotions over the course of writing your book. You will go from exciting, productive days when the words just flow like a waterfall and you are full of confidence, to days when you sit in front of your computer, staring at a blank screen, convinced that you can't drum up even a sentence and the end is nowhere in sight. You don't need to bang your head against a wall at these times; instead just take a little break and come back to it when you're feeling less frustrated. Remember that there are ups and downs with everything in life, and the journey of writing a book is a roller-coaster ride. However, you can help to ground yourself by maintaining your discipline and writing on your predetermined schedule, thus following one of Hemingway's rules for writers, which was to "apply the seat of the pants to the seat of the chair." The millions of books in the world symbolize the time management success of all those authors before you, and we have faith that you, too, can enjoy the same success once you find the strategy that works for you and put it to good use.

·**Finding the time to write and having the discipline to fill the time sitting at your computer is one of the most challenging parts to writing a book.**

·**Try different time management strategies until you find one that fits both your schedule and the wiring of your brain.**

CHAPTER 3

Generating a Genre

We make decisions every day, which can range from whether we want juice with breakfast to deciding whom we want to marry. Sometimes we make impulsive decisions that leave us with a good story, but wondering *what in the world* we were thinking. As you probably know by now, the best decisions are usually made after considering the spectrum of options. Now that we have convinced you that you *can* find the time in your schedule to write, it is valuable to think about all the possible writing genres and even do a short "test drive" before the grand launch. In this chapter, we will discuss the process of selecting a genre and why you shouldn't be afraid to try more than one. We will also give you examples of how certain successful authors decided on their literary niche. With careful evaluation and self-examination you can ensure that the time you spend writing your book is enjoyable, empowering, and enlightening.

When deciding on a genre, remember that your book is an extension of you; it is a representation of your interests, knowledge, and creativity. It may even be a window to your soul. Therefore, you should choose a topic and genre which ignite your passion. The words will be powerful and direct like darts hitting a target and your passion will be present on every page; in every sentence; in every word. Similarly, writing about a subject of which you have some knowledge, or a desire to do research on, in your strongest writing style, is likely to result in the best finished product and will make the process much smoother for you. You will enjoy completing the manuscript more if you write what truly inspires you, and, since your passion will be infused into every page, you are more likely to please your readers. Also, we are often able to communicate much more clearly and easily that which we understand or are at least enthused by.

As Arielle Eckstut and David Henry Sterry note in their recently-published book, *Putting Your Passion Into Print*, which we highly recommend for a potential writer of any level of experience, the key to choosing your genre and topic is to avoid "should" books. The authors point out that we often convince ourselves that we *should* write a certain type of book because it is rooted in our day-to-day profession or we think that it will help to build our visibility and platform, when in reality, a passion for the subject and style should be by the far most important factor. "Should" books are often less saleable because readers can sense that you are emotionally disconnected from the material. They are also incredibly difficult to finish and see through the publication process because it feels more like work, rather than an enjoyable activity that can add balance to your life.

But, on the other hand, sometimes a "should" book might be just right for you, if the "should" is a result of a passion for a subject that you have building up inside of you. Or, perhaps it's an acceptable "should" book because writing it helps you to work through a problem in your own life and shed light on a possible solutions for others in a similar situation. This was the case for Kim Koeller, who, after learning that she had severe food allergies, thus making it difficult to eat meals outside the home even though she had to travel over 1 million miles as part of her job, decided that she needed to find a solution to her own problem. Writing a book was going to be a big part of that solution. In the course of her research for *Let's Eat Out! Your Passport to Living Gluten and Allergy Free* and the design of her website (www.allergyfreepassport.com), she discovered that over 300 million people in the world have celiac disease or food allergies and have special diets to help control their ailments. As a result, they leave much of the world around them unexplored because they are fearful of having meals prepared in places where the chefs aren't sensitive to their food needs. Through her extensive marketing plan, which included incorporating many medical associations and groups catered to allergy prevention around the world, Koeller has been able to help millions to be able to travel safely again through her "should" book and continues her efforts today. According to Koeller, her philosophy from the get-go has been in line with Ralph Waldo Emerson, who said, "If I have helped just one person in exploring a new location, be it in the city or countryside, within their own country and/or on foreign lands, I will feel as though I have succeeded."

While it's not advisable to write in a certain genre only for its selling potential, you do need to keep your potential readers in mind when choosing a genre. If you want to reach as many readers as possible, you'll want to ask yourself how engaging your material is, when presented in one style versus another.

Bestselling author Robin Cook, as a medical doctor, had a desire to educate the public about current medical issues. Cook, who started writing when he served on a ballistic missile submarine, faced a major decision with his work. Nonfiction would have been the obvious route to take, but Cook felt that fiction was the best vehicle to achieve his goal of reaching the masses. Novels such as *Toxin*, which centers around E. coli poisoning in restaurants, and *Vector*, which deals with bio-terrorists spreading anthrax in New York City, have helped to establish him as a leader in the medical thriller genre. Although it was perhaps riskier to write fiction rather than nonfiction—with the increased difficulty of acceptance by a publisher due to the unpredictability of fiction sales once a book is released—one can't argue with the results over the past 30 years. His merging of medical information and suspenseful storylines leaves masses of readers eager to turn the pages, while indirectly teaching them about cutting-edge issues in medicine.

Even if you have a genre in mind (perhaps you already post stories or commentary in your own blog on the Internet) you might be worried about whether you are a good enough writer to write an entire book and not just a few scattered pieces. However, as you well know, writing covers a wide spectrum of art forms; from poetry to scientific treatises to romance novels. There is an almost endless list of topics to choose from in nonfiction and you are bounded only by your imagination in fiction. You may be better at one type of writing and not even know it because you haven't tried it yet.

Remember also, that your book can be as long or as short as you want—from a 30,000 word collection of poetry to a 150,000 word biography. In fact, successful books can exist in any size. Consider *The Prayer of Jabez*, the pocket-sized book with less than 100 pages, which found itself in the #1 spot of the *New York Times Bestseller List* for several weeks and then the mammoth, *John Adams*, which managed the same feat.

Choosing the length of a book is just part of the creative control that you enjoy as an author and it allows you to write your book as you see fit. If you are a very visual person, you can choose to enhance your book with pictures, figures, or artwork. If describing Revolutionary War battles is your forte, diagrams of battlefields can bring your words to life and help to reinforce the material. A book about a specific home improvement project will most likely be much easier to follow and safer for the participant with pictures of each step in the process. And what would a book about Renaissance art be without the scaled-down prints of Michelangelo and Da Vinci?

Still, you may be apprehensive about sitting down and trying a new style, even if it piques your interest. But what is the worst that can happen? If it doesn't work out in that style, you simply pitch the paper after a few hours. Big deal! There's no waste of time in scratching it out and starting over—you are simply practicing the art of writing and honing your skills as an author. In addition, you are taking the necessary steps in refining and conceptualizing your book idea. Take a moment and consider the thoughts and apprehensions of those authors before you. How do you think the best-selling authors felt when they sat down to write *their* first book? Most likely the task was no less daunting for them. They probably experienced the same feelings of anxiety, but since you are reading their books today, they were obviously able to overcome their fears and self-doubts about their chosen genre and writing style. And so can you.

Looking into your literary future, you may also fear that selecting a genre today will pigeon-hole you into that niche for the rest of your literary career. Many authors of all levels, including Neil, write in a number of different genres—often with great success. For example, John Grisham, most famous for his best-selling legal thrillers, has shifted to other genres with two of his works, *Skipping Christmas* and *Bleachers*. Humorist Dave Barry, well-known for his weekly syndicated column (which ended recently) and nonfiction humor books, has augmented his fan base by branching into novels with the publication of *Big Trouble* and *Tricky Business*, and even children's books, such as *Peter and the Starcatchers*. The point is that you are bound by nothing once you decide on a genre for your first book; you can reinvent yourself and use your creativity, imagination, and knowledge-base for a completely different type of book in the future.

Genre selection aside, you may be interested in a subject or have a certain storyline in mind, but you lack the knowledge to write about the subject or to create enough background information for your story or narrative. This challenge is frequently faced by new authors and you shouldn't let it stop you. In fact, famous diplomat Benjamin Disraeli once noted, "The best way to become acquainted with a subject is to write a book about it."

Sebastian Junger, author of *The Perfect Storm*, became interested in a storm that ravaged the Northeast in 1991 after he read a newspaper article. His curiosity led to months of research and personal interviews, in order to complete his best-selling book. Mark Bowden, author of *Blackhawk Down*, heard about the unfortunate events in Somalia in 1993 on the news and in several newspapers. He followed up on his interests in a similar fashion— by reading extensively and by tracking down those who could share their firsthand experiences. Neither of these authors had much of a knowledge base in these topics prior to writing their best-selling novels, but they had the necessary ingredients: a passion for their subjects and a writing style with which they were comfortable. They simply filled in the rest with a little research legwork.

Luckily the remedy for increasing knowledge in a certain area is right at *your* fingertips as well, and it has been used for centuries. All you will need to do is head to your local bookstore or library or search the worldwide web to put it to good use. *Reading*: It's an excellent way both to find new ideas and to learn more to enhance ideas already circulating in your mind.

Reading has advantages that go beyond the content of the material. You can pay closer attention to different styles of writing, which may trigger a new slant to your style or give you insight into the approaches that have captured the attention of the masses. Reading, like writing your book, is meant to be a pleasurable experience and you should read anything that interests you. If you like romance novels, the world of Danielle Steel is at your disposal. If political commentary is your cup of tea, pick up a copy of a Bill O'Reilly or Michael Moore book. It doesn't always have to be books. Grab an issue of *Time, USA Today,* or *People* and find out what is going on in your world.

You never know what might happen once your brain starts processing the information in front of you. What you choose to read on a regular basis might give you insight into which kinds of books are suited to your skills, interests, and knowledge base, but don't be afraid to explore genres outside the ones you typically enjoy; inspiration for your work can often come from unexpected places. You just might find innovative and unique ways to improve your work in progress, not to mention a previously unexplored genre of books to add to your reading list. Many writers even go so far as to consider time spent reading to be essential to the craft of writing. Often they read each work critically and examine every element of the composition. Stephen King probably put it best, when he said, "If you don't have the time to read, you don't have the time or the tools to write." The value of reading to improve your writing has even become the subject of a recent popular book, *Reading Like a Writer: A Guide for People Who Love Books and for Those Who Want to Write Them*, by Francine Prose, a successful author, who has been a finalist for the National Book Award and has taught literature and writing at the university level for many years.

The day your nonfiction book is published is the day you become viewed as an expert on the topic of the book. You become a magnet to people who are interested in the topic and they often teach you more about the subject. If you write a book about a small species of South Pacific jellyfish, you won't likely attract a large readership, but you will likely be granted something which might even be better than a PhD: expert status! Your book might find its way to biology library shelves throughout the world; international jellyfish experts are likely to read at least sections of *your* book and to hold you in high esteem; they may track you down, comment on your work, ask your opinion on a related issue, and/or give you more information on the topic. They might also invite you to speak on the topic at an international meeting...

paying your expenses and giving you a fat honorarium. Perhaps you'll even end up being interviewed on *Animal Planet* as an authority in your field. These are just a few of the spin-offs that can result from even a book with a small readership. All of these added bonuses represent what marketing guru and best-selling author, Harry Beckwith, had in mind when he championed in his book, *What Clients Love*, "Publish. Anything can happen."

However, you don't have to cater to such a small niche audience to reap these types of rewards. It is certainly possible to be considered an expert in a narrow area that is very popular, and therefore also have a widespread readership. In addition to the many doctors (Dr. Atkins, Dr. Phil, Dr. Laura) who have become household names, there are others, such as John Hope Franklin, who are not only well-known, but have also helped shape a social movement. Franklin, a distinguished professor who has won countless major awards and has received 100 honorary degrees, has had his book, *From Slavery to Freedom: A History of African Americans*, go through eleven editions since 1947. It is regarded as one of the best—if not *the* best—books about the history of African-Americans, and it is a result of a lifetime of study, which continues to this day. He is recognized as one of the most preeminent scholars in the field for this, and other influential books, many of which appeared during the social upheaval of the 1960's, and became an integral part of the Civil Rights Movement. As a result of his work, he is a frequent lecturer and has even been recognized by Former President Clinton for his efforts.

On the other hand, you may decide to become an authority on the home front. For example, if you wanted to write a book about your family tree, most likely only your family would want to read it, unless of course your last name happens to be Kennedy or Rockefeller. Your accomplishment would not be that your book becomes nationally known, but rather that you would be able to create a literary family heirloom and share your family history and creativity with the spreading branches of your family for years to come. Plus you would be completing a book that is personally important to you without the pressures of mass marketing and distribution. As we mentioned earlier and will cover in depth later, the availability of print on-demand presses make it more affordable for anyone with a topic, broad or narrow, to self-publish and to end up with a professional-looking finished product that will last for generations.

If you don't feel comfortable embarking on a book which will involve a great amount of reading to research, you can write about a topic on which you are already an expert—yourself! It can also be a healthy way of coping with changes in your life. For example, you might work through a personal problem by fashioning a character in your own image, who triumphs where you feel that you might have done better. Or you might write a nonfiction advice book about how you made it through a particular challenge in life, which can help others in the same position.

How about if you are one of those people who has lots of ideas and a genre in mind, but you just *insist* that you can't write? Well, we've got an answer for you, too. We call it *collaboration*. You might be knowledgeable about a subject or have great creative ideas, but are lacking in writing skills. Your collaborator may not have the creative ideas, but may have the technical know-how to get the letters, spaces, and dots on the page. If the chemistry is right, a collaborative effort can give birth to a successful book. Even if you have a few collaborators/partners in mind, before you commit to working on an entire book, try collaborating on an article or a chapter or two of the book. You'll want to determine if there is good synergy between you and your business partner.

The collaboration may be a truly equal partnership, with both authors sharing the researching, writing, editing, and ultimately the space on the cover, or it could be more of a ghostwriter relationship—common among celebrities and business figures, such as Donald Trump, who have principles in mind to present or the auto-biographical information and want the credit for the book, but still need someone to do the bulk of the writing behind-the-scenes.

You may never have noticed, but many of the great books in the market today are collaborations, for example, the best-selling *Chicken Soup for the Soul* series, by Jack Canfield and Mark Victor Hansen. Putting together their series of over 30 books involved compiling hundreds of stories on a variety of subjects, and through collaboration with each other, and a team of other authors and editors, they were able to share their workload and produce a more engaging final product.

Another benefit of collaboration is something that we'll call *access*. Any time two or more people work together on a project, each person has their own key to unlocking the creativity and knowledge of the others. If one co-author has a creative block, the other can reignite the creative flames. Furthermore, each collaborator contributes their own resources relating to publishing and promotion; putting two or more heads together can give rise to an extensive list of contacts…whether it's access to publishers, printers, bookstores, or even corporations which would purchase bulk quantities of the book. The collaborators might even come up with a list of "insiders" in the movie industry who would potentially be interested in making a film based on the book.

If nothing else, collaboration can be a good starting point for new writers, who can benefit from linking up with someone who has successfully been through the process. In the business world, this would be analogous to a new salesperson pairing up with a more established one when meeting with their first few clients. Even though the "rookie" may have an idea of what they want to say and what they hope to accomplish in the meeting, it helps having someone working with you who knows the pitfalls and can keep the process flowing smoothly. In publishing, an experienced collaborator can keep the project moving along and offer advice and moral support that is often needed by newer writers.

Carl Hiaasen, perennially at the top of bestseller lists, began his literary career at Emory University where his wry sense of humor began to emerge in the column he wrote for the student newspaper. It was also at Emory where Hiaasen began his path to becoming a novelist. Neil, also at Emory at the time, had ideas for books, but was just developing his writing skills. Once they connected, there was synergy. Neil and Carl collaborated on Neil's first two novels. Both went on to write many more books. Later as a columnist for the Miami Herald, Hiaasen researched and wrote about "hot topics" high on his agenda about his home state—issues relating to the environment and unscrupulous real estate developers. Other novels such as Strip Tease and Basketcase, combine his wit, imagination, and biting humor, with his desire to make a difference in his part of the world, as he develops unforgettable characters and a gripping, Florida-based plot.

Get Between the Covers is another example of how two writers coming from different backgrounds and writing experience can work together to blend their styles into a finished product when they have a shared interest and common goals for developing the subject. Neil, with his many years of experience in the publishing industry relating to successful authors, publishers, and agents, is aware of the various pitfalls and the variety of paths to success. Eric, who is just a few years out of college and is new to the publishing game, understands the anxieties, fears, and desires of new writers reading this book. He can also draw on his sales, marketing, and entrepreneurial background to help find the best words to communicate the message of the book, which includes giving you a fresh perspective on ways to promote and market your books, in addition to explaining the cutting-edge trends in the publishing industry. Our aim is to take the experience of the "aged" and the creativity of "youth" and launch you as an author.

COLLABORATION ON A LARGE SCALE

We obviously believe in the power of collaboration, because, as the saying goes, the whole is better than the sum of the parts. Truly great works can be written when more than one mind combines to form the finished product. To that end, as part of furthering the idea of thousands of new people writing books, we have created a website, www.cRADIANCE. com. With help from some of the top web designers in the world, our site will serve as an online creative community that facilitates a number of collaborative writing programs.

Using cRADIANCE, we plan to run novel writing contents at over 100 universities, experience sharing opportunities (wherein groups of 20-100 people submit around 1000 words on a topic that we choose, which is then collected and arranged into an entire book), and even to link seniors who have stories and knowledge to pass on with students, who have the desire to write and are looking for interesting material to put onto paper. In all of the programs with schools, associations, and corporations, we have secured funding from partners to help us edit, package, and distribute the books through various publishers, with the proceeds coming back to the organization.

As this movement grows, we will keep you updated through cRADIANCE and through the book's website (www.getbetweenthecovers.com) for the latest publishing projects. In sales, you always want to meet the prospect "where they are at." In layman's terms, if you want someone to write an entire book, but they've never tried, they are far from your objective on Day 1 if you are trying to convince them. But, if you can get them hooked on writing by becoming just a fraction of a published book (which might only take them a few hours), there is a high probability that they will see the value of writing and take the reins themselves the next time around on an entire book of their choosing.

If, at this point, you have more than one idea for a book, it may be helpful to create a Top 3 or Top 5 list and then narrow it down, as you start to brainstorm what you would like to write about. Consider factors such as your enthusiasm for each potential project, the resources available on the topic, how long it will take to complete, etc. Of course, you may eventually write all of the potential books on your list, but you've got to begin somewhere. In the next chapter, we will offer you advice on how to approach certain types of writing and offer some successful strategies of notable authors in different fields.

So now, there's only one thing left to do; get off of your tailbone, jump into a genre, and try your hand at it! You can always hit the delete button or throw away the pages if your first choice doesn't work out. Once you settle on the right fit and get the first forty pages hammered out, you are likely to experience a euphoric momentum, which can propel you to the final pages.

·Choose a genre that interests you and that showcases your best writing, not just one you think sells the best.

·Don't be afraid to try your hand at different styles until you find the one that works for you. Remember you will improve over time as you research, write more, and read other books in your genre.

·Collaboration can be an excellent way to work through the obstacles of writing and publishing, and to increase your ability to network and market your book.

CHAPTER 4

From Concept to Completed Manuscript

Uniqueness—it's not only a buzzword that causes most teenagers to hide their head in the sand—it is a fact of life. No two people have the same set of fingerprints or identical strands of DNA (at least according to each weekly episode of *CSI: Crime Scene Investigation*). Everyone has had different experiences over the course of their life, and each person's imagination, because it is shaped by everything that they have ever seen, done, or heard, is one of a kind. Deciding on how to approach a topic once you have chosen a genre makes use of your unique imagination, which only you have the key to unlock. After all, who knows what is in your mind better than you? It is simply a matter of "self discovery," followed by strategizing, and ultimately putting in sweat equity in the form of outlining, researching, writing, and finally editing.

Perhaps the best starting point for you on any book, before you even get to working on it, is to sit and reflect on why you want to write the book in the first place. Is it to entertain? To educate? Is it just for a few people to read, or do you hope that thousands will get a chance to share your gift? How are you connected with the idea for this book that drives you to want to write it? These are just a few of the questions that you might want to ask yourself, and, as many writing experts have noted, the answers can help you to figure out your own angle on the topic, as well as a definitive approach to the outlining, researching, writing, and editing. Determining how your book will be different from others in the marketplace and unique to your person will help set the tone and style of your writing…not to mention that it will also allow you to better pitch it to a traditional publisher or an agent as being a fresh new perspective on a subject or a unique variation of a particular creative genre.

Since there are so many genres, with a nearly infinite list of topics and storylines within each, and a limitless expanse of ways to combine all the elements, it would be impossible to tell you *exactly* how you should go from an idea to a completed manuscript. In this chapter we will offer you some general suggestions and advice on how you might approach certain types of writing. Beyond that, we refer you to books (and the publishing experts who wrote them) that go into more detail in specific areas related to completing a manuscript.

The majority of the chapter will give examples of approaches used by successful authors. The four authors highlighted in this chapter achieved considerable success, yet had little writing background, and didn't have the benefit of a research assistant or an editor helping to guide them before submitting their manuscripts, since as a first-time author or as an author writing in your spare time, you may choose not to receive these services or may not have the money to afford them yet. We will outline some of the strategies they used, and hopefully these examples will open your mind to the limitless number of creative ways of getting from an idea to a finished manuscript and will show you how *your* book can fit its own mold. The next several chapters will also offer advice to help you as you develop your book from an idea to a typed manuscript: from unblocking writer's block, to seeking help from peers, to the basics of editing and where to go to improve your grammar, vocabulary, and sentence structure.

In the previous chapters we discussed choosing a topic and genre and finding the time to write, but once you decide what to write, based on your interests and background, an important next step is to plan the process. The exact amount of planning will differ based on your work habits, your topic, and whether or not you have collaborators. There will be some overlap with the time management strategies that we discussed in Chapter 2, but those were more geared towards freeing up the time to write. This chapter is designed to give you an overview of some of the major steps in writing a book and offer you advice on how to tackle them.

All of us have probably heard enough advice about planning in relation to different elements of our lives, but noted insurance salesman, Howard Wight, who publishes a newsletter filled with useful tips, has a simple approach to planning. He calls it the *1% Solution*, and the premise is that you should devote 1% of your day to planning the other 99%. One percent of the day is about a mere 15 minutes, which almost everyone can find in their schedule, and if it is used to plan the rest of the day, it will lead to success in the other 99%. You will then be focused, organized, and prepared, rather than chaotic and expending needless energy.

The *1% Solution* is also a great tool for the process of writing a book. The hardest part of any process is taking the first step—especially true of a large project like a book. If you try to attack the whole 100%, without having a plan of attack, it's like being at the base of Mount Everest without hiking boots, picks, rope, or cold weather gear. Adapt Howard Wight's philosophy to your book and spend at least 1% of the total time that you devote to the project to planning and outlining. Whether you are the type of person who likes to lay out an intricate plan or you like diving right in and making decisions along the way, this approach can help you. In fact, you may find yourself inclined to devote even more than 1% of your time to choosing which block to dive in from, how many laps you are going to swim, and which stroke you'll use.

As you plan, it is important to note that we all have a stream of ideas that flow through our minds each day, especially when working on a creative project like a book. We've all worked on projects in our lives—at school, at work, in our homes—but tackling a book is a different beast and it requires more organization. Since you will create and recreate perspectives, alter your strategies, and reconsider your ideas for the book constantly, it is valuable for you to devise a system of note taking. Otherwise you may forget your own wisdom and miss a chance to capitalize on a really great creative idea. Carry a digital voice recorder or tape recorder with you or keep a pad of paper and a pen handy to jot down ideas when they come to you. This is especially important when you're away from your normal writing area where you may store all of your notes. Don't judge the ideas as they come to you, even if they seem tangential to your project; simply record them. Evaluate the viability of them later. World-renowned leaders, inventors, and artists make a point of writing down key thoughts as part of their daily routine. You can always put the thoughts into a more elaborate, structured document later, but for the time being, you'll be sure not to miss any inspirations or revelations related to your work if you jot them down, even if they are in a rough or fragmented format.

While you're recording and collecting your spontaneous thoughts, you might begin to research your book. As we've previously suggested, and will reinforce throughout this book, get your hands on anything that you can read related to your intended book: whether it's a feature article in the newspaper on your topic, a novel with a similar plot or theme, a research article with scientific data in a scholarly journal, or a website/blog in which people offer feedback or thoughts on the subject. Consider visiting your local library or even a larger library at a nearby college and identifying the research tools you have at your disposal. Librarians are some of the most helpful people in the world for those researching and writing books, and they can usually point out the best sources (which also have the added bonus of being free).

Beyond locating printed research tools, you can also consult with others in your field. Even when writing fiction, consultations can offer you good background information for your character and setting development. In addition to being able to interview others for valuable firsthand information, you will also start to build a network within that particular area, and one contact might provide a bridge to another one. Thousands of authors around the world use this to their advantage, and we think that you will likely find that the authorities and experts in certain areas, or even simply the residents of a town that you want to set your novel in, are often willing to help. Just be sure to give them a quick "thank you" in the beginning of your book. To find appropriate advisors ask around and contact authors of articles or books that you are researching (and also the authors who are referenced in their works). Also run searches on Google or Yahoo using various keywords.

THE GODFATHER OF PUBLISHING

For advice and assistance in working on any aspect of writing, completing, publishing, and promoting your book, a great point person qualified to offer you advice on everything from A to Z is Dan Poynter. His name is known by just about every self-published author, publishing expert, and publishing house editor. For the past 30 years or so, Poynter has led seminars and given public lectures, written numerous books on writing and publishing, offered book consulting services, written articles for every major publication about the publishing industry and its future, and basically has established himself as one of the world's foremost experts on publishing.

Through his website (www.parapublishing.com) Poynter's full range of products and services are made available to any would-be author, in addition to numerous author success stories, book publishing statistics, a history of the book publishing industry, and articles on various publishing-related subjects. Poynter also has an e-newsletter that goes out to over 26,000 people in the publishing industry, which you can sign up for (free of charge) at his site. Perhaps the most useful service that Poynter offers to you, also at no cost (he's a generous guy), is a chance to post a 100 word listing in another of his e-newsletters, in which you can present the subject of your book and your contact information, and ask individuals to submit material to help you create the book. We used this to our advantage in our research on *Get Between the Covers* and were put in touch with some of the most interesting and successful authors from a diverse array of backgrounds. Many contributed to the building of this book.

Whether you read one of his books or solicit his personal services, Dan's expertise can help you organize, research, and effectively write, regardless of the topic or the intended audience. His words echo our sentiments and motivation for writing this book, when he says, "I don't want people to die with a book still inside them." We highly recommend visiting his site. Normally, in a book of this nature, we wouldn't aggressively promote one particular individual, but, quite frankly, when it comes to sources of knowledge and assistance, Dan's the man!

Depending on your past writing experience, you may already have accumulated a collection of polished writings, beyond just notes and ideas, which you would like to piece together into a complete book. Thousands of individuals around the world have written short stories in their spare time, posted daily entries on their own blogs, written news articles as part of their job as a journalist, or compiled elements into a thesis to complete a school program. If you are in this group, then you may already be well on your way to a completed book. Learn a lesson from Khaled Hosseini. His hugely successful book, *The Kite Runner*, was expanded into a complete novel from an original short story that he had written and shelved in his house before a family member read it and thought there was more to be written. The key for you will be determining how to add material to make the book long enough, while not losing the overall essence of the story and without the transitions being too choppy. Of course, you could always opt to publish a book which is a collection of short stories or articles, rather than expand one of them into an entire book—something which many notable authors have done in the past.

In general, in terms of work flow, as you sit at your computer or in your work space, do your best to stay focused on the task at hand—that way you can not only stay productive and efficient, but still have plenty of time for the other important things in your life like your family and friends. Certainly with the millions of sites on the Internet, with all of the programs that you could be watching on television, and with family members or friends calling you or emailing you constantly, it's really tough to get in "the zone" and keep working. Distractions are a part of life—they plague employees in every business sector—so much so that there are annual studies about the number of minutes each day that are lost (and what that means to productivity) when distractions reign in the work environment. As much as you might like to keep checking the latest score on ESPN. com or see how you're progressing in your auction on Ebay, remember to gently refocus when you stray off target, because you are technically in *your* work environment. Our culture makes it easy to develop Attention Deficit Disorder…the goal is to make you ADD "functional."

FICTION

People often say that you should write what you know, but in fiction you simultaneously write what you can imagine and are therefore less constrained than you may be in other types of writing. In fact, Peter Matthiessen, winner of the National Book Award for nonfiction with his 1978 book *The Snow Leopard*, and also a critically-acclaimed novelist, describes writing nonfiction versus fiction as being the difference between making a cabinet and creating a sculpture. In nonfiction you have constraints because of the burden to present the facts, but in fiction you don't always know where the material will take you when you sit down to write, even if you have a rough outline.[1] If you develop the characters well, they may "take over" and write the rest of the book for you.

Even though some of the best fiction writers have described elaborate scenes and created unbelievable imagery with their writing without ever having seen that which they are describing, you will likely need to do a considerable amount of research to add substance to the people and events you dream up. Many successful authors, including Elmore Leonard, bestselling author of *Out of Sight* and *Tishimongo Blues*, and Tom Clancy, author of all things military, spend considerable time observing the real people, places, and happenings which are the backdrop of their highly-successful tales. Of course, they also find themselves sifting through material in various libraries or doing research online to supplement their "real-life fact finding." But perhaps your personal connection to your work

---

1   www.bookpage.com/0002bp/petermatthiessen.html

may be enough. Bestselling author Barbara Seranella, writes crime novels, such as *No Human Involved*, which incorporate much of what she had already learned from experience, as a troubled teen with a "wealth" of run-ins with the law before turning her life around. She uses the memories of those experiences to fuel her insightful fiction. She doesn't necessarily need to research her novels because she's partially lived in the world she writes about. We mentioned earlier that there is a piece of you in everything that you write and it couldn't be more true for novelists, as there is always a character, a plot twist, or a theme that is described in a certain way because of the life experiences of the person penning the passage.

Because of the complexity in trying to help you to format your novel and approach the writing of it by providing advice in a succinct fashion, there are several other sources catered specifically to walking you through the process and improving your writing, which we highly recommend. Author/literary agent, Noah Lukeman's books, *The Plot Thickens: 8 Ways to Bring Fiction to Life* and *The First Five Pages: A Writer's Guide to Staying out of the Rejection Pile* are both great reads and cover everything from character development to creating suspense to narration styles. Our sentiments mirror Lukeman's, when he says, "There are no rules to assure great writing, but there are ways to avoid bad writing." With his help you can steer clear of the pitfalls that many less experienced writers sometimes fall into, such as having a really great first 40-50 pages: where the characters come alive, the drama is intense, and the conflicts have been exposed, only to lose steam in the remainder of the book. In the struggle to maintain the evenness of the pacing and to keep the storyline consistent, it's easy to lose sight of how engaging the tale is.

For general help in laying out your ideas, there are several books which give you "the basics" for writing any book, but a novel in particular. *What If?: Writing Exercises for Fiction Writers*, by Anne Bernays, contains many exercises that can help a new fiction writer to put together a novel. *How to Write a Damn Good Novel*, by James Frey, is one of the most successful instructional books for fiction writers, and provides practical, easy-to-understand advice. *The Marshall Plan for Novel Writing* and *The Marshall Plan for Getting Your Novel Published*, both by Evan Marshall, are great resources for new fiction writers. They cover all of the basics—from building characters to developing plots—and the former even includes a blueprint that you can fill in with thoughts and ideas for your novel, in addition to giving you advice about publication. Another helpful book is *Write in Style*, by Bobbie Christmas (www.zebraeditor.com), which has won numerous literary awards in the past couple of years. All of these sources are valuable and can help you to conceptualize and organize your work. However, bear in mind that every book project is different, and thus advice from a general source can only go so far. As W. Somerset Maugham comically notes, "There are three rules for writing the novel. Unfortunately, no one knows what they are."

Once you come up with themes and plot lines, you have other decisions to make. Do you want the narrative to be in first person perspective, so you can be part of the action, or do you prefer third person, which allows you to tell the story from the outside? Will your story be told in present or past tense? How will the events unfold? One hit of action after another or slowly drawn-out over time? How will the characters develop? These are not always easy questions to answer and perhaps the best way to get ideas is to follow the advice of best-selling author Clive Cussler, author of *Atlantis Found* and *Vixen 03*, who recommends that you start out by copying the styles of some of your favorite authors to get your feet wet. Don't forget, it's just the style you are adapting—your masterpiece is still an original story. That which you find interesting as a reader—both stylistically and plot-wise—may give you truthful insight into the type of writing that you would like to pursue and which you would most likely excel at.

On a final note about planning for a novel, your approach for writing it will probably be different if you are trying to write a more commercially successful novel vs. one that could win the National Book Award. Many of us have picked up a copy of a typical commercial novel and thought that given the opportunity and time we might be able to write something similar. While the plots and romances are intriguing and keep millions of fans in eager anticipation, few would say that the actual writing, vocabulary, and structure is engaging them on a highly-intellectual level—rather, their brain is being given an escape or a rest—hence the appeal to the masses. Many authors—in fact the bulk of novelists—prefer this type of novel-writing style because it's easier to sell to the average person. There is always the chance to make it big (however slim it may be), and it's easier to write. An example would be Ian Fleming, author of the James Bond series, who recognized that he could captivate the masses with stories of secret agents, beautiful women, fast cars, and exotic locations. He found he preferred to capitalize on his success with writing mass-produced novels, rather than trying to write novels regarded by the critics as being literary masterpieces.

On the other hand, if you have aspirations to be the next John Updike, Susan Sontag, or Charles Frazier, all we can say is *good luck*. Their novels are critically acclaimed, contain complex plots and verbiage, and are generally regarded as classics, even though *The Centaur*, *In America*, and *Cold Mountain*, have only been out for a few years. It's a rare gift to be the next William Styron or Reynolds Price, but who knows? You may be that diamond in the rough who makes the next grand contributions to the literary world and takes home The Pulitzer Prize.

LESSON IN SUCCESS: FERROL SAMS

A common misconception is that everyone who writes successful novels was born with some kind of special writing ability or spent years perfecting their craft, but there are many stories that remind us that everyday people with little writing experience can write a novel worthy of praise. Ferrol Sams, a medical doctor, has written several bestselling novels over the past twenty years, including his first one, *Run with the Horsemen*. He started with little or no knowledge of the publishing industry or how to write a book, but simply found time to write in his schedule and took advantage of it.

Sams, who describes his story as a "Cinderella" one, took over a year to write his first novel, a process that included writing the book longhand and enlisting the help of his sister to type it. Once he completed it, he was clueless as to his next move, but he began by letting his family read and edit it. They convinced him that he should show it to an "outsider," after being impressed with this early version. He decided that the "outsider" would be a friend who was an editor at the *Atlanta Journal-Constitution*. The editor was a little hesitant because he wanted to give him an honest appraisal and was afraid he might have to tell Sams that his efforts had been in vain. However, three days later he called with his critique: "You've got a real son of a bitch here." To this day, Sams believes that this is the highest compliment anyone has ever given his work.

After letting several "publishing insiders" read it, he received more praise and was urged to seek out a mainstream publisher in New York. He eventually opted to go with a smaller publisher, after he met the president of the company and found her to be the helping hand that he needed to walk him through the publishing industry. In Sams' words, "I was like a child led for toilet training." The book eventually ended up on best seller lists for almost two years and was nominated for a Pulitzer Prize.

The biggest lesson that he learned in his tutelage with the publisher was how to edit his own material—possibly the most valuable lesson for any new writer. "I revised and revised and revised that manuscript and began to get better at the skill over time." His approach to writing his second novel was more organized after his initial experience. To augment the core knowledge he already possessed, he researched World War II history and pursued a strategy of including a poetic style in his passages. His imagination was also functioning on a higher level as a result of his work on the previous book and he found that it was easier to channel creative material from his mind to the paper.

Despite his incredible success, Sams remains humble. According to Sams, "I just look at what I have accomplished and think…not bad for a country boy." He is excited about the prospect of encouraging people to write books and believes that he is a perfect example of how "anyone can do it." His advice for budding writers, especially fiction writers struggling to get started: "Just let your writing flow and keep writing. You can always go back and make changes."

TRADE NONFICTION

Browsing in a bookstore or searching Amazon.com, it becomes obvious that there are an almost infinite number of topics which evolve into nonfiction books. From computer guides to cookbooks to celebrity biographies, anyone with an interest in anything can become an "instant expert" once they've written a book on the topic; however, there is an art to making a topic into a good read as a completed book. Luckily, as part of this art, you have a number of techniques at your disposal. You could enlist the help of noted authorities, provide additional sources as evidence of your claim, or do innovative market research or laboratory experiments to support a new theory that you are proposing. For example, Malcolm Gladwell supported his assertions in his successful book *Blink* by taking part in or observing many of the psychological tests that he used as evidence. Another approach could be to write the book from a unique angle or, much like many of the most successful writers, relate how you are personally related to the work that you are presenting. A notable recent example would be John Crawford's critically acclaimed *The Last True Story I'll Ever Tell*, which recounts his time spent serving our country overseas in Iraq.

No matter how you decide to write your nonfiction book, like any other type of book, planning should always be a top priority. In addition to increasing your organization by combining research with outlining, there are a few other suggestions you may want to consider as you proceed. Judith Appelbaum, in her successful book, *How to Get Happily Published*, recommends that you survey some of your acquaintances to gauge their level of interest and comprehension of your subject. This will help you to determine the best approach for presenting your material—to avoid telling people too much of what they already know or assuming that the reader already has the knowledge and not telling enough. She also recommends telling all sorts of people about your book-in-progress because you just never know who might be able to help you find new sources for research, to give you direction in your project, and even to promote it to others both before and after publication. Lastly, try to figure out how you fit into the puzzle of this nonfiction subject, in terms of your background, and why you decided to write about it. All of this input should give you the core that you need to get started and will help you to proceed effectively.

Here's another way to help you conceptualize the vastness of your options, even in only one genre or topic. Within the genre of "pop" psychology, consider the single subject of how to cope with life changes. There are thousands of books written on this topic each year. Spencer Johnson, best-selling author of *Who Moved My Cheese?*, wrote his short book about the need to embrace change in life or face the consequences of being left behind. His approach to teaching the lessons of life was to use parables in which the imaginary characters were mice, who served as examples of common human personality types. Johnson's book, incredibly simplistic at first glance, was highly successful in conveying a message that so many people generally find difficult to embrace. Dave Barry, a famous humor columnist, has also written books about major changes in life, such as turning 40 and dealing with parenthood. His approach capitalizes on his unique wit and sense of humor; instead of simplifying the lessons of life, he helps people to laugh at them and learn to accept them. At the other end of the spectrum, the serious advice book *Life Strategies* by Phil McGraw, is based on psychological theory, and took a hard-line stance similar to the persona that Dr. Phil presents in his television talk show. Each of these authors, realizing that there is no "right" way to deal with their subject, found a tone, angle, and presentation style that suited their writing skills and personalities. You too can do the same! Once you have chosen your subject and done your research, put a little of your own personality in the writing; it will lead to the best finished product and will help to solidify the intimate bond between your words and your readers.

LESSON IN SUCCESS: JOE DABNEY

Joe Dabney has written successful nonfiction books on a variety of subjects and uses the same basic approach with each project—starting with a credible idea and then backing it up with a plethora of research. His major works include *Smokehouse Ham, Spoon Bread, & Scuppernong Wine*, which won him the James Beard Kitchenaid Cookbook of the Year award in 1999, and *Mountain Spirits*, a book about moonshining in the South. The marketing of these books garnered national attention and landed him on notable television shows like *The Today Show*. As a former long-term employee of the aviation manufacturing company, Lockheed, Dabney even wrote a book about the C-130 plane, entitled *Herk, Hero of the Skies*, which has seen ten printings.

He did not agonize long and hard about choosing his topics; he simply dove into whatever tickled his curiosity. For his ground-breaking look at the life of moonshiners, it was a visit to a museum in Dawsonville, GA that originally piqued his interest. His extensive personal contacts related to writing *Mountain Spirits* indirectly led him to the writing of his award-winning cookbook. And his book about the C-130 was born as a result of the respect for and interest in the field of aviation.

Once Dabney concocted a clever idea large enough to fill a book, it was simply a matter of diving into the research. Later he would approach the actual writing and ultimately the business of getting his book published. According to Dabney, "I wasn't interested in worrying about marketing each book right off the bat. It was more important to do the research and get the book set up and written in a presentable form first. The rest would come later." Research took different forms with each project. For *Mountain Spirits*, which he researched over six months in the mid-1970's—back in an "ancient" time before public access to the Internet—he spent hours in the library. He also interviewed and interviewed and interviewed: from Treasury Department officials (there was no ATF at the time) to third and fourth generation moon-shiners in north Georgia. By the time he was finished, he had 50-60 cassettes of interviews and more than enough information about a subject of which the public knew very little.

Even with the availability of the worldwide web to help with research, Dabney still chose a very "hands-on" approach when working on his cookbook twenty years later. He compiled recipes from anywhere he could find them—personal recipe collections, culinary formulas in books published decades ago, and even wild game recipes discovered at the University of Georgia for cooking bear and opossum! Without the personal contacts who "learned him a lot," his book never would have been born.

Extensive outlining followed months of research on each subject; in the case of his cookbook, which has more of a "folklore approach" than a traditional book of recipes, outlining was more important than one would expect for a cookbook. For his work on *Herk, Hero of the Skies*, he detailed the setup of each chapter, before ever writing a word in the manuscript. He went into *Mountain Spirits* with less initial planning, but allowed the constant assimilation of new information to continually reshape and reform his manuscript. Flexibility was crucial in the development of the book due to the nature of the content. The key for him with each project was customizing the format of the books after he learned more about the topic and brainstormed a bit. Overall, Dabney's words of wisdom for any writer are simple: "The big thing is persistence. Try it a different way if it doesn't work for you the first time, as you move through your manuscript. Keep going. Don't give up on your idea; just find a new way to present it."

CHILDREN'S BOOKS

If a picture is worth a thousand words, then a single illustrated children's book has the capacity to speak in volumes. But while there is a great scope of potential in merging two forms of creativity—the written word and the visual rendering—the process requires some extra thought and consideration. In terms of moving the process along, the writing may drive the story and inspire the illustrations, or conversely, the art may be the driving force of the text.

In addition to juggling the artwork/writing relationship, the style with which one approaches a children's book can vary greatly, depending on the target age group. Rhyming, for example, can have the power of holding the attention of younger children, who might otherwise lose interest in the words. Dr. Seuss' images are bright and fun, but this alone wouldn't have gained him such popularity if he weren't also a master of rhyme. Take into account the use of appropriate vocabulary for each target age group and do not use too many words that surpass the target child's level of linguistic development. Simplicity of language does not limit the ability to create stimulating stories.

In addition to young children's books, there is a huge market of books for young readers—as J.K. Rowling can surely attest. There is a great degree of crossover between these types of books and adult novel writing, since the author is creating a fictional tale and crafting an engrossing plot without the benefit of pictures. Certainly the intended readership can end up being much greater than just the "tween" market—many parents often end up getting just as wrapped up in these tales as their children (after their kids go to sleep and no one is watching of course).

In fact, because the processes are so similar, there are a number of authors, such as Julianna Baggott, author of the national bestseller *Girl Talk* and also author of *The Anybodies, The Somebodies*, and *The Nobodies* (under the pen name N.E. Bode), who write books for both younger readers and adults. However, Baggott, who currently has one of her books for younger readers in development with Nickelodeon, prefers to write for children, even though she enjoys writing no matter who the intended audience is. According to Baggott, "They need no hand-holding the way adults do. They're always ready to leap with you -- arms wide -- into any adventure." Part of her enjoyment of working with this crop of readers has to do with the influence that she can have on their lives: "Reading works the soil of the imagination, and our most underprivileged children, especially, need to imagine futures 'blooming and fruitful' that they can walk into."

When dealing with children's books or books for young readers, simplistic presentation doesn't prevent depth of content; children's stories can be a great vehicle for education, as well as entertainment. Since children tend to be more receptive than adults to blatant, undisguised moralistic teachings, children's books can easily reinforce lessons or messages which parents or teachers want to impress on their kids,. You can play around with interesting ways to convey a message through the fabric of the story or you may choose to also state it clearly at the end of the story, as in the classic fables of Aesop. On an interesting side note, there are also innovative ways to expand on children's books of the past. *Disabled Fables: Aesop's Fables, Retold and Illustrated by Artists with Developmental Disabilities*, was put together by the members of L.A. Goal, a nonprofit center that assists those with disabilities. It contains a foreword from actor Sean Penn, who spent time at the center preparing for his role in *I am Sam*, and it is a collection of each contributor's interpretation of Aesop's fables. The book has become one of the hottest and most innovative ones in the marketplace.

An important consideration for books targeted at younger children is that for almost every child there's often an adult leading the adventure by doing the reading. Anyone who has spent time reading to children knows that young kids always have certain favorite books that they like to have read to them over and over again. The best kids' books are the ones that appeal universally to all ages, so that the parents or babysitters don't have to inwardly groan at the tedium of reading them yet again every time they are pulled from the shelf.

A.A. Milne is a great example of a writer whose work has achieved that universality. His Winnie-the-Pooh series is clever and fun on so many levels, that it's equally entertaining for adults. Milne incorporated humor that appeals to a child's sense of silliness and imagination, while appealing to an adult's appreciation of the endearing way that children see the world. He often used techniques like including childlike misunderstood and made up words and expressions spelled out like they sound, such as the "heffalump" that Pooh is hunting down, which is visually depicted in Pooh's imagination as an elephant.

Furthermore, there is a lot of room for creativity in the placement or layout of the text and images on the page in children's books, so that the text can visually reinforce an idea.

If, for example, one of the characters is falling

      D

         O

            W

               N

it can be illustrated in the lettering. In fact, A.A. Milne was also very playful with his placement of text in the Winnie-the-Pooh series. Other common strategies involve using pop-up tabs or making the whole book die-cut in an interesting shape sure to catch the eye.

With all of the options open to you in creating a children's book, you may find that cost is your biggest constraint. Whenever printing in color, the publishing expenses increase, as they do when printing die-cut or pop-up books. Unless you already have the financial backing of a publisher, you may or may not want to commit capital to enhancing your children's book in these ways, especially if you think the writing and basic artwork can stand alone. On the other hand, adding these special features to the book can contribute to its initial appeal. If the first book is a success, then there might be a demand for a sequel. Ultimately, this could make a more complex design for a finished product worth the time, money, and effort.

Lesson in Success: Sibley Fleming

Sibley Fleming, who has won such awards as the Family Channel Seal of Approval, been named Outstanding Writer by the National League of American Pen Women, as well as received the title of Georgia Writer of the Year by Georgia Writers, did so by writing both children's books and, more recently, an adult nonfiction book. Her newest book, *Celestine Sibley: A Granddaughter Reminisces*, is about her grandmother, who was a well-known Atlanta newspaper columnist for over thirty years. This book has netted her significant praise; however, the main thrust of her writing career has been children's literature. Several of her children's works have been quite successful...included in her repertoire is *Under the Backyard Sky*, co-authored with Neil.

According to Fleming, the key to success in writing a children's book is to "see the world through a child's eyes." With any book she takes on, she tries to adapt this mentality first and foremost. "Children believe anything is possible. Their minds are like open sponges and their belief is suspended much easier. Adults should keep this in mind, try to approach their audience from the audience's perspective, and avoid being too preachy."

Fleming has always found that the best way to see if her storytelling is on the level with children's interests and perspectives is to test her material before anything is ever written down. In much the same way that Jay Leno tests out material in Los Angeles comedy clubs before using the best punch-lines in front of his national television audience, these trial runs give Fleming some insight into what is working in each story. She originally developed this skill as a mother telling stories to one of her sons when he was a little boy. She would tell the story, covering her intended storyline for a book, and add material, making it wilder and more unbelievable, based on her son's facial expressions. To further her insight into what "works" in her children's books, Fleming has even done similar live storytelling events at local schools, and has found it useful and enjoyable because with live story-telling you can experience the audience's response immediately, instead of writing something down and wondering if it will work later on.

Once the trial runs are complete, Fleming is ready to tackle the actual writing of the book. Her general approach is to start with a set number of pages or words, tell the story, add the art, and then do serious editing. Since the artwork often makes the story come alive, ideally artists are involved in the creative process from the get-go. On the other hand, it should be pointed out that sometimes Fleming and the illustrator never meet, but instead work through an editor at a publishing company. Under these circumstances, the editor often selects the artist after receiving the first draft from the author.

Fleming views each book as collaboration between art and writing and often finds herself trying to solve the conundrum of which comes first: the images or the words. Sometimes the artist will read the words and create pictures that follow them, and other times, the artist may work ahead, following their own creative vision, leading Fleming to change part of the story to fit her collaborator's new ideas for the project. In either case, the ultimate goal is to have the images flow like a movie, with each one leading to the next.

But if you ask most children's book authors, including Fleming, the real challenge of writing for children is the wording. Every word has to invoke an image in the child's mind, as the ultimate goal is to tell a fascinating story with a transparent message, using a limited number of words. While this may seem like a constraint, she views this as the reason that the field of writing children's books is wide open. Though the message may be universally conveyed again and again, there are *always* new ways to tell stories when dealing with suspended belief. And what better way to get in touch with your own inner child!

TEXTBOOKS

Textbooks, much like trade nonfiction, are a wide-open field in terms of what is available to write. The world of academics is always in motion. History, science, politics, philosophy, and economics (to name a few) are continuously evolving. The need to adapt our education to the constantly changing global society is becoming more and more imminent. In fact, almost all subjects must be continuously updated, creating the necessity for the development of an up-to-date, diverse array of textbooks.

Your approach will obviously be different depending on what type of text you plan to author, as a scientific text might involve laboratory or environmental research, while a historical textbook might only require you to read scholarly journals and texts, and a theoretical math text might require you to solve complex problems. Bearing this in mind and also with the assumption that you know more about your subject than we do, the best general advice is to be thorough in your research, get help with information and editing from colleagues, make sure to check facts and cite all sources, and always keep your audience in mind (e.g. high school students vs. graduate students). Those who read your book will be starting with varying levels of knowledge on the topic and few will have the core knowledge-base which you will have acquired through the writing process.

If you are a teacher or a professor, study the works of your peers who have written textbooks, particularly the ones which have been successful. What approach did they take towards your subject? Which sources did they consult to compile the information? What was the approximate educational level of those to which the text was geared? You may want to consider modeling your own work on parts of their approach or style, depending on your desired goals for your project. Just be careful about how much you rely on the information and style of others, as some well-known figures have run into trouble with plagiarism in recent years. To find more information on academic research and writing, consult The Web of Resources in the Appendix, and use the databases and sources which are specific to your field.

Perhaps the most important part of the process is to involve others, as it will ideally lighten your workload, increase the quality of your work, and expedite the process. You may want to seek out the authorities in your field, even those who have not written textbooks previously, as they may be an untapped wealth of knowledge. If you are an active teacher or professor, your students can offer helpful suggestions, particularly stylistic ones, as you work towards completion.

On a final note, we should point out that by no means are you limited to just one field or only your particular area of expertise. Joy Hakim, sometimes referred to as the J.K. Rowling of textbooks, is best known for her *A History of US*, a history text used in thousands of classrooms nationwide. Recently, however, Hakim has turned her history lens onto the field of science, and completed *The Story of Science: Aristotle Leads the Way*. She found she had such an interest in this area that she plans to continue researching and writing in the scientific realm in the future.

LESSON IN SUCCESS: JOEL COLTON

Joel Colton, a professor in Duke University's History Department for over forty years, has been involved in textbook publishing for several decades. Colton, who has won the Mayflower Award, as well as prestigious fellowships such as the Guggenheim, Rockefeller, and National Endowment for the Humanities, is perhaps best known for his work, *A History of the Modern World*. The text, which has gone through nine editions, has been translated into six languages, and is used at hundreds of colleges and universities nationwide, was the result of collaboration between Colton and R.R. Palmer, a noted historian and former president of the American Historical Association. Several of the more recent editions have been written with the help of a third collaborator, Lloyd Kramer, a history professor at the University of North Carolina. The textbook has been so influential that *The New York Times* named it a classic in its field.

According to Colton, the most difficult part of putting together the textbook was keeping it updated over time. The original edition, which first appeared in 1950, was too difficult for college students to navigate, prompting the authors to try a different angle. From 1956 on they have tried to attract student interest and also track new developments in the field. This was initially accomplished by adding family, social, economic, and intellectual history to the political history they already had in place. They also had to update the language in the text, as have many other scholarly text authors. For example, among other things, there has been an increase in gender sensitivities.

Every year new articles and books come on the market that approach historical subjects and events in a new way or unearth new evidence, which can be both useful and overwhelming when researching for new textbook editions. Because their text covers such a broad base—European and Western history from the Middle Ages to the present—Colton finds that doing research can be difficult and very time-consuming. In order to expedite the process and help filter through the new material that will ultimately end up in *A History of the Modern World*, Colton and his collaborators rely on professional journals in their field, such as *The Journal of Modern History* and *The American History Journal*, as well as on reviews of books in *The New York Times* and other major critical sources.

Once the authors have researched and chosen what they will add to a new edition, they present the text to their publisher for commentary. The copy editor goes through it and evaluates strictly for style, making suggestions before sending it back. The authors are ultimately responsible for the content and for making the book reader-friendly for their target audience. Because the publisher is only evaluating from a stylistic viewpoint, the burden is on the authors to verify the facts presented, which can be a tedious task, but one that is obviously important. The authors make sure to include a bibliography, not only to accurately acknowledge where they obtained their information, but also in the words of Colton, "to let students know that there are other sources of truth beyond ours." Improper citing of sources and questions of plagiarism have plagued other prominent experts in their field, making Colton and his co-authors extra careful when putting together the finished product. One task in the area of content research in which the publisher does help is visual aids. Typically, the publisher assists the authors in finding maps and tables and may even enlist a photo research agency to track down relevant photographs.

Even though the job of completing a textbook, especially one with such a broad subject, is a challenging one, Colton sees the intrinsic value. In addition to the personal satisfaction which comes with completing such a monumental achievement, he believes that it helps a professor to advance their standing, and often leads to promotions, academic distinctions, grants, and sometimes even higher compensation. While he concedes that many texts are "stillborn and never really catch on," Colton is convinced that if you work hard, pay close attention to details, and keep up-to-date in your field, you can successfully complete a textbook that is meaningful in the world of academia.

No matter what the intended book is, a certain amount of organization, structural planning, and the discipline of sitting down to actually write on a regular basis are always necessary components…all the rest depends on the nature and scope of the project, as well as the ability of the author to develop core skills. With a little guidance, it *is* possible for you to get better at certain aspects of your writing and to unlock your creative spirit and translate your ideas to paper. Of course there are great writers of the world who have done it all on their own. No one told them which sentences should go where and how they should formulate their plot, make their arguments, or weave in symbolic elements. They just did it. If you are not one of the self-propelled great writers of the world, consider the advice that you've read here and brainstorm about how to fulfill your vision for your book.

CHAPTER 5

Unblocking Writer's Block

Everyone deals with obstacles in life, and many people probably encounter a certain one at least five days a week: *traffic jams*— another of life's little ways to send us on an emotional roller coaster. One minute everything is moving along smoothly; you feel relaxed and in good spirits. Suddenly you turn the corner and cars are jammed into an ugly gridlock. Your glow of contentedness transforms into the heat of frustration as your stress level skyrockets. Every minute seems like an eternity when you're trapped motionless in your car with a burning desire to get somewhere. In the literary world, the *somewhere* is finishing your book, and you will most likely encounter cerebral traffic jams or *writer's block* along the way.

In his critically-acclaimed historical novel, *Arthur & George*, which deals with the lives of two men—one of them Sir Arthur Conan Doyle—Julian Barnes describes Doyle's lack of letting writer's block stand in the way. "He is too professional and too energetic ever to suffer from writer's block for more than a day or two. He identifies a story, researches and plans it, then writes it out." Oh, if it were only that simple for us mortals who aren't writing about detectives living at 221B Baker Street.

Luckily, there are a number of ways to triumph over writer's block, but the key to successfully navigating the momentary slowdown of your creative output is to understand that the *best* solutions are the ones that work for you. Keep trying to work your way around the block until you discover which way is most effective. Remember you are not alone in facing this problem. Even winners of the National Book Award have taken years to write follow-up novels because writer's block of various degrees stood in their way.

The mental state of thinking "I have writer's block" makes the task of overcoming it even more difficult. It conjures up an image of an immense Berlin Wall-like barrier separating you from your goal. In this chapter we will help you to put a positive spin on the slow-downs in the writing process and avoid cerebral gridlock.

For Sharon Singer, a writer, poet, and creative writing teacher, looking at the brighter side involves being accepting of oneself during a fallow time in writing and using "softer" terminology to describe writer's block. She prefers the term *pause* to *block*, because *pause* is non-evaluative, whereas the word *block* carries a hefty backpack of judgment! In her mind it is all a matter of perception. "So much depends on how we perceive what is happening. Call it a 'block' and we are apt to produce conflict and fear that only further stymies the creative impulses. Be allowing and kind with oneself during a 'pause' and the resulting space oxygenates and is more conducive to engaging the creative energies."

Susan Page, author of *The Shortest Distance Between You and a Published Book*, also believes that writers are too hard on themselves during periods when they struggle to find the right words or to get started on a literary project. She is quick to point out that the slowdown of output or the failure to achieve an initial launch is not due to procrastination or an unwillingness to sit at the computer and hammer out sentences. As she notes, "Procrastination is putting off something that you *don't* want to do— like writing an obligatory thank-you note, or cleaning out the basement."

The problem may actually be caused by acedia, which is essentially a mental and emotional block that often faces us when we *want* to do a creative project. It may sound bizarre, but because we are so interested in getting started on a project, we actually have trouble making it happen and often get caught up doing other things unrelated to writing, which is often misconstrued as procrastination. Subconsciously, we want to put our best foot forward in our literary effort, owning to its personal importance to us, and this creates even more pressure to sit down and perfectly capture the shining jewel of an idea in our mind. The mental pressure of perfection can be so debilitating that it can stop progress completely.

So whatever the cause of your block, even if it is as simple as feeling intimidated by all of the great writing found in the books of your favorite authors on your bookshelf, once you make peace with your temporary slowdown or struggle to begin, you are left with how to overcome it. Sometimes what you need most is to take your mind off the task at hand. Just do something you really enjoy and forget about the book for a little while. If you like to read, it can be an excellent way to relax and may even help you come up with new ideas. Read material both in and outside your genre--you may stumble upon ideas that can remove the block. Another strategy is to organize your notes for your project or reread some of the old material that you've already produced...you will be amazed at how straightening up or revisiting old notes can open the creative channels in your mind.

Beyond reading or rereading there are many everyday solutions. Stay in touch with your friends by writing emails because it will get you writing again and allow you to regain confidence in your creative abilities. Exercising is another great way to stimulate the mind, plus it has the added bonus of improving your health and reducing that waistline. Step on the treadmill and let your mind wander! Turn on the tunes, play with your dog, plant some flowers—do anything to get your mind off your book for a little while. If you take a short break doing something that you enjoy, you will be amazed at how refreshed you are when you return to tackle your writing.

Certain pastimes, however, we wouldn't recommend as highly. Many authors, including famous ones such as Hemingway and F. Scott Fitzgerald, are said to have turned to drinking excessive amounts of alcohol for inspiration and to help keep the words flowing. While the two managed to rack up quite an impressive list of novels and accolades, this might be one method you want to skip when tackling writer's block. Though you may get some euphoric highs under alcohol-induced inspiration, it's safe to say that the resulting hangovers will likely hamper your overall efforts and could cause lots of non-publishing related problems.

Your "inner critic" may be the biggest part of your writer's block problem. The "inner critic" is essentially the desire you have to make each sentence and every word perfect because, in your mind, most of the things that you've read and enjoyed have lived up to this standard. You *do* want your writing to be polished and to read well, so, on some level, being able to critique your work is helpful. But giving full reign to the "inner critic" during the initial drafting of the manuscript can be detrimental because it causes you to get hung up on one sentence or word and lose sight of the big picture, thus slowing your progress and increasing your frustration.

Put your perfection-driven mind at ease by taking a stroll through culinary history. Once upon a time, in the days before microwaves, people used an appliance called a waffle iron. You are probably used to the prepackaged variety of waffles, which is a good thing, because the waffle iron had one problem. The first waffle batch never came out right; it always stuck to the iron. With subsequent batches, it stuck less and less, until eventually you got the perfect waffle. Writing a book is similar. The first draft *isn't* going to be perfect, but each successive rewrite should leave you with a better product. Override the "inner critic" in your brain by remembering the waffle-making analogy.

Another approach for quieting the "inner critic" involves putting on "writing blinders." Turn off your computer monitor or, if you happen to be using the antiquated machine known as a typewriter, simply close your eyes. Then just WRITE, let loose, and continue typing without looking at the words. The grammar will most likely be off and typographical errors will abound, but this process can often help you get over your mental block. Remember, you can always go back and fix mistakes. It may seem absurd to type without being able to see the words, but it should keep you from "over-focusing" on a single sentence. Jonathan Franzen, author of *The Corrections*, reportedly used a similar method with great success. He had just quit smoking and was having difficulty concentrating, so he blindfolded himself to write parts of the first draft of his award-winning novel.

Sometimes, especially when first getting started in writing, we just need some informal writing practice to help build confidence and be able to channel the creative impulses. *The Moving Pen*, a method coined by Natalie Goldberg, author of the highly-successful *Writing Down the Bones,* helps to develop this skill. It simply involves "free-hand" writing for a certain amount of time without stopping the pen and it is often referred to as stream of consciousness writing. The key is to not analyze the thoughts that come to mind; you simply must write them down on the paper in front of you. Your choice of topic can be as random as "My Slipping Stock Portfolio" or "Why North Dakota is Paradise." You may have a lot to say about one subject and not much about another. Even if you end up writing "I don't know what to write" or "All work and no play makes Jack a dull boy" over and over for twenty minutes, that's okay. This is just to free yourself from gridlock and to allow yourself to drift closer to your own innate creative flow.

Sharon Singer uses this method in her creative writing classes and it typically works with everyone from teenagers to the elderly. She recommends practicing it in ten minute intervals once or twice a week, then gradually increasing the sessions to thirty minutes. Think of it as a tool that you are refining each time, which you can keep in your "mental toolbox." The point is to make time to write with no judgment involved. Though a lot of what comes out will be meaningless drivel, this practice can also unearth some colorful gems of creative thought. You already have the creativity, imagination, and memories necessary to write a book; the objective is simply to get them from your brain onto paper.

Neil and Eric also struggled with writer's block while putting together this book. Although there have been many books—covering every facet of the publishing industry—written to help current and future authors, we wanted to write something unique and captivating. Ultimately our agonizing paid off. We came up with the concept of short, concise chapters, filled with motivating stories, which would lead someone just like you from INSPIRATION to sharing your gift with the literary world and collecting royalty checks. As we toiled to complete this book, if one of us experienced a "block" we would take a step back, have a conference call with each other, and get reenergized by talking about our mission with *Get Between the Covers*—to encourage millions around the world to write books and to change our literate society globally. Once we were excited about the project again, we would then discuss a specific issue... the next chapter to be written, how we would approach it, which authors to include, what anecdotes would be appropriate, and what kind of motivational language would captivate the reader.

Considering all of the attention that we have given to writer's block in this chapter, you may be surprised to learn that some people don't even believe that it exists. Instead, they believe that writer's block is merely a manifestation of the same thing that keeps you from fixing the clog in your drain. It's not that you *can't* find a way to get the water flowing, it's just that you simply don't feel like fixing the problem *right now*.

Life moves along in cycles—with emotional crests and troughs in every aspect from job responsibilities to your "love life." Unfortunately we can't always control the rises and falls; the process of writing a book is no different. There are wonderful times when the material seems to flow effortlessly, and by all means you should keep the ball rolling during those times. Then there are other, frustrating times, when you can't even put together a sentence. A momentary stoppage isn't the end of the world and it doesn't have to be a major obstruction in your path to completing your book. Try to keep a healthy perspective and use any trick that is effective in helping you to navigate around the block; you can turn writer's block into a pebble in your path, instead of a show-stopping boulder! Remember, your brain doesn't always THINK in sequence, so just because you don't know what's going to be on the next page, it doesn't mean you can't jot down ideas for the next chapter. Maybe you'll wake up in the middle of the night with a great idea for that next page.

·Writer's block is an obstacle that almost every writer faces when attempting to complete a book —from the novice attempting their first book to the Pulitzer Prize winning novelist.

·Remember to stay positive and try to avoid being judgmental of yourself and your progress during times of low writing output.

·Try the strategies presented in this chapter or any "home remedies" that you discover.

CHAPTER 6

Edited-Down Advice on Editing

E ven though the books of most successful authors are distinct in their own way and share few characteristics with other works—apart from writing that enthralls or educates many readers—there is typically one written acknowledgement that they have in common. If you look at the beginning of each book, where the authors thank family members, friends, and contributors for their support, you will often find an additional "thank you" to an editor or a team of editors. These editors, completely unbeknownst to the public, work behind the scenes helping to transform a rough version into a polished finished product. As readers, we see only the jewel that is the finished copy, crediting the author on the cover, without the benefit of witnessing the metamorphosis the manuscript went through from first draft to final copy. The value of editing, therefore, cannot be expressed in mere words, and if it could, it would require several drafts.

Of course, a good writer is generally a good editor of their own work, and it's been said that the best writers are actually the best "re-writers." Kurt Vonnegut is reported to have edited each manuscript up to twelve times and would go through it page by page until each one was perfect in his mind. Ernest Hemingway is said to have edited *The Old Man and the Sea* over **200** times! These are two of the most critically acclaimed writers of the 20th Century and no one would doubt their raw talent as writers, yet editing was necessary even for them to achieve a certain degree of readability and structure with each work. Successful authors, who enjoy longevity in the publishing industry, learn quickly that almost *every* written work needs a certain degree of touching up before it's ready to hit the bookshelves.

Jack Pendarvis in his hilarious collection of stories, *The Myterious Secret of the Valuable Treasure,* has one of his characters who is a greenhorn writer full of confidence, when talking about changing and editing his material, say, "Normally I do not approve of such changes. Revision and 'rewriting' are, to me, signs of weakness or low self-esteem in a writer. I highly doubt that the great authors of the past, such as William Faulkner and Isaac Asimov, spent their free time in such a piddling and self-indulgent fashion." While the character's take is humorous and reflects the thoughts of many writers (of all skill levels) who simply believe that they did "everything right" the first time, the reality is that editing is the most crucial element to getting a book ready to be put into the hands of the public.

So, recognizing the importance of editing your book, how do you get started? Well, that is not such an easy question to answer. There's grammar, structure, syntax, consistency, development of characters, plot…the list goes on. Kevin Ryan, author of *Write Up the Corporate Ladder* and a writing consultant to many large corporations, notes that there are actually two types of writing rules that are being evaluated: stylistic and mechanical. Mechanical is much easier for you or an editor to review, since it deals with spelling, punctuation, and grammar—the so-called "science" of writing.

The more stylistic type of evaluation deals with such things as the use of the active voice, the necessity of every word, and the degree to which the writing can pull the reader in and keep them engaged. This is the more subjective form of editing, and it's the one that writers struggle with the most—with each having to develop their own system for spotting areas to be improved. Author Elmore Leonard sums up his approach, "If it sounds like writing, I rewrite it."

Every person who edits, professionally or otherwise, tastes and gets a sense of what works. If you gave a few paragraphs to ten editors you might get ten completely different revisions. Beyond just personal preferences, fact checking might be a major part of your editing if you are writing nonfiction. However, if you are writing a fantasy novel, the information about characters and plot are (or should be) figments of your imagination. You can get into trouble if you write fiction in a non-fiction book, as several recent authors can attest. On the other hand, if you write fact into a fictional tale, the "real" character may drop a libel suit on you.

Typically, the easiest place to start editing is to correct the grammar and spelling, making frequent use of your computer's spelling and grammar checking features. You still need to also look for "typos" because a wrong word spelled correctly will not always be picked up ("an" instead of "and," for example). To really learn how to edit from true experts and receive in-depth instruction on grammar and usage, consult *The Elements of Style*, which has been around since the 1920's and has been used by millions to improve their writing. Lynn Truss's *Eats, Shoots, & Leaves: The Zero Tolerance Approach to Punctuation*, which recently became a runaway bestseller, can be incredibly useful for improving one's grammar. We also like this book because it reinforces a point that we make throughout *Get Between the Covers*—that even a seemingly narrow topic for a book, which at first glance wouldn't seem that marketable, can enjoy significant commercial success. In addition to these two choices, pick up a copy of anything written by Richard Lederer, co-host of NPR's *A Way With Words* and author of twelve best-selling books and a weekly column, "Looking at Language." *Self-Editing for Fiction Writers*, by Renni Browne and Dave King, is another valuable resource to check out.

If you have trouble finding the right word or knowing how to use it in a sentence, refer to *Bryson's Dictionary of Troublesome Words: A Writer's Guide to Getting it Right*, a helpful guide by best-selling author Bill Bryson. Another approach is to read successful books similar either in genre or topic to your own, in order to study the structure and/or the flow of the plot. Go a step further and look at how individual sentences are composed; examine the mastery of punctuation, the use of vocabulary, and the selection of the appropriate length. Thousands of successful authors, as we mentioned in earlier chapters, have used this approach to vastly improve their writing and gain a better understanding of how to produce a truly great manuscript.

Once you understand the basics of editing, one strategy which may be helpful for you is a formula that Stephen King proposes in his book *On Writing*, and uses himself when working on his novels. His formula: 2nd Draft=1st Draft minus 10%. The basis for the formula is simple—we almost always use more words than necessary in the early drafts of our manuscripts. Shorter sentences cut straight to the point and may enhance your book stylistically, particularly in the case of drama/suspense stories. By keeping this in mind, King is more efficient at spotting sentences to be rewritten, without sacrificing any elements from the gripping storyline. If you choose to adopt this strategy, go gently on your manuscript. Remember, the goal is to eliminate unnecessary words—not just any words. Once again, balance is the key to your success! Work on getting the manuscript in as clean a condition as you can without turning the "inner critic" up too high and spending years finishing your book. If your "inner critic" is in overdrive it might influence you to take out the good stuff too.

As a matter of fact, sometimes the "fatter" the book, the bigger the rewards and popularity for the author. For example, the famous French author, Alexandre Dumas, creator of all things Three Musketeers, was actually paid per line for his famous work *The Count of Monte Cristo*, which led to him loading up the book with extra character dialogue and descriptions. In this case not only did he rake in the loot, but he produced an end product that is a fantastic novel.

In terms of editing in general, a strategy that many writers of books (in addition to writers of school papers, business proposals, and personal correspondence) use is to print out a hard copy of the material and do the edits in hand, before making the changes on the computer. It may sound like a mundane piece of advice, but you would be surprised at how many people try to read through their material quickly on the computer screen as their "editing session" and not only miss the obvious grammatical errors, but fail to make the more stylistic structural changes that could improve their work. For whatever reason, we often seem to process material better when it's seen on a piece of paper versus on a computer screen, not to mention that it's a lot easier on your eyes. You can also make notes in the margins to figure out where to move material and rearrange pages, as you read through.

Beyond just having an external record of your work (which is never bad in the event of a catastrophic computer crash), there is an intrinsic value in seeing the actual number of "physical" pages that one has typed, as opposed to seeing a page count at the bottom of a Microsoft Word document on your screen. It's great to see the visual fruition of a day, a week, a month, etc.

So the bottom line is to make a slightly larger investment in the toner for your printer and put it to good use if you want a "cleaner" manuscript.

Of course, it should be noted that if you are planning on self-publishing, editing could be an especially important consideration because you won't have the benefit of the publisher's professional editor to review your manuscript before it is available to the public. For this reason, it's not a bad idea to hire a freelance editor to look over your work. If you have aspirations of gaining acceptance with a traditional publisher, it could also be crucial because of what we call the "paradox of editing." This concept, which thousands of writers have experienced, works like this: you need a well-edited, polished manuscript to get accepted. Once accepted by a publisher, you will have an editor or a team of editors working with you to improve your work for publication. So, you "get" an editor AFTER you have submitted well-edited material that impresses an acquisition editor. If your writing hasn't been carefully edited before you submit, you likely won't be accepted, thus closing the "door" of the publisher's editor to you. To put it simply, you need to be edited to get edited.

Visit www.freelanceonline.com or ask around at your local library, writers groups, newspapers, and English departments at secondary schools or universities. Family, friends, and neighbors who are avid readers may also be very helpful (not to mention that their fees may be 0). If paying an editor, consider hiring the editor for the first chapter, as a trial run. Don't commit to the entire project until you determine if he or she is the right fit for you and your project.

Even after heeding the advice in this chapter, using the resources listed and undergoing a number of editing sessions and progressive rewrites, you may still end up not totally satisfied with the manuscript. You may always feel like changes could be made in order to achieve "perfection"; however, sometimes you have to let go! You are not incompetent or lazy by taking that step; it simply means that you are human. In fact, a number of Native American tribes throughout history developed the practice of purposely making a mistake in each rug, bead design, or article of clothing produced. These intentional mistakes were viewed as acts of humility to identify the items as human made and to keep them from approaching the perfection that they observed in nature. While, we don't recommend purposely creating errors in your manuscript as you strive for the best finished product, if errors do occur in the final version or if you notice later that things could have been reworked differently, be accepting of yourself and let them serve as a lesson for your next book. Do your best to avoid the plight of Johann Wolfgang von Goethe, famous for his novel *Faust,* who completed the first draft when he was 25 years old and proceeded to revise and edit it until his death at the age of 82.

If you struggle with editing at first, don't worry. Remember you become a much better writer and editor the more writing you do, just as you become a better swimmer the more you jump into the pool, or a better public speaker the more you find yourself behind the podium. It is simply a matter of practice! Each time you rework your manuscript, you are honing your skills and will ultimately be able to proceed with greater ease. Once you think you have your manuscript as polished as a showroom car, it's time to benefit from some constructive criticism. Turn the page to learn to how.

·**Editing is one of the most important parts of the writing process and is what separates a polished manuscript that reads well from one that is choppy, contains errors, and is hard to follow.**

·**Use the resources recommended in this chapter to learn how to better self-edit your work and be sure to read the next chapter.**

CHAPTER 7

Improve Your Manuscript Through Peer Review

You have a unique perspective on the world because your individual life experiences, knowledge base, and memories are yours alone. When you complete a manuscript, you have managed to share a piece of yourself with your audience. Unfortunately, unless people can read your mind as well as your book, certain parts of your manuscript which might be clear to you, will not necessarily be clear to others. Remember, you have the entire story, with every bit of nuanced background in your head. Your readers do not have this background, and for that reason, things that may seem obvious to you, such as character motivations or plot twists, may not be easy for your audience to pick up on. You face the same challenge in nonfiction when trying to convey the full picture of your knowledge base to the reader.

Furthermore, authors are often blind to their own grammatical and typographical errors. When reading your work over and over again, it can be hard to remain critical and to notice every small error, which is why traditionally-published authors are usually pleased that there is a team of editors working behind-the-scenes to take care of the details. For these reasons, as well as having the opportunity to creatively connect with others, network with important contacts, and to simply make new friends, peer review and critiques from other writers and writers groups can often help an author.

Before you conjure up images of disillusioned expatriates sitting around, sipping wine, smoking, and discussing the latest issue of *The New Yorker* or senior citizens knitting and reading poetry around a fireplace, perhaps we should explain what constitutes a writers group. Members of writers groups write in all genres, come from all walks of life, and have different levels of writing abilities. They usually meet once a month to listen to guest speakers (publishers, editors, other authors) and help each other with their respective works. These groups convene in most cities, and there are often multiple groups in the larger metropolitan areas, ranging in size from small, intimate 3 person gatherings to much larger public meetings. Many of them have critique groups that operate autonomously within the larger writing group, with each focusing on a different genre, allowing each member to receive more customized assistance and meaningful feedback.

In addition to having your work critiqued, there are many other benefits of attending a writers group. Meeting with other writers can give you ongoing motivation or a boost of inspiration to help keep your "work-in-progress" on the move. You may also develop contacts, perhaps even ones that could lead you to a publisher or advise you on successful ways to self-publish. Many writers groups offer creative writing courses on the mechanics of putting together a "good read," and attending these courses may teach you some new writing skills, stimulate your creative juices, boost your confidence, and pump up your enthusiasm. It's great for the morale to have a room full of people rooting you on as you move towards your goal of completing a finished work. To find a writers group in your area, ask at your local library or bookstore, or try an Internet search.

Beyond local writers groups, you can join larger writing associations for publishing contacts and support, such as the American Society of Journalists and Authors (www.asja.org) or the Women's National Book Association (www.wnba-books.org). These are just two of the numerous national and regional groups that exist, catering to specific genres, writing occupations, or the demographic backgrounds of the authors. These associations typically have hundreds or thousands of members, a wide spectrum of seminars, periodical publications, and interactive, professionally-designed information websites. Most of these associations have annual or semi-annual meetings (like the large publishing industry conventions such as BookExpo America or the Canadian Booksellers Association) and facilitate the interaction of writers from a wide range of backgrounds. It's another opportunity for you to connect with the right insider to help mentor you with your book.

If you do not want to join a writers group or don't have the time or desire to attend association meetings or writing conferences, you can always tap the brains of friends and family for feedback. Of course, no matter who is reviewing your work, don't take it personally. Everybody has a bias and there is no absolute authority. Many an experienced editor at the most reputable publishing house has turned down books which became runaway bestsellers. In the real world, as opposed to the academic world, there are no grades and no teacher with the final say; there is merely a spectrum of response to creativity. There will be some people who love what you've written and others who will hate it. You are the final arbiter. You select the advice which you agree with and want to use to improve your manuscript, and pleasantly discard that which you disagree with. If you try to please everyone, you'll end up with a truly problematic work.

When sifting through the reviews and advice relating to your work, try to shrug off any hurt associated with rejection. It may be tough, but try to react objectively and without emotion. Even if the reviewer uses words like "flat, boring, and tasteless," simply reflect on why the reader reacted with such emotion and see if there is something in the writing that you are missing. If you feel that some points are worthy, it's better to rewrite now before submitting your book to the sometimes "brutally honest" publishing industry, where the bottom line is either yea or nay.

In addition to family and friends, it's wise to take your manuscript to the "experts," including reviewers who may not share your opinions. It's never bad to see things from a different perspective. For fiction, almost anyone can give you feedback on the plot, structure, character development, etc, but you probably also want someone with knowledge specific to your plot and subject to check facts and descriptions, in order to ensure that the backbone of your creation is accurate. This is especially important if you are a budding Tom Clancy or Michael Crichton and the story is based on highly technical material. At the other end of the spectrum, if you are writing a children's book, consider reading to the kids in the neighborhood to observe how they react to the story and artwork.

With nonfiction, you simply must find someone who is knowledgeable on the topic, in addition to everyday readers who can comment on how the book reads overall. If you are a student, a professor or teacher might give you an insightful appraisal, and, as a result of their experience, might be able to steer you in the right direction. A professor or researcher may also refer you to their colleagues. This will help ensure that your manuscript is checked for accuracy—a key component of scholarly writing. A cookbook writer might benefit from getting his/her manuscript into the hands of a master chef. A fashion historian may want to give Ralph Lauren and Kenneth Cole a call. The list of suitable peer reviewers is as endless as your choices of topics.

Other writers could certainly give you good advice about your manuscript, since they have had to edit and improve their own works. They might offer insight about what to do with the manuscript once it is completed. They also understand better than anyone else the emotional aspect of writing a book and can help you through the highs and lows. Many successful writers were mentored by colleagues in the literary world, such as Ernest Hemingway, who spent time with F. Scott Fitzgerald, during the years he was writing. Even James Joyce, one of the most skillful writers of all time, learned Norwegian so that he could communicate with and learn from his idol, Henrik Ibsen, perhaps the most famous playwright in history after Shakespeare.

HAVING A GOOD HEART GETS YOU PLACES

Virginia Brucker, a long-time teacher, is the author of *Gifts from the Heart*, a book that is meant to help bring friends and families closer together.

Her tale demonstrates that being magnanimous can do more than just help others in the world around you. Often the more you give away, the more you get back. Sometimes what you "get back" is a publishing deal.

After being inspired by cookbooks offering a portion of their royalties to help various charitable causes, Brucker came up with the idea of creating a "recipe" for families to form a tighter bond particularly around the holidays, especially Christmas. As part of her project, she decided to give all of the proceeds of her book to helping fight cancer (Note: So far she has raised an amazing $100,000 for various charitable organizations). Her dedication and generosity was recognized with awards from the Canadian Center for Philanthropy and the Canadian Cancer Society.

Despite not having much of a writing or speaking background, Brucker has managed to speak to all manner of groups and to audiences as large as 400 people. Her book is such a hot item at these events that she routinely sells hundreds of copies, including once selling 50 to one person, who bought one for every employee in his company. She has also had numerous media appearances and an impressive number of interviews.

With all of the attention that she received, not only for the success of the book, but also for her generous actions taken with the fruits of her success, she was delighted to find out that another Canadian author had included information about her in a recent book. When the two exchanged emails, they realized that they only lived 100 miles apart and quickly became friends. Not only did they establish a bond, but the other author, while visiting her publisher in Toronto, mentioned *Gifts from the Heart*. A few days later, Brucker found herself staring at a contract from a traditional publisher for her originally self-published book, which will be re-released in 2007. Being a good person will always take you far in life, but it doesn't hurt to network either…there's no telling where it could lead. Her advice for new writers, "It takes a lot of hard work to write and market a book. Don't focus on being rich or famous. That doesn't often happen. Write a book because you believe you truly have something to share with others. Do it because you want to write a book that makes a difference. Books can change lives. Mine did!"

While working on *Get Between the Covers*, we solicited a lot of feedback during the process, even when our concept for the book was not fully developed. We not only let various publishing insiders/experts see our material, but also individuals who were interested in writing books and had read a number of the other writing resources in the marketplace, so they could help us to compare our work from an objective angle. After all, these were the people that we hoped to move to action for years to come with this book and its accompanying marketing plan, so why not test market our approach? The commentary that our readers provided was invaluable, and it offered us a chance to make improvements to the writing, reorder chapters in a more logical fashion, and find new authors who had compelling stories to include in the book.

Consider peer review. Don't be shy! Don't be afraid to allow other brains to react to your writing. Don't be intimidated by other people criticizing your work. You're not obliged to agree with what they say. Make the changes that you agree with after giving the comments an objective look. The important thing is to do whatever it takes to improve your book. Try not to let your ego get in the way and be sure to keep an open mind!

·Peer review is a great way to not only improve your manuscript, but also to network with others who share your passion for writing or who have connections in publishing.

·Contact people who are experts in your writing genre. Consider joining a local writers group or national writers association to make it easier for you to connect with the people who can help polish your manuscript.

·Don't take the feedback personally; use it wisely to propel your book forward.

CHAPTER 8

Somebody Will Want Your Book

O nce you have begun writing your book or even while you are still just considering tackling the project, there is often the fear that you won't be able to publish it (if you don't already have a publishing deal) or that no one will want to read it when it hits the market. Therefore, it's reasonable to not want to put all the effort into fulfilling your goal of completing a book if no one else will ever enjoy your finished product. Ten years ago, this would have been a valid concern, given the uncertainty of acceptance by a traditional publisher and the high costs of self-publishing. But with advances in the publishing industry and thus the availability of new options, which we will deal with later, the fear of your work never seeing the light of day should no longer bind you.

We've already dealt with the actual writing of your book in the previous chapters—from finding the time to write to how to get organized and approach different styles of writing, and we've even briefly touched on the some of the psychological factors, like overcoming writer's block. However, before moving on, we thought that including this chapter would be important. In the coming chapters, we will deal with more of the business end of publishing, covering all the publishing options and some great steps to success that you can take post-publication. In the meantime, trust us, in most cases there *are* people who will be eager to read your book…it will just be a matter of finding them.

As you will learn in this book and through your own experience, when dealing with the traditional publishing industry it's important to realize that receiving rejection letters is just part of the process of getting a book published. You shouldn't take it personally. Agents and publishers are simply making judgments based on what they feel is right for them or their company at the time. You simply need to find the "right fit"…somebody who is interested in your topic, likes your style of writing, and has a built-in mechanism to get your book to the right market. Getting your book published is simply a multi-step process of which rejection is a matter of course.

It's very rare to find that key contact on the first, second, or third shot. This is why J.K. Rowling, the billionaire author of the *Harry Potter* books, which have come to dominate the literary world and more recently the silver screen, was rejected by the first several publishers that she approached. Dr. Seuss was rejected 27 times before the 28th publisher accepted his first book and sold 6 million copies. All he did from there was win The Pulitzer Prize, sell hundreds of millions of copies of his books, and have numerous movies made from his popular titles. Even Robert Frost, regarded as one of the most influential poets in history, initially failed to get many of his lines of verse published.

THE BLACK SWAN IN PUBLISHING

Eric's colleague, Nassim Taleb, one of the most brilliant minds in the world and the author of the *New York Times Bestseller, The Black Swan*, spends his time illustrating the impact of the highly improbable and the randomness of events in the world around us, of which the publishing industry is a perfect example. In his book, he defines a "black swan" as an outlier (meaning it lies well outside the realm of what is expected), something that carries and extreme impact, and in spite of its outlier status, we as humans come up with explanations for its occurrence after the fact, making it seem explainable and/or predictable (Note: the name comes from the fact that until the discovery of Australia, which has black swans, people thought all swans in the world were white). It's important to note that "black swans" can be positive or negative; however, in the context of publishing, black swans are generally positive (e.g. when a new author becomes a runaway bestseller around the world. Although, it should be noted that if a publisher paid a big-name author a $10 million advance and then his novel went on to sell 1,000 copies, rather than several million, this would technically be considered a negative "black swan," since it was completely unexpected and had a negative impact on the bottom line.

Examples of "black swans" in life would include September 11th, the rise of a company like Google from a garage to the highest-trafficked site on the Internet, and, of course, any kind of runaway bestseller. In the first two cases, we look back and say that this terrorist group was doing X, Y, and Z and so we *should* have known that planes could be hijacked and flown into buildings. For Google, people always think "Of course having a search engine that is so accurate it can return the most relevant results in fractions of a second would become a huge company." What they forget is that there were companies like Google already (many of which have fallen by the wayside) doing the same thing since the mid-90's.

In publishing, as you will learn, traditional publishers don't always get it right. In fact, sometimes they get it very wrong and pass on a hit because they have no idea just how many "somebody's" out there will become engrossed in your work. Books like *The Da Vinci Code* or the Harry Potter series truly are "black swans" because no one saw them coming, they've had an astronomical effect on book sales, reading, and even religious and scholarly discourse. Also, looking back in hindsight, people (both publishers and everyday readers) always say how they can see *why* these books did so well. The reality is quite the opposite. Very few saw the value in the works originally…they were merely well-written books that were a long shot unlikely to pay off for an acquisition editor or the publisher.

As you will learn in this book, part of the reason that publishers reject so much material is that the odds are stacked against them that they will find that positive "black swan" in the pile of manuscripts. Instead, they will lose money on many new titles. But what keeps them searching for new authors and titles is the knowledge that the next "big thing" is out there somewhere, ready to be accepted, published, distributed, and read by millions for years to come. They therefore diversify by investing in hundreds of titles a year hoping to find that one diamond in the rough whose revenue can swamp the small losses incurred for the other titles that didn't pan out.

As you read the coming chapters, remember that if you can't get a traditional publisher to take your book, there are many alternative routes to getting a book published and making it available to anyone in the world, and who knows, it might just take off. Self-publishing by going to a printer is more practical; it's less expensive than it used to be and there are more avenues for sales and distribution. Another affordable and accessible approach to publishing books is to use print on-demand publishers on the Internet. You will learn more about these avenues in the "Paths to Print" section of this book, but for now just know that you have plenty of options for your book to see the light of day.

Another fear slowing you down today may relate to the popularity of your book. What if you do find a way to get it published, but some people don't like it? Let's say you've written something and are pleased with the finished product; should you just keep it to yourself, rather than put it out there for public scrutiny and take the chance that someone might not feel the same way about it as you do? The answer is simple; there is no book in the world that captivates every reader. This is true without exception... liking or disliking books is simply a matter of taste. Some people don't like certain types of books because they are too scholarly and wordy. Others may find a book is too racy or over the top, or offensive to their morals or religious beliefs. Maybe you don't like a fantasy novel simply because you only read courtroom thrillers. Or you can't dig your teeth into a humorous book because it doesn't appeal to your sense of humor. Even the most celebrated works do not meet universal approval, such as James Joyce's *Ulysses*, often named as one of the top ten novels of all time, which was recently criticized by several literary insiders who felt it was far too long. There will always be people who can't connect with your writing no matter how much time you spend perfecting your book, so don't let that stop you.

On the other hand, will *anyone* be interested in and enjoy reading your book? **Yes.** The trick is just finding the right target market. For example, Tom Brockaw's books about the World War II generation are probably not marketed as heavily on college campuses as they are to veterans' societies and associations for senior citizens like AARP, since few students were alive during any of the events which he chronicles, and probably wouldn't be as interested as the generation who are the subject of his series. If your book is just for your family and friends, you have a sure market that can easily be reached. However, if you want to attract a wider audience or a targeted one that is spread out around the world, we will help put you on the path to finding the individuals who are interested in your book. They may be editors, literary agents, or simply a loyal following of readers.

Ultimately, there will be a number of "someone's" out there who want to read your book. Though television and movies occupy many people's spare time, books still have a unique place in our society. The books we read can have a tremendous influence on our lives—often without us even being aware of it. Different books and authors "speak" to different people in distinct ways. Nonfiction books, such as *Fast Food Nation* by Eric Schlosser, or *Missed Fortune 101* by Douglas Andrew, are more transparent in shaping our minds, actions, and futures, but even novels can change the way we view life. For examples, look at *The Grapes of Wrath* by John Steinbeck, *The Invisible Man* by Ralph Ellison, or *The Catcher in the Rye* by J.D. Salinger, which has sold 60 million copies since its release in the early 1950's and remains one of the most read books in the American public school system. Even further, books can offer us a much needed break from our lives. For this reason, the United States, during the recent conflict with Iraq, restored a reading program from decades ago wherein troops received special editions of classic novels and plays to read on the frontlines.

Bear in mind two things as you work on your book. First of all, a small idea of yours can potentially touch many lives, even if you don't start out with that intention. Lalita Tademy, who had never even written a short story, originally wrote the novel *Cane River* for her family, since it traced their roots in Louisiana. But the hands of fate intervened, and it became a bestseller and a selection of Oprah's Book Club. Secondly, the timeliness of your books can also be a big factor in helping you find readers. In the wake of the September 11th tragedy, there were a slew of books released—everything from compilations of notable presidential quotations to photo collections of the courageous rescue personnel of New York City. While Rudy Giuliani's *Leadership* and *The 9/11 Commission Report* were by far the most successful of these books, each one touched a nerve or caught the attention of a certain group of people. While this was an event of incredible magnitude, there are countless smaller current events and hot topics cropping up at any given time. If you are able to launch your book in a timely fashion, you may reach many more readers than you ever thought possible.

At the end of the day, there *will* be people who want to read your book, even if it is just a few family members and friends who, in addition to being interested in the topic of your book, may be star-struck by you being the only real-life author that they are close with and will want to learn more about what makes you tick. The possible number of readers of your book or all of the books that you may write over your lifetime is incredible…anywhere from a single person to Agatha Christie's numbers (over 2 billion copies of her books have been sold in 103 languages). If you desire to reach a larger audience than those in your inner circle, we will give you advice on how to market yourself and your project successfully in the coming chapters.

After reading the chapters in Part 1, ideally, you are now pumped up to sit down and start composing your book, if you haven't already begun. There are readers out there just waiting for a book like yours to come along to entertain them, educate them, and possibly to change their lives. It's time for you to learn more about your publishing options, so that your gift to the world can emerge.

Part 2

Demystifying the Mighty Giant: Welcome to the Publishing Industry

Navigating the
Publishing Industry

Most women could probably attest to the fact that it is much easier to get to your destination when you have a map and actually use it. On the other hand, it may be a stereotype, but most men may prefer to navigate their own course through life without asking for directions, and are far more likely to end up lost on a deserted road. While some of your more interesting and unusual experiences may have occurred by wandering aimlessly, in general, your life is much easier if you have a guide to your surroundings.

The quest to publish a book is no exception. You may eventually reach the goal of having your book in the bookstores by stumbling from one lesson to the next, but wouldn't you rather have an idea of a good portion of the course and its obstacles before you start? The next several chapters in this section of the book provide a map of the publishing industry, and like a roadmap, they will cover the basic information, how to get from point A to point B, and the major points of interest along the way. Once you have the "helicopter" view of the industry, Part 3 will detail different options for getting your book into print, including ways to publish a small quantity of books just for family and friends. Beyond that, we offer a collection of chapters in Part 4 to help you with specific elements of the publication process (submitting material to an editor, marketing, understanding rights, etc.).

Considering the high rate of manuscript rejection in this industry, it's surprising that around 75,000 books are published by traditional publishing houses in the United States every year. Many people would certainly say that this is a great deal of material to be published, especially when also taking into account the approximately 100,000 books that are self-published every year; however, after reading Part 1, you've probably ascertained that we feel exactly the opposite. The annual production of books is just a small fraction of the total knowledge base in the world at one time, comprised of six billion brains experiencing, thinking, and imagining! Not to mention that there are tens of millions who feel that they have a book in them waiting to be written. So if you're ready to commit to putting a little piece of your brain in between the front and back cover of a book, read on. We hope this overview will give you a better understanding of the publishing industry and will lead you into it with greater ease.

CHAPTER 9

ON THE INSIDE: *How a Traditional Publisher Operates*

They can be found in a towering skyscraper in the heart of New York City or in a humble, one-story trailer in Idaho. They can range in size from an international conglomerate, with thousands of employees, which annually publishes catalogues full of titles, to a local publisher, possibly run by one person, which puts out one or two titles yearly. Some only publish biographies, while others publish everything from business books to Star Wars novels. There's even a publishing label (linked to Pocket/MTV Books) founded by ultra-famous rapper, 50 Cent, which specializes in stories about the rough life on the streets of the inner city. Essentially, in the world of traditional publishers, just about anything can be a particular house's specialty, and it seems the only thing that they all have in common is their basic output: *books*.

What you probably don't realize is that there are around 85,000 publishers in North America, yet incredibly six publishing houses, known as the Six Sisters, account for about 80% of the sales in the industry. Even though the majority of authors end up going with one of the thousands of smaller publishers, the biggest ones have the most famous authors listed among their ranks, and hence sell the most books.

This unequal distribution of literary wealth may still seem impossible, but a basic understanding of the layout of international conglomerates should make things clearer. Within each of the conglomerates, a parent company owns many publishing companies, which in turn control smaller publishing companies. In many cases, the parent company at the top of the chain isn't even an American company, even though the bulk of its operations are in the States. An example of this is Random House, the largest publisher in the world, which is owned by Bertelsmann Book Group of Bertelsmann AG, a German corporation. Random House owns other publishing companies (Ballantine, Bantam, Broadway, Dell, Knopf, etc.), which publish different types of books, from novels to children's books to self-help guides, thus serving to expand the markets they reach, to sell more books, and ultimately make them profitable. The next time you pick up a copy of the week's bestseller list, check out which publishing imprints are represented among the highest sellers. Most will be the major publishing companies or their sister companies.

Some of the major publishers are tied to the entertainment industry. Time Warner, a mogul in the television, movie, and magazine industries, owns Warner Books. The parent company of Simon and Schuster is Viacom, the media giant which also owns CBS and MTV. Rupert Murdoch's News Corp., famous for its Fox TV among other things, controls the publisher HarperCollins. And Disney, the king of theme parks and animated films, owns the publishing company Hyperion. Since these publishers have a built in connection to the mass media, theoretically they are able to market and promote their books more easily than other publishers. They supposedly have easier access to movie and television program decision makers. Also, the parent corporation can funnel additional funds to one of its publishing companies from another division if need be—a considerable advantage over a stand-alone publisher which may rely solely on book sales.

Despite differences in the scale of their operations, both small and large publishers, like almost every company, are primarily motivated by the bottom line: *profitability*. It must be conceded that some publishers, including university presses, will occasionally publish a book even though it may lose money, because it fits into the company's vision or agenda. However, in general, profit margin is the name of the game. Publishers end up "in the black" when the revenue generated from the sales of their books or book rights exceeds the expenses of running the company, such as employee salaries, printing, publicity, and advertising. Publishing books requires capital up front, with expenses such as paying the author an advance and covering the cost of printing before any revenue from sales is received. Accepting manuscripts becomes a risky proposition with all of these expenses on the line, since book sales are not guaranteed.

In terms of profitability, it truly is amazing how much the highest selling books matter to a publisher's profit or loss. Yearly estimates vary, but according to Nielsen BookScan, somewhere around 90% of titles published sell less than 1,000 copies. Obviously the returns (positive or negative) for a book that sells less than 1,000 copies varies depending on a number of factors (e.g. initial print runs, advertising costs, advances paid to the author, etc.), but what this generally means is that a publisher losses money or barely breaks even on the vast majority of its titles. It relies on the big sellers (the positive "Black Swans" that we discussed in Chapter 8 and also its A-list authors with huge markets of millions of fans) to outweigh the losses. In this sense, publishing is very much like venture capital (a comparison we make throughout the book)...it's tough to get funding (accepted) as a new company (author), most of your investments as the venture capital firm (publisher) lose money, and you hope that you just funded the next eBay or pharmaceutical company with a breakthrough drug (runaway bestsellers from literary newcomers).

Most publishers are interested in finding a book which fits into the genre they publish because they have established approaches for reaching their particular readership. For example, a publisher of weight-loss books may have a catalogue, a book club of avid readers, and even access to special displays at Jenny Craig or Weight Watchers or a national chain of gyms. They would also maintain an updated list of magazines and newspapers which review books in that genre. Publishers constantly look for angles to get more exposure, such as contracting a celebrity to write a foreword or tying a book's release into a specific event or news story. We will touch on marketing strategies in future chapters, but the bottom line is that the publisher is not only looking for a well-written book, but also one that it can successfully market to recoup its money and turn a profit.

No matter who publishes the book, the company's point person for the author is an assigned editor, an individual who has a good overview of the writing process and the publishing industry, often from experience as a reader or assistant editor. Because of the many activities that they must coordinate, the editor is usually quite overworked, and in keeping with the popular expression, they are generally underpaid relative to the responsibilities assigned to them. They move the book along, coordinating with all of the various departments within the company, as they support their authors through the writing process and help them cope with the traumas of bad reviews or poor book sales. In fact, editors have even been referred to as "mini-psychologists," because they so frequently end up nurturing and counseling their writers through the emotional rollercoaster ride of giving birth to a book.

Editors negotiate the contract for the legal department, arrange for royalty payments with accounting, connect with the PR department and the Publicity Director in planning promotional activities, and establish deadlines for submission and review with the production department. They also pitch the book to the sales force at sales meetings before the salespeople hit the pavement to start knocking on booksellers' doors. The editor is sometimes even the final decision-maker concerning the title of a book and how the cover will look. Editors often rely on "outsiders" such as literary agents to help them screen incoming material to reduce their workload as they search for new authors. Remember, there are thousands of new authors published every year, and in order to expand the publishing company and maintain profitability, editors must constantly juggle their time between working with existing authors and scouting out the newest up-and-coming writers.

From the start, the editors in the company are the author's advocate. They attend committee meetings, where they present manuscripts which they feel are marketable and well written. The committee usually includes the vice president of public relations, the vice president of sales, the editor-in-chief, and all of the other editors, and in these meetings, they decide which manuscripts to publish. In the case of novels, because they are riskier investments, the editor may have to gain the approval of someone as high up as the president of the company.

Just as in the rest of the business world, there is a hierarchy among editors within the same publishing house, even though all of them are essentially trying to find the best manuscripts to accept and to ultimately turn their earnings into a profitable revenue stream. In a business or law firm, one might rise through the ranks by bringing in the best clients, who end up making the firm a substantial amount of money. The employee in this case might have the relationship that keeps the client doing business with the firm and, as a result, the firm chooses to reward that employee with a bump up in title. In publishing, depending on the size of the company, the situation can be very analogous. Bringing in the next "big thing" and nurturing that relationship has led many editors up the ranks, sometimes all the way to editor-in-chief over time.

EDITORIAL POINTS OF VIEW: LARGE AND SMALL

Bob Pigeon knows a thing or two about editorial responsibilities in publishing companies of differing sizes. Formerly, he was the owner of a small niche publishing company, which specialized in World War II and Civil War nonfiction. When his company was sold to a larger publisher, he became an editor with that publisher. The change was tough for him at first, because even though he had personally reviewed manuscripts in the past, he had never dealt with fiction or juvenile books. He also had to adjust to a corporate culture, which encouraged him to accept mainstream manuscripts and avoid risky or peripheral ones. The author-publisher relationship, which he found to be warm, friendly, and hands on with a smaller publisher, was somewhat more removed within a company with a larger scale of operations, and it took some getting used to. The upside of a larger publisher from his perspective; however, is that authors have a much better chance of getting books sold due to its augmented resources.

Although he has never written a book himself, as the owner of a small publishing company, Pigeon dealt with everything from reading the manuscript to picking the right book jacket. From his experience, he knows how powerful the feeling is to eventually have a hard copy of a book with your name on the cover. He also understands the difficulty of the process, and his advice for new writers is simple: Take a step back and look at the big picture. "Keep in mind that the ultimate goal is to become part of our legacy and our culture by sharing thoughts that only you had before." If you are persistent, endure the process, and find the right editor for your manuscript, you will eventually be able to accomplish this goal.

Depending on the size of the publisher, there are various divisions within the company, such as production, marketing, and sales. The more visible side of a publisher's operations, which you come across every day, are publicity and marketing, both of which we will discuss in Chapter 10.

Structural editing, meaning major changes to the manuscript such as character enhancement or plot clarification, is usually done by an editor in the editorial department, but another type of editing must occur before the book is ready for publication. Copy editing is typically performed by an editor in the production department of the publisher, and this entails ironing out grammatical or typographical errors—the little things that we all miss on the first and sometimes the second proofreads of our material. Also, these people sometimes verify facts, an important component of staying clear of a lawsuit. Essentially copy editors want to ensure accuracy and make the manuscript as "clean" as possible. There are also line editors, whose job is kind of a cross between a copyeditor and a structural editor—they critically evaluate individual sentences, in addition to fixing mistakes, and try to make things more readable without re-working large passages.

The people in the production department contract with printers for the publication of the book and also set all of the specifications such as spacing, column width, and book jacket design. They also deal with graphics or artwork that needs to be included—a weighty task—since they must find the most economical printer for the size of the job and reserve space in the printer's busy schedule, once they have created the design. It can take several months for the book to be printed by a printing press and there can be thousands of dollars lost if the printer with the most efficient equipment for the job is not used. For example, if a publishing company only wanted to print 100 books as advance copies it might be less expensive to use a smaller printing company with smaller presses. But when the publisher wants to print 100,000 copies of the same book, it might be more efficient, and therefore profitable (in terms of cost per unit) to use a printer with a bigger press.

Sometimes the print jobs even run into the millions. Both Bill and Hillary Clinton's recent books had over a million copies in their first printings, and J.K. Rowling had a staggering 8.5 million copies in the first run of *Harry Potter and the Order of the Phoenix*, exceeded only by the 10.8 million copies printed of *Harry Potter and the Half Blood Prince* in 2005. Overall, knowing the niche of the different printing companies allows the production department to minimize costs and to reduce the amount of time it takes to get the book out to vendors.

The sales department is also an essential ingredient, and in large publishing companies, the sales force is often divided into subdivisions, each with a different target group of potential buyers. Small publishers, on the other hand, sometimes contract with an outside sales company because they do not have the resources to pay sales employees full-time. The function of the employees in a typical sales department is to knock on doors, in a sense, and convince bookstores, libraries, and wholesalers to carry their books.

The range of potential purchasers of their books can be from a small mom-and-pop bookstore in Wisconsin to a buyer in North Carolina who purchases for national accounts such as Barnes & Noble or Borders. Larger publishers have separate sales forces for independently owned bookstores, major bookstore chains, libraries, etc. Prospective buyers are shown the publisher's catalogue, which is typically produced one to two times a year. These catalogues, much like the ones from clothing stores that may be stacked on your coffee table, contain all of the items, in this case books, which the company has to offer for sale.

Since the members of the sales force are the ones who physically try to sell the book to vendors, wholesalers, and libraries, they often have a say in which books are accepted, because they are attuned to what "the market is looking for." Usually two times a year, the publishing editors, various in-house marketing and promotional experts, and the sales force will meet to discuss the new books for the season. The response of the sales force at these roundtable discussions can have a major influence on how hard the push will be to sell a particular book.

Larger companies also have ancillary rights and premium sales divisions. The ancillary rights division tries to sell the additional rights to a book, including movie rights, mass paperback rights, electronic rights, serial rights to magazines, and foreign rights. These are all ways for the publisher to make additional profits from the original book, and we will discuss all the types of rights in Chapter 21. The premium sales division usually sells books to companies or organizations that don't sell books, but give them away as promotions for their products, include them in employee benefit packages, or distribute them at training programs. This division might sell a high blood pressure book to a pharmaceutical company, whose sales representatives would give the book away to doctors. Or perhaps a *Fortune 500* company would be interested in purchasing 10,000 copies of Dale Carnegie's famous book, *How to Win Friends and Influence People*, because they plan to give it out to their employees during the Holiday season.

After reading this chapter, you hopefully now have a clearer picture of the behind-the-scenes workings of a publishing company. Try not to be intimidated by the size of some of the publishing houses or the volume of submissions that they receive. Think of a publisher like a popular New York City restaurant on a Saturday night: many people want to get in, not all will make it to a table, and those who do will likely have to wait a little while at the door. The upside is that there are many restaurants where you can eat in New York and if nothing seems appealing, you can make your own meal instead. After reading the "Paths to Print" section of this book and later learning how to submit eye-catching material, you will have the confidence to approach publishers until you find the right one. You will also be aware of innovative, accessible, and affordable options for self-publishing should that fit your needs and objectives.

CHAPTER 10

THE MULTI-FACETED GRAPEVINE: *How Publishers Let Readers Know About Books*

People buy romance novels, cookbooks, biographies, self-help books, children's books, and everything in between. Sometimes a buyer happens across a book with which they are unfamiliar and purchases it, but the most successful books are usually sold to buyers who have read reviews in local or national newspapers and magazines, seen the author's name or book title listed on a bestseller list, seen or heard the author on a radio or television show, or even more simply, spoken with someone who read the book. Behind many of these appearances, newspaper articles, and reviews is the publishing company itself—spending time and resources—to ensure that its books, in which thousands of dollars have already been invested, generate revenue for the company. In this chapter, we will cover the basic ways in which publishers promote authors and their latest titles. Later, in Chapter 20, you will learn how authors of all levels can promote themselves and their work, you will get advice from some of the leading publishing sales and marketing experts about successful promotional strategies, and we will impress upon you why you should always have a heavy hand in marketing and promoting your book, whether you are going through a large publisher or self-publishing. Never leave your sales up to Fate alone. Even if you are planning on self-publishing, read this chapter carefully because the behind-the-scenes activities of a publisher promoting titles may give you some do-it-yourself ideas for your own marketing efforts.

To begin with, you may wonder why a publisher doesn't make a heavy marketing push for every book to create a "buzz," if word-of-mouth, the end result of all marketing strategies, is the key to big sales. It is simply a matter of time and money; each publisher has many new books to share with the world at any given time, and, in general, these companies don't have a large enough staff and can't afford the financial risk of heavily promoting more than a few. These few are usually written by authors who have a track record and a built-in audience of thousands of readers who are salivating in anticipation of the next novel. Thus the publisher must spread its most concerted efforts across the top books for the season, not only for time and monetary considerations, but also because there are a limited number of PR spaces available in print, radio, and television. This kind of publicity is invaluable to publishers because it's free—as opposed to sending out materials and placing advertisements, which fall under the category of marketing and cost significant money up front. This is not to say that each publisher only makes an effort for a handful of books and ignores the rest; rather, the publisher must first focus on several top titles, and then use the remaining resources for the vast majority of their other titles. Even when the publisher does heavily promote a book, it's typically only for a three month period, unless sales are favorable. Oftentimes the three months isn't really enough time to jumpstart the sales because it's such a limited timeframe for readers to find out about the recently-released book.

Given that only certain books will get a high level of promotional attention, how do publishers determine how much money and energy is directed at marketing each book? A wave of excitement within a publishing company has a major influence on how much money is invested in the promotion of a book, in addition to the business predictions made by management as to what kind of returns can be expected from the book. One of the principal ways that they determine the potential sales is by figuring out the size of the target market for your book and what kinds of sales have been witnessed with other similar projects in the past. When you are accepted by a traditional publisher, you often fill out an author questionnaire, which contains information about you and your professional background, the specifics about what your book is about, what makes it unique, and why you think there is a viable market of readers for your work. All of this information helps the publisher estimate the sales levels, but, of course, there can be a significant margin of error in these calculations, since no one is ever 100% sure how the public will respond to a product.

Typically, publishers must take into consideration that they'll lose money on a certain percentage of the books published. However, this does not negate the budding enthusiasm of editors, sales representatives, and executives. The real driving force behind any wave of excitement can be ignited by quotes and praise on the back cover of the book from celebrities (actors, newscasters, talk show hosts, and other authors) or from a gut feeling that the book presents a hot topic, is the launching of the next big author, or is a literary masterpiece destined for a literary award.

Advance reviews, in popular publications or from celebrities or notable individuals in your field, are also a consideration in deciding how much money to put into promoting a book and can often act as a gauge for the publisher as to the book's eventual appeal. Critics, who may be free-lancers or full-time employees for a magazine or newspaper, receive more mail from publishers than celebrities do fan mail, but somehow they find the time to review books. Because of the volume of submissions they receive, critics typically prioritize the books to be reviewed by starting with the bigger name authors and the larger publishers, but they also will review the books from smaller publishers that present a unique idea or have generated a buzz with coverage in smaller publications. The degree of difficulty in getting a book reviewed by a prestigious source, like the *New York Times*, leads many smaller publishers and newer authors to attempt to have local and regional publications review their books, and then work their way up the limelight ladder, as they build a name. In terms of obtaining blurbs from celebrities or notable individuals, if you don't already have a target list in mind, you should ask the publisher's publicist for some suggestions and/or network with your friends and relatives. You are only six degrees of separation from a great quotation for your book jacket. It's always a good idea to be proactive and help your own cause by seeking out cover blurbs, since, in addition to reading the description of the book, many readers make purchasing decisions based on a quick glance at the book jacket or back cover for quotes from individuals whose names they recognize or for positive reviews from major publications.

At the time of the book launch, most large publishers send out press releases and copies of the book to the major publications around the country. Popular national magazines and newspapers, or specialized magazines that target the topic area of the book, can have a major impact on book sales if they give it a positive review or spin an engaging story about the book or the author. Many of these publications, such as the *New York Times,* the *Washington Post*, and *USA Today*, are considered leaders in public opinion. As you well know by now, the "buzz" generated by others is a major motivating factor in us trying a new product, whether it's going to a new release at the theater, using a new razor, or test driving a car. The word-of-mouth that these publications create can validate a literary work in the minds of purchasers, which is particularly useful for a newer author, since few readers know what to expect when they pick up a copy. A review in *Publishers Weekly* can be especially valuable to sales promotion, since most bookstore buyers, libraries, and even movie producers subscribe to it. But don't forget that the major publications typically thought of in association with book reviews are not the only place a sales-boosting review can appear. Reviews can be found in all kinds of publications and media. The *Library Journal* reviews books; radio shows review books; websites (both writing-related sites and also the blogs of everyday people) review books…the list goes on.

Occasionally an author wins the "PR lottery." A publisher can sometimes get a review or feature article on a book to run over the newswire if it has a finding of news value, such as something scientific or scandalous. So, if you catch a major politician setting up a secret bank account in the Cayman Islands to launder money or if you discover a new diet pill, and then you write about it, the buzz inspired by your book may sweep the nation! Anytime you can spark discourse on a subject (e.g. steroids and baseball, global warming, etc.), you may have the news stations scrambling to have you on air, sometimes without even knowing much about your book other than the subject and a little bit about your background, simply because they want to capitalize on a hot topic and bring in the most viewers or listeners possible. When this fortuitous situation occurs for an author, as in the case of *The Da Vinci Code* by Dan Brown, you will often see the publisher respond by mobilizing resources and personnel to heavily market the book. Author Malcolm Gladwell describes the seemingly miraculous phenomenon in his successful book, *The Tipping Point*, wherein a product (e.g. a book) or author suddenly reaches a point of saturation and acceptance where it or they are on the tip of people's tongues everywhere. The publisher always tries to keep in tune with the pulse of breaking news opportunities. Capitalizing on this can provide instant access to a market of potential readers.

Advertising in major magazines and periodicals tied to the publishing industry is also an option. Some examples of monthly and weekly publishing-related periodicals include: *Publishers Weekly*, *Book*, *Booklist*, *Book Links*, and *The Bookseller*. To call attention to the ad, the publisher will be sure to include eye-catching information, such as whether or not the author has had a best seller, won an award, or is well-known in a specific field. The next time you pick up a copy, observe how the publishers have chosen to present authors and build up their credentials.

Advertising, if placed in periodicals with large circulations, is very expensive, and it is therefore usually only reserved for the biggest name authors; however, publishers sometimes advertise for lesser-known authors in smaller publications or in trade magazines or association newsletters, because the cost is significantly lower. Many times they will approach book clubs to advertise in their monthly listing and mail-outs for new books (in addition to trying to convince the book club buyers to purchase copies). They also structure agreements with the national bookstore chains in which they pay the bookstore to promote several of the publisher's titles in a co-op advertisement or to promote an author's visit to particular stores around the country. With the advent and rise of Internet retailers, advertising options have expanded considerably in the past several years, with the ability to update information in real-time online and with millions visiting Amazon. com and BarnesandNoble.com daily.

Face-to-face marketing plays a large role in the sale of books, particularly if the publisher and the author continue to market a book over an extended period of time. Book tours are probably the most common type of in-person marketing, with the author making appearances on local, regional, or even national television and radio programs, while visiting bookstores in major cities across the country. Depending on the author and the subject of the book, publishers may also arrange speaking engagements at libraries, universities, *Fortune 500* corporations, non-profits such as AARP or the American Heart Association, and other venues where there are large audiences. We will explore speaking at bookstores and other locations in greater detail in Chapter 12 and Chapter 20, since it is a common activity for authors of all levels of publishing. In general, while they allow you to look your readers in the eye as you promote your book and sign and sell copies, book tours in and of themselves are not an end all. Likely, you will need to combine other elements of marketing and publicity to effectively sell your book in quantities. We will help you with the other elements in the coming chapters.

Besides arranging book tours and speaking events, representatives of a publisher, as well as the major authors published by the company, often attend the larger publishing conventions each year. Two of the largest are BookExpo America (www.bookexpoamerica.com) and the American Booksellers Association (www.bookweb.org), but there are also numerous regional and local conventions around the country and the world, such as the Maui Writers Conference (www.mauiwriters.com) and The Frankfurt Book Fair (www.frankfurt-book-fair.com). These events facilitate networking between editors, publishing executives, authors, literary agents, publicists, and graphic designers. These events keep the publishing company's name in the spotlight and enable them to keep abreast of the latest literary trends and the projects that may become the next big thing. These conventions are usually open to the public for a registration fee and can facilitate networking with publishing insiders and successful authors, in addition to helping you get a tan or brush up on your German.

Of course, not all large publishers or literary divisions within publishers use the same methods of marketing once a promotional budget is established, notes Laurie Rosatone, an editor with John Wiley, a large publishing house in New York. Her division of Wiley publishes only higher education textbooks, meaning that many of the more commercial means of publicity and promotion do not apply because they would prove to be less effective in reaching the targeted market of people in the academic fields. Most of their authors are professors or individuals with advanced degrees, so Wiley sends them to national professional meetings and conventions for academic groups, rather than to publishers' conventions, so they can get more visibility among scholarly peers from around the country. Since many of their buyers are professors or deans shopping for books to assign their students, Wiley mails textbook brochures directly to any professors or decision-makers who might require them for their courses. The publisher even organizes specialized workshops around the country aimed at promoting the discussion of curriculum development. These tactics allow them to showcase their materials to the audience most likely to purchase them—a crucial ingredient to having success in any kind of sales.

In addition to the mainstream ways to market books, some publishers have attempted more innovative ways to reach the masses. For example, several publishers have been offering advance copies of upcoming releases by popular authors to select resort destinations around the world. Guests of the hotel have the opportunity to read the latest works before they're available to the general public, while soaking in the sun in an exotic locale. Publishers hope that these individuals will spread the word when they arrive back in the United States, giving sales a jump start when the books are officially released.

Penitentiary Promoting

Sometimes publishers and creative publicists are able to set up in-person promotional events for authors at unconventional types of venues, which at first glance may seem like unlikely settings to increase book sales, but may actually fit well with the theme of the book and lead to bigger publicity in more conventional sales markets.

Ejovi Nuwere, author of *Hacker Cracker*, got the opportunity to appear on CSPAN-2 to promote his intriguing book, but he didn't find himself in a bookstore or in a library talking to average citizens. Nuwere presented his book and answered questions from the Orange County Correctional Facility in Orlando, Florida, where he was surrounded by a room full of inmates. His book traces his childhood in the tough Bedford-Stuyvesant, New York neighborhood, and his early stint as a computer hacker, before ultimately becoming a kickboxing champion and a security specialist for a large financial institution. The story struck a chord with the inmates, who could relate to his rough childhood and the mistakes that he had made in the past. Not only was he able to speak directly to an appreciative audience, but more importantly, he also received publicity and attention on a popular channel with viewers who read books on a regular basis.

How the "Little Guys" Make It

Smaller publishers generally use the same approaches to marketing as do large publishers, but they are typically working within a tighter budget, so they can't advertise heavily or send authors on national book tours. As a small business, they cannot afford to take as many financial risks as a larger publisher. There is also a lot of competition even for something as simple as book signing venues, with bookstores often choosing the bigger name author, who typically is published by the larger company, if there is a scheduling conflict. A small publisher may not even have the means to hire a full-time PR person, and they will instead hire an outside public relations firm to promote their books on an as-needed basis.

Based on what you have read so far, you might think that smaller publishers would not be able to sell any books, but don't despair if you are planning to use a small publisher; there is always a silver lining! The key to the success of smaller publishers is doing more with less, also known as "guerilla marketing." In Chapter 20 you will see that there are plenty of inexpensive, creative ways for authors to sell books—whether you go through a large publisher, a small publisher, or take the self-publishing avenue.

According to Barbara Witke, Director of Sales and Marketing for Peachtree Publishers, even though smaller publishers may not always have the resources and must make what they have go further, the personal attention that an individual author receives can more than make up for the shortage of funding. Peachtree is a smaller publisher which puts out mainly children's books, parenting guides, and self-help books. As a result of publishing so many children's books, the publishing staff is heavily involved in sending the authors to regional elementary schools as frequently as possible, in addition to setting up special local events for kids. In these sessions, the author reads to the children and makes contacts within the school system with those who might be interested in buying a large quantity of books. At a minimum, the author creates a "buzz" about the book among kids, parents, and teachers. These events also can potentially generate newspaper and television coverage locally and even nationally. It's not out of the realm of possibility for a book published by a small company to garner big media attention. In fact, this was the case with Peachtree's *Helping the Child Who Doesn't Fit In*, written by Stephen Nowicki Jr. and Marshall Duke, when they received media attention from Oprah, which, as any Book-of-the-Month author can attest to, is never a bad thing for book sales.

Publicity is cumulative, which often makes major network shows and articles in the *New York Times* the last stop, rather than the first, unless you are already a famous author or you have written about a hot topic in the news. Every time you see an author on a major television talk or news show or hear them on National Public Radio, there has likely been much legwork behind the scenes by a publicist, either from an outside firm or from within the publishing company. Publishers of all sizes, like most businesses, try to use media publicity to their advantage, since this is often the most economic way to quickly reach a large number of people. Sending out press releases and advance copies of a book to potentially interested radio and TV stations, in hopes that they will get coverage, is relatively inexpensive in relation to the thousands of dollars that it costs to place even a small advertisement in a national paper or a 15 second announcement on a syndicated radio show. Not to mention that appearing in the media in modern times seems to be a more effective way to market a product than simply advertising, which many viewers, readers, and listeners have learned to tune out.

Clearly there are many ways that a traditional publisher can promote and publicize an author. Not only do they have some financial resources, but they also have the know-how and the contacts necessary to be successful. While having the backing of a publisher can put you at an advantage in certain respects, you need not rule out your own potential for self-promotion; doing your own PR may even open up a whole new realm of creativity for you and can increase your chances of higher sales by supplementing the efforts of the publisher.

·**Marketing a book is a time-intensive and expensive process for a publisher, and because of the number of titles they produce every year, they cannot put resources into heavily promoting each book.**

·**There are a variety of ways publishers can promote books, including: having reviews and articles written in all sorts of publications, booking authors on radio and television, sending authors on book tours and to publishing conventions, and placing positive cover blurbs from celebrities, other authors, and relevant experts on the front or back cover of the book.**

CHAPTER 11

LITERARY AGENTS: *The Matchmakers of Publishing*

When you hear the word *agent*, perhaps visions come to mind of the smug and smooth-talking wheeler and dealer who represents a famous athlete or a major entertainer, who graces the cover of every sports or glamour magazine from coast to coast. The agent in this example negotiates the terms of a contract with either a sports team or with companies looking to offer endorsements. Unless you have the dunking ability of Michael Jordan or the face of a supermodel, you will probably not be requiring the services of this type of agent in your lifetime, at least not in your waking lifetime. Literary agents, on the other hand, are more accessible, represent all types of writers, and can help even a literary newcomer to become successful. Many, such as Lynn Nesbit, who has represented Michael Crichton for over 30 years, even develop long-term working relationships with their authors and help advance their careers. And, just like in the world of sports, the bigger name agents typically represent the bigger name authors, with the end result being that they negotiate extremely lucrative contracts for their A-list people.

You've probably read about various literary agents in passing, but if you are new to the publishing industry, you may be wondering what the exact responsibilities are for a literary agent. In the simplest sense, a literary agent presents an author's book to editors at publishing houses, with the ultimate goal of having it published and negotiating the most favorable contract for the author. Many literary agents have worked for publishing companies in the past, typically as acquisition editors, and they use their experience to the author's advantage. In return for their services, they typically receive 10-20% of the author's income from the sale of book rights.

How many times have you heard, "It's not what you know, it's who you know"? Probably enough times to believe it's true. However, in the publishing world, the "what" and the "who" are equally important, and literary agents have access to both: an extensive knowledge of the publishing industry and an impressive list of contacts at publishing companies. With all of the downsizing occurring in publishing companies, editors are increasingly relying on literary agents to screen manuscripts and only send them the most promising ones, to avoid being flooded with material. In fact, many of the largest publishing houses will only accept "agented" material because of the volume of submissions. It is reported that nearly 80% of all of the books that are published by traditional publishers come through agents.

Earlier we used the analogy of trying to land a traditional publishing deal as being as difficult as trying to get into a popular restaurant in New York. To further this idea, as many of us have experienced, knowing the right people in life can open doors that we sometimes can't open for ourselves for any number of reasons. In the publishing world, having the best literary agent for you and your project in your corner can make all the difference between getting a chance to sign on the dotted line or dealing with rejection letters.

So, there are many ways for you, as an author, to benefit from having a literary agent. First of all, they are tuned into individual editors' likes/dislikes and the current literary needs of different publishers, as a result of their relationships with acquisition editors. This enables them to send your manuscript to the publishers most likely to accept it. Conversely, the editors are familiar with the reputation of various agents, their tastes and interests when accepting new projects, and with the caliber of the authors and books that they represent, which can give you and your book credibility if you are as yet an unknown in the literary world. Agents are usually on top of the publishing industry—tracking trends and priorities—in order to best position your manuscript. They are more likely to get it read quickly than if you just sent it in yourself. Some agents will even offer their clients advice on how to improve their book proposals and manuscripts and help them to reframe their ideas before submission—a service that may be particularly important, because they have a good sense of how the manuscript must look in order for it to be accepted and for it to be marketable once it is released to the public.

Once a manuscript is accepted by a publisher, literary agents can handle the business side of dealing with the publishing industry as well. Even if you have sent in a manuscript on your own and had it accepted, you may still want to employ the services of a literary agent. Again, they understand author-publisher contracts, and their goal is to achieve the most lucrative deal for the author. In fact, Stephen King has admitted that, because he didn't have an agent in his early days, he was making millions of dollars for his publisher, and relatively little for himself, without even realizing that someone could have negotiated a much better deal for him. If you choose to go it alone in negotiations, the same may end up being true for you, even if you are dealing with much smaller dollar figures. This is particularly true if you have no negotiating or legal background.

In addition to royalties and advances, literary agents also market some of your subsidiary rights. Often they have working relationships with agents in other countries and can sell the foreign rights to your book, and sometimes agencies have different people who work on separate rights concurrently. One agent, for example, might try to get the manuscript accepted by a publisher in New York, while at the same time, another tries to sell the movie rights in Los Angeles. William Morris Agency, ICM, and Creative Artists, which represent actors, authors, screenwriters, and directors, are examples of large agencies with agents who specialize in different rights. It's possible that the agency might even approach a producer or an agent representing an actor such as Mel Gibson, Julia Roberts, or Tom Cruise, to determine if they would be interested in starring in a movie based on the book.

Once the book is available in bookstores, agents can do still more for authors. They can negotiate financial bonuses for the author from the publisher if their book wins certain awards, from smaller regional ones to highly prestigious awards such as The Pulitzer Prize or the National Book Award. A similar bonus may be secured for the author if the book makes one of the best-seller lists. Royalty checks can take a while to be sent out by publishing companies, and literary agents can track payments and ensure that they are made in a timely fashion, which could be particularly important if you are counting on the money. Even one step further, agents can also often convince the publisher to do more publicity or advertising for the book if it has good sales, thus keeping it in the public's eye and generating more income for the author.

INSIDE ADVICE FROM AN AGENT AND AN AUTHOR

Michael Larsen is one of the principals of the Larsen-Pomada Literary Agency (www.larsen-pomada.com) and also the author of several notable books for writers, including *Guerilla Marketing for Writers* (co-written with Rick Frishman and Jay Conrad Levinson), *How to Write a Book Proposal*, and *Literary Agents: What They Do, How They Do It, and How to Find and Work With the Right One for You*. As a well-respected literary agent who has worked with numerous successful authors, Larsen is one of the more qualified people to offer advice, especially since he's an author himself and can see things from both sides.

Like us, Larsen recognizes that even though writers are often the best promoters and sellers of their books, there are many reasons to hire an agent. They can help the author to package the book into something saleable, find the right editor and publisher that fits the subject, leverage their relationship with an acquisition editor to land the best deal from every angle, and ultimately guide the author along throughout their literary career.

As an agent, Larsen looks for books that have literary, practical, and commercial value, especially those with enough "promotional ammunition" to attract the larger New York publishers. He recommends following the advice on the formatting of submissions that he's offered in his power-packed books. Larsen, as an agent, is also attracted to books that lend themselves to a possible series, which the author would enjoy working on over the course of several months or years…many of the most successful books are part of a series, since the author becomes well-known for specializing in a certain market.

The following are his words of wisdom to all authors, even those with little experience.

> *You can write a book. It will probably take longer and be harder than you can know when you start it. Read what you love to read and write what you love to read. Become an expert on the kind of book you want to write. The editor who buys your book will be. If you get a lot of knowledgeable feedback as you write and learn from your mistakes, you can do it. The faster you fail, the faster you'll succeed. If you don't accept failure as an option, the only option left is success. You only fail when you stop trying.*

Although they provide valuable services, literary agents are not for everyone. A writer who is independent and self-reliant may not want another person negotiating the sale of their finished product for them, and instead may choose to approach publishers and negotiate contracts on their own. Perhaps a writer just doesn't want to give up a percentage of their income from the book to pay an agent, since their income often is already small if a book only targets a small market with a limited group of interested readers. Also, if your target audience is small, it may be an uphill battle to land an agent, since they tend to represent mainstream literary works, although they do occasionally focus on a specialized area. The reason that agents with a number of existing clients focus on the more mainstream, commercial ideas and themes is that they are working on commission in a way (taking percentage of your cut from the book). They are, therefore, reluctant to take on a project that they don't feel is widely saleable or that they aren't passionate about, knowing that they could spend a lot of time, but receive no income for their efforts if it doesn't sell.

So how do you find an agent who has the key to your success in the literary world? Literary agents operate within the local, national, and even global literary communities, although many tend to be clustered in New York (so they can "do lunch" with editors), and each agent specializes in representing certain types of literary works. The *Guide to Literary Agents* and *Writer's Market*, which are updated each year, are the two best resources for finding an agent who could potentially be the right match for you and your book. Both books offer listings of hundreds of literary agents and present the pertinent information about each literary agency. For example, you can find out about an agency's openness to submissions, their location, recent sales, contract terms, contact information, and which writer's conferences they attend. Checking the indices in each book, you can search for agencies by the subject material that they represent.

The two guides also offer information about pitfalls which writers can fall into with literary agents. In particular it is important to read the description of each agency carefully, so that contractual stipulations don't creep up on you. For example, a writer should find out whether a literary agent charges a "reading" fee. This fee, which can be as high as $500, must be paid even if the agency decides not to represent the manuscript and is essentially just a payment for the time spent evaluating it. Some agents who charge fees may give better feedback about a manuscript to the author, but the presence or absence of a reading fee does not necessarily reflect the inherent value of the agent. Just be aware so that you don't unwittingly commit yourself to needlessly spending your hard-earned money! Other expenses can include a critique fee and office expenses relating to marketing the manuscript to publishing companies.

Writer's Market and *Guide to Literary Agents* also list a number of agents who are members of the Association of Author's Representatives (AAR). Agents in this voluntary organization follow a code of ethics that keeps them from charging any kind of reading or consideration fees. New writers are encouraged to approach agents in this group with their material, since there is no initial financial obligation for the writer to fulfill, and thus less risk of expensive misunderstandings.

Finally, the two guides list contract terms for the agencies. This is important information, since some agencies only offer exclusive contracts with authors, meaning that by signing on with them, you agree to retain them as your agency for a set period of time or for a certain number of books. They also list the percentage of the proceeds, both domestic and foreign, that the agency receives for representing a writer's work.

For further information, check out *Guide to Book Publishers, Editors, & Literary Agents*, by Jeff Herman, and *Literary Marketplace* in print or on their website (www.literarymarketplace.com). Another great site, run by the witty and irreverent, Gerard Jones, is Everyone Who's Anyone (www.everyonewhosanyone.com), which has a listing and even a ranking of all of the agencies and agents. Agent Research & Evaluation (http://agentresearch.co.uk) lists several hundred notable agents and provides a match service for a fee, which can help narrow down the agents best suited to represent your book.

Beyond researching websites and print resources, you should always be looking for ways to meet agents in person—at speaking events, writer's conferences, or even directly through a mutual friend or business contact. Many authors have landed an agent as a result of a face-to-face meeting because it gave the writer a chance to have a dialogue with the agent in question, rather than the interchange being limited to an impersonal query or proposal. A personal encounter gives the agent more insight into who the potential client is—everything from their business demeanor to their passion for their projects, which is often a crucial ingredient for success with any literary work.

Once you have selected several potential agents or agencies to submit to, it's important to follow their guidelines for submission, not only to impress them with your professionalism, but also because most agencies only accept a small portion of the number of submissions received, and they may not even look at your work if it is not in the requested format. For example, some agencies only want a one-page query initially, while others may want a more elaborate proposal or even the manuscript. Read over the guidelines for each agency in the resources we've listed, and use *Writer's Market* for assistance with how to format your submission. Pick up a copy of *Author 101: Bestselling Secrets from Top Agents*, by Rick Frishman (who we feature in Chapter 20 in relation to marketing) and Robyn Freedman Spizman. Also, be sure to read Chapter 19 carefully, as it discusses how to impress an editor—a process that is very similar to that of convincing a literary agent that you should be their next client.

Overall, as you approach agents, be sure to not only follow their specific guidelines for submission, but to keep track of the dates when you send in material and the agents and agencies you've approached. It's best to start with just a few, perhaps 4-5 at a time, and give them a chance to respond, rather than taking the "shotgun" approach and spreading your material all over the publishing industry. Another key to success is to personalize your submissions to the agents. Always research the agent's name (Google seems to work nearly every time) to find out about other books and authors which they have represented. Explain why you would be the ideal next client for them to take on with your book, using this background information as a "warm" introduction. You can also find similar information and the details of recent publishing deals in the industry publication, *Publishers Lunch* (www.publishersmarketplace.com/lunch/free).

Overall, your research shows that you did your homework and are taking the process seriously, that you aren't necessarily just sending it to every agent whose name you come across, and that you know exactly what type of material typically appeals to that agent—all of which greatly increase your chances of acceptance.

If you do decide to employ the services of an agent, it's important to find one who believes in you and your proposal/literary project and is ready to go to bat for you, especially since you may develop a long-standing working relationship. Remember to be patient in your search; it is often just as difficult—if not more difficult—to find an agent who wants to represent you as it is to find a publisher for your book.

·**Deciding whether to enlist the help of a literary agent depends on your priorities for your book, how big a market you think it might attract, and how confident you feel about handling the business aspects of publishing and marketing your work.**

·**If you are interested in submitting to a literary agent, reference** *Writer's Market, Guide to Literary Agents,* **and the websites www. literarymarketplace.com and www.everyonewhosanyone.com.**

·**Be sure to follow the agent's guidelines for submission, do your homework on some of the recent works they have represented and the subject areas they are interested in, and read Chapter 19 for help in making your submission shine.**

CHAPTER 12

Booksellers and the Retail Market Under the Microscope

You are probably aware of the many venues in which authors and publishers sell books, from the independent bookstore in the basement of an old duplex to the modern mega-store offering you coffee and your favorite DVD's and CD's, to old-fashioned book clubs, to Internet sites such as Amazon.com and BarnesandNoble.com, and even to national supermarket chains and large retailers like Wal-Mart or Target, which sell millions of books per year. If you want to make the transition from a reader of books to a writer of books, then it will be valuable for you to know a little more about the sales process and how retailers work behind the scenes. Even though we all drive past our local bookstores and surf the web sites of the large Internet retailers, few of us are aware of the many steps involved in selling the more than 2 billion books—just in the United States—purchased by consumers each year. The Internet age has certainly reached the publishing industry with close to 50% of all books sold being processed through one of the many online retailers.

Libraries, schools, and associations, while not typically considered part of the retail market, are not to be overlooked. They are huge potential markets for bulk order book sales. In this chapter, which is meant for any writer, regardless of their chosen path to print, we will give you the inside scoop on how the retail industry operates, and, to keep you in the loop with the changing face of technology, we have added a section on Internet retailers.

For starters, how do retailers even know which books are available to sell? Booksellers typically purchase books from a publishing company after looking through the publisher's catalogue for that season and determining which ones they would like to carry. This is why it's especially important to work with your publisher to ensure your book is listed under the right subject or subjects in the catalogue, since many stores might only be interested in purchasing a certain number of titles from each genre or subject area. In the case of the large chains, the decision to carry a book in all the stores is made by a national buyer for the company. The publisher's sales team attempts to convince the buyer to purchase their books.

As is often the case in sales, landing a deal with the chain is difficult. There is a short time to pitch each of the publisher's books for that season, and therefore the salesperson must boil the entire book down to a few words, much like a salesman might make an "elevator pitch" to an executive. The publisher's sales team is often forced to describe it as "like" another book or as a cross between this author's work and that author's work. A funny mystery writer might be described as a cross between Jerry Seinfeld and Mary Higgins Clark, and the next big self-help author, may be compared to Deepak Chopra, Ken Blanchard, or Stephen Covey. Unfortunately, a book which has a complex plot or a unique theme, written by an up-and-coming author, might be tougher to describe, especially in a limited amount of time. But that's the nature of the publishing business. In terms of purchasing books, smaller, independent booksellers, as opposed to the larger chains described above, usually only have one person—the storeowner in many cases—who makes decisions about which books to buy and because of limited resources, may have to be very selective in the titles the store chooses to carry.

According to Susan Driscoll and Diane Gedymin in their book *Get Published!*, bookstores decide what to stock based on 5 principal criteria: the book's quality, its cover design, the plans for any marketing or publicity campaigns surrounding the book, the author platform (essentially how well known the author is and their access to speaking or media outlets), and the track record, either for the author's other titles or if this is a new genre for the author or the author is a first timer, the sales for similar titles by other authors.

Booksellers typically purchase their books from the publisher at a 40-50% discount off the cover price and generally obtain them on consignment, meaning that they have a certain amount of time in which to return any unsold copies that they don't wish to carry any longer, without having to pay for them. Usually the store has 90 days to return hardbacks and trade paperbacks or to return the torn off covers of mass paperbacks (the more common type of paperback). Since the mailing expenses may exceed the cost of printing the inexpensive mass paperbacks, the bookstore is requested to only return the cover, which guarantees that the book can't be sold. In an effort to minimize losses and prepare for the next round of titles that will hopefully make them money, publishers will even remainder some of their titles, meaning that they sell them to retailers below the 40-50% discount, and the retailers in turn deliver it to you, the consumer, at a fraction of the original list value on the cover.

Bookstores will only shelf a book at full price longer than 90 days if it is continuing to sell; otherwise, they return the remaining copies within the grace period or, in some cases, offer steep discounts to ensure that consumers purchase what's left of their supply, rather than returning them to the publisher. With the limited amount of shelf space in any store and hundreds of new books coming in, they must allocate space based on which books are selling. As you may have experienced, the customer can still order the book via the computer database in the bookstore, but they won't come across the physical copy when they are browsing. Some titles stay on the bookstore shelf for years, while others may only last a few weeks, depending on sales and ultimately decisions by management.

Consignment purchasing was a practice that, like Welfare and Social Security, was established during The Great Depression and has lasted until today. The rate of return on books has generally been 20-30% and fluctuates to reflect the state of the American economy. It comes as no surprise, then, that the return rate in the year 2001 reached as high as 40%, given the slumping American economy in the wake of 9/11.

We've talked about what happens when a book doesn't rake in the profits for a bookstore, but what happens if a book does really well and the bookstore sells out of it? In this case, the bookstore typically contacts a book distributor or wholesaler, who stores copies of the book in a warehouse. Or they may choose instead to go directly to the publisher, depending on the timeframe for receiving the needed books. While the terms "wholesaler" and "distributor" are often used interchangeably, the principle difference between distributors and wholesalers is that distributors are more proactive in trying to place copies of the books they carry in bookstores and they make use of a sales force. Many times bookstores will also purchase their first run copies of books from book distributors, such as Ingram Book Group or Baker & Taylor, instead of from the publisher. However, distributors are particularly useful once books start selling in the store, after the launch from the publisher. Booksellers opt for distributors and wholesalers so they can save on orders by buying in bulk, can combine orders for books from a variety of publishers, and can have them faster than they would by contacting the actual publishers. Ingram, the largest wholesale book distributor in the U.S., has millions of books in storage, and can immediately ship on demand.

Even self-published authors can have their books handled by distributors who warehouse the book at one location and sell it to a larger distributor or to bookstores; however, the author has to pay certain fees such as for storage and shipping and has to give up a certain percentage of the profits to the distributor. In addition, some distributors will only take you on as a client if you publish a certain number of titles per year. If you are a self-publisher, the advantage of using a distributor is that it's a more cost-efficient way to reach a larger sales base than if you had to cold call individual bookstores. For further assistance in working with wholesalers or distributors, be sure to visit the website for Ingram (www.ingrambook.com) and for Baker & Taylor (www.btol.com), which specializes in schools, libraries, and independent bookstores. For a more comprehensive list of distributors and wholesalers, go to www.literarymarketplace.com (or pick up the print version) and also try marketing expert John Kremer's website (www.bookmarket.com).

In addition to the raw sales figures, determining how many of each type of book to order and where they should be positioned in the store is an important issue in many of the major retail chains. Bookstores typically provide premium space near the entrances to the store for new releases by the more popular authors. The publishing company of each author often pays the bookstore for this space; therefore only the biggest names or the hottest books are given this advantageous position. To this end, Borders, the second largest retailer, has even started doing aggressive market research using focus groups, polling, and exit interviews. Currently, all bookstores can really do is track inventory, but they hope that this new information will help them determine which books to group together and how they can adjust pricing to fit demand. Many Internet retailers, such as Amazon.com, are already similarly tracking the buying trends, and during the checkout process, online shoppers are shown lists of other titles that might be of interest to them.

Beyond helping to determine inventory size and the placement in prime locations in the stores, tracking sales of individual books provides the necessary information to create bestseller lists. Publications, such as the *New York Times*, the *Los Angeles Times*, *USA Today*, and many other large publications, rely on a few thousand bookstores and several wholesalers nationwide to generate their weekly lists. After collecting the numbers from these sample stores each week, they weight these sales based on the location of the stores to try to come up with a national representation of total sales. The bestseller lists are tallied from sales for only that week, which is how books in their first week of release often take the spots of those which have been on the list for several weeks. In regional publications, the data may only come from the stores in that geographic region, meaning that if you can start to build an audience and a sales record on a grassroots level, you may get the title of "Bestselling Author" sooner than you think. Local or regional accolades gain you instant credibility and create a ripple effect that could quickly help you become a bestselling author in another, larger publication (you can only hope that it will eventually be the *New York Times*).

Many stores and internet retailers even have their own best seller lists; Amazon.com and BarnesandNoble.com rank every book on their sites and update these lists nearly continuously. In a smaller bookstore the posting of top books, based on sales in that individual store could be significant. The popularity of the book just in the hometown independent bookstore could lead to greater attention from the literary world beyond. The customers who find out about it may generate hype by emailing, calling, or writing to friends or acquaintances to rave about the book, which could lead to the book being sold all over the country or the world. Tracking sales and understanding the laws of supply and demand are crucial in the business world—they become major factors in the decision-making process for where resources should be allocated, which products should be heavily marketed, and even what types of ideas the company should be looking to bring to market in the future. The publishing world is no different, with each house tracking sales of books using Nielsen BookScan (www. bookscan.com), which is basically like the Nielsen ratings that we hear so much about in relation to *American Idol* or *CSI*. However, this website is exclusively for the literary community.

In order to create a "buzz" for themselves and not just the authors whose books they sell, and also to find out about new advances in the industry, many booksellers attend national association meetings, such as the American Booksellers Association, as well as smaller, regional events. These gatherings allow them to find out about new books and meet authors, publishers, agents, and editors. Regional outlets of large bookstore chains often have a community relations person who, apart from attending conventions, sets up local events to attract customers, such as book signings or workshops with authors. Usually the community relations people approach local and regional authors for local book events, but they may occasionally be able to get a bestselling author to sign books at the store while they are in town on a publicity tour for a book. Independent bookstores similarly approach authors, though they tend to host smaller events and focus almost exclusively on showcasing local authors.

RESHAPING THE RETAIL MARKET FOR THE NEW MILLENNIUM

Over the past five years or so, the Internet has had a dramatic impact on how books are purchased. Most people are familiar with the biggest Internet retailers such as Amazon and Barnes & Noble, which also sell a plethora of other products, but there are also many others like Alibris (www.alibris.com), which sell millions of books. Ebay hosts the auctions of thousands of books, new and used, between individuals, bookstores, and wholesalers. It even recently featured an auction for charity, wherein bidders could bid on the opportunity to select character names that would be appearing in upcoming novels of notable authors. All of the print-on-demand companies sell their books on their websites, in addition to partnering with the largest Internet retailers. Even the larger traditional publishers are in on the act, with the majority becoming aggressive at boosting their own website hits, in order to sell their books directly to consumers.

Aside from the world's movement towards the Internet in general, why the rush to sell books online? It is simply a matter of benefits over costs, and every party involved in purchasing and selling books on the Internet benefits in some way. As an individual consumer you have the convenience of being able to purchase books from your home and have them shipped to you in a few days. The search engines provided on the largest retailers allow you to find the book or type of book you want with the greatest of ease. The selection of books is generally larger, since, as we mentioned, Internet retailers and publishers are not constrained by shelf space. Also, books can stay in print longer, and therefore remain available for purchase.

Selling books on the Internet, with all of the electronic versions or scanned pages that can be placed on websites opens up a whole new realm of possibilities. Many of the largest Internet retailers are rolling out plans to sell books to readers by the page. Stephen King was perhaps one step ahead of the curve, when he sold individual chapters of one of his books one-at-a-time on his own website several years ago. Essentially, these changes to the structure of the retailers are allowing readers to "virtually" browse books by paying a nominal fee for a few pages, rather than buying the whole book at once, having to pay for shipping, and then waiting several days for the product to arrive. So, like your counterparts whose books are selling in the "physical" bookstore, make sure that your first few pages are captivating. Readers can now make "virtual" snap decisions about whether to purchase your work, as most of us do in a Barnes & Noble or a Borders store when we snatch up a book by an author with whom we are unfamiliar.

All authors benefit considerably from selling their "physical" books on sites like Amazon.com, BarnesandNoble.com, or Alibris.com. First of all, any author, even a self-published one, can have their books listed and made available to the global marketplace, a feat that was nearly impossible ten years ago. Many self-published authors who have their own websites (or even those who are traditionally-published, but want to promote themselves through their site), choose to sell their books on their own site, but do so by providing links to the major Internet retailers. In essence, the author is drumming up the business, but wants the retailers to handle the monetary and physical logistics side of things (credit card processing, shipping, etc.). This setup is a particularly wise option for the author who is just beginning in the publishing industry. Of course, some authors run their websites as an extension of their business and may be set up to accept and fulfill orders, therefore cutting out the "middle man."

For authors desiring to learn readers' opinions of their work, many retailers' sites offer buyers an opportunity to rate and comment on the book. Internet retailers even rank the book sales on their site, so that an author or buyer can know how a book is selling relative to the rest of the crowd. This is an innovative feature, but one that could have both positive and negative effects on you. You'll either simply check in once in a while and appreciate knowing how your book is selling or you will sit in front of your computer, hitting the refresh button every few seconds, tracking your progress constantly. For your own sanity, try not to fall into the latter category of response!

Even further, when trying to get a book published or to create a unique spin in a press release and garner some attention, the websites of Internet retailers are an excellent tool to help you determine which competing titles are out there, so that you might emphasize the unique aspects of your work. In most types of business including publishing, differentiation is often the key to turning heads and selling copies.

Publishers also profit for many of the same reasons. Purchases and payments are easier to track on the Internet, meaning that publishers get paid faster and they are notified immediately when changes of inventory occur—a crucial component of eliminating the lag...when there is a high demand, back-orders, and more books need to be printed. Keeping track of inventory used to be a Herculean task for traditional publishers (and still is to some degree), but instant computerized feedback has lessened the burden and lowered the costs. Retailers selling books on the Internet also open the door for innovative and aggressive marketing campaigns, with the publisher being able to strategically place advertisements on the high traffic pages of the site or in areas where certain readers with special interests are likely to browse.

LOST AND FOUND ON THE INTERNET

Self-published authors appreciate Internet retailers like Amazon. com because they provide an easily accessed portal for selling books to readers all over the world. Buyers use Amazon.com because they can select from hundreds of thousands more books than they could ever find in a major bookstore. But sometimes this relationship can have hilarious consequences. The following story comes from Karen Smith:

My husband Pete and I were busy in our real estate careers in the late 80's, when he got the idea that he would try his hand at writing a novel. He had never written anything of this length before, but I encouraged him to pursue it. Every time he had an open house to showcase to potential buyers, he would spend the down time working on this novel. The book was titled The Chiffon Strangler and it had a complicated plot loaded with intrigue, murder, and love affairs.

After he finished it, he paid a couple of thousand dollars to have about 2,000 copies of it self-published. I read over the completed version and quite frankly I was a little frightened. Some of the plot mirrored our life and I wasn't sure whether I was the girlfriend or the wife. I honestly thought that he might be leading a secret life. Needless to say, we were reluctant to show it to our four kids, even though they knew about it, because we didn't want them to know that their father had written the steamy scenes...

He sold a few copies here and there over the years and sent out about 200 to movie stars and Hollywood producers, hoping that maybe they would make a movie out of it. He never heard back from anyone and the remaining copies mostly just stayed in a few boxes in the garage, which unfortunately made the trip each time we moved into a new house. Finally, I told him that he needed to get rid of them, but rather than just throw them away, he donated them to a charity halfway across the country in Boston, thus ending the saga of <u>The Chiffon Strangler</u>*...or so we thought.*

Just recently, quite a few years after donating them to the charity, we got a phone call from our son. I almost dropped the phone when he said, "Mom, guess what I'm reading right now?" Apparently his wife wanted to get him something special for his birthday, knew about the book Pete had written, did a little searching on Amazon.com—and presto—the long lost book was in the hands of our son after we thought it had been sent to its "literary grave."

As a self-publisher or a traditionally published author looking to boost sales and increase your revenue stream you should focus on bookstores and other retailers. Having your book listed on Amazon.com, BarnesandNoble.com, and other such sites is fairly simple, and there is information on each website that details how to submit and set up an account. This is also true of most wholesalers or distributors that you will come across.

If you want physical copies in local bookstores, approach the smaller ones first. Bring at least ten copies and try to convince the owner or manager to allow you to keep them shelved for a month or two—at least enough time for you to get sales rolling and pay for the original cost of printing the books. Try to keep any "pitches" that you might give to the staff to stock your title to less than a minute...the so-called "elevator pitch." If you can't encapsulate your work in a minute or less, the bookstore staff certainly won't be able to do it for a customer who asks about your book down the road. Come prepared with ammunition for your "pitch." Explain why there is a need for your book, why you are the person to write it, how your book presents a fresh perspective, and even about special promotions that you could work out with them that would benefit both parties.

Once you are in the door, establish the system for you to get paid for the sale of your books (usually you have to wait 90 days to get paid). You are now ready to start marketing your books to readers, since they can now find them and purchase them. Be sure to check back with the store to ensure that they don't run out of copies. After building a base in the smaller stores, try your hand at the larger chains. Also, don't forget to pursue other retailers such as drug stores, gift shops, and pet shops, especially if you have a book that might appeal to their customer base.

If the book retail industry appears slightly more complex to you after reading this chapter, don't be concerned. If someone were to explain to you how Coca-Cola runs their corporation, they would give a more in-depth answer than just "they make soft drinks." Often, the backstage activities are more complicated than what the customer sees upfront; however, once you get into the thick of the operations, it becomes more understandable.

In the case of Internet retailers, try not to be intimidated if you don't consider yourself to be a "technical" person. Remember, good writing, clever ideas, and unique creativity, which everyone possesses, are the backbone of writing and selling a book. The same positive attitude and attention to detail that help you in other aspects of the publishing industry will also allow you to overcome any challenges on the way to getting your books in the bookstore, whether physically or virtually!

·**Booksellers vary in terms of size, organizational structure, and whether they are physical or "virtual."**

·**By following the advice in this chapter and persisting, you *will* be able to get copies of your book placed in bookstores and listed on Internet retailers, and you will be on your way to finding readers around the globe!**

·**Visit our website (www.getbetweenthecovers.com) and use the Important Links section to access Amazon.com and BarnesandNoble.com. For any click-through revenue that is generated, we pledge to donate 20% of the proceeds to multiple literary awards and grants for students in both secondary schools and colleges and universities, as part of the programs that we are establishing within those institutions.**

PART 3

PATHS TO PRINT

Now that you have a better general understanding of the writing process and how the publishing industry functions internally and externally, it's time to move on to specifically how to publish your book. After all, that is likely one of the principal reasons you are reading this book in the first place. As previously mentioned, you are fortunate to come along at such an ideal time in the evolution of the publishing industry. Instead of there only being "two paths diverging in the woods," as poet Robert Frost noted in a famous poem, there are many different ways to publish, with each one offering advantages and also challenges for the author.

Even if you already have an idea of which "path to print" you would like to pursue, we recommend that you read every chapter because you might just learn something new about another option, which changes your mind. Or, even if you don't use an alternative route to publish this time, you may for a future book project. Once you have read each chapter and understand the advantages and disadvantages of that respective option for publication, you can make an intelligent decision as to which one is right for you at this time. You will likely need to do a little more research from there, which is why we have referenced other sources in these chapters that are catered to those avenues for publishing. Also, remember that if one path does not work out, the publishing process does not need to end. There's always another option to try out. Over the years, thousands of authors have continuously attempted alternative approaches until they got their material into the hands of the public. Tenacity pays off...eventually you will have success and may even end up being able to publish using your original "first choice" of publication options.

Even though we've listed the options in a particular order, bear in mind that it has nothing to do with which one is better or worse for you. Only you, the reader/future author can decide which path fits your goals and objectives, and then time and fate will help determine the direction the process will ultimately lead you. To help you compare the key points of each option, we have included a table summarizing the paths to print at the end of this section. Also, it should be noted that we haven't included audio books as a form of publishing, even though over 20 million Americans listen to them while doing such things as driving or running on a treadmill. We consider this an ancillary right, which is a product of you getting your manuscript to market using one of the forms of publication that involves written words.

CHAPTER 13

TRADITIONAL PUBLISHING:
A Tradition Like Many Others

They travel by air, land, and sea. *Thousands* of them migrating every year from one location to another. Their sheer numbers alone make it extremely difficult to settle at their destinations and causes many of them to return to where they started. It is a matter of available space, and there is simply not enough of it for all of them to find a new home. Who or what are *they*? They are not Canadian geese or Northerners headed to Florida for the winter; *they* are the manuscripts, queries, and book proposals of writers who hope that they can find a place in the traditional publishing industry.

But why the rush to the path of greatest resistance, as compared to the other publishing options? Traditional publishing, although sometimes difficult and frustrating, does have certain inherent advantages over the other paths to print. It has a great success rate in helping you achieve your goals, whether you want to reach a small, scattered market of people or whether you desire to sell copies to masses and generate a considerable source of income from your book. Not to mention that traditional publishing, like many other long-standing, established institutions in our society, is what the everyday person is familiar with, since its output represents the majority of what they see in Barnes & Noble or Borders. In general, people haven't yet realized that books are published in numerous other ways beyond the traditional publishing company route. Even though there are a number of alternatives to traditional publishing, it will likely always remain at the forefront of the publishing industry, and, with so many publishers out there, you have plenty of opportunity to find one who wants your book and can give you the personal attention that you need.

With a positive attitude and a certain degree of persistence, you may be able to pursue this type of publishing as your path to print. In the next few chapters you will learn about all of the ways to publish your book, and if things don't work out in traditional publishing, there are others paths for you, especially if your book is meant to target a smaller audience or if you want to have more control over the project.

As a starting point, one of the biggest advantages to traditional publishing is that you do not have to invest any money for printing, as you would in other forms of publishing. This can be a significant consideration for you. In addition to you not having to make any withdrawals from your bank account to cover expenses of the book, in some cases, publishers may even offer you a cash advance against your royalties upon acceptance of a book proposal, depending on your publishing track record, the book itself, your professional background, and the size of the publisher. You will receive a percentage from the sales of each book, in addition to a cut of the money that the publisher or your agent can obtain for the sale of other rights of the book, such as foreign language, magazine excerpt, or even movie rights. With a traditional publisher you have a much better chance of selling these ancillary rights because someone with experience and contacts is taking the lead for you. In traditional publishing, you may even be offered a multi-book deal once you have had some initial success, and, in fact, this is the case for a number of authors. Everything essential to know about rights and publishing deals will be covered in Chapter 21.

Another advantage of going with a traditional publisher relates to *reaching your target readers*. If you are only writing a book for your family and friends to enjoy, marketing is not a difficult task; however, reaching national or even international readers takes a sizable effort. Even though in Chapter 10 we offered that most publishers do not have the resources or time to heavily market every book, because of the financial cost and time constraints, traditional publishing will increase your chances of getting your book reviewed in newspapers and magazines or landing TV, radio, and print interviews. A traditional publisher will also help in the arranging of signings in bookstores that allow you to connect locally with readers and fans. Your publisher will include your book in their seasonal catalogue and a sales force will push your book to national bookstore chains, local stores, book clubs, and wholesalers, ensuring that there are many ways for readers to find and purchase your work. But, by no means, should you just turn in your manuscript and rest on your laurels. Stay actively involved in every aspect of the project, particularly the marketing and promotion, if you want to end up with the best finished product and reach more readers.

Having a better chance of getting exposure and reaching your target readers is obviously advantageous. If your goal is to educate others, it means that your knowledge will likely be imparted upon more people. If you want to increase your sales and generate significant income, traditional publishing may be your answer. A corollary to this would be that if you have hopes of your book becoming a best seller—a slim chance using any type of publishing—then traditional publishing is your best bet. However, don't be dismayed if you are planning on self-publishing. It's not only traditionally published authors who make it to the "big-time." There are hundreds of stories of authors who have self-published books that garnered media attention and sold a significant number of copies. So, if having more control draws you to the other paths to print, but you still want to be successful with the book, don't despair. It is absolutely possible to self-publish and achieve the success; it just means that you must rely more on yourself to make it happen.

Another benefit of traditional publishing is that the publisher handles the business—everything from printing to shipping to billing, and the company has a team of individuals who are knowledgeable about the industry, including editors, PR specialists, publicists, and sales people. While these people have the power to reject manuscripts and may reject yours, which may leave you with a feeling that they are anything *but* knowledgeable, just remember that accepting or rejecting manuscripts is nothing personal. They are simply making decisions based on what they feel they can sell, in order to recoup their upfront production costs and operational expenses. Think of it this way: you can benefit from any rejection by using the feedback or commentary to help you improve your manuscript. You don't have to agree with all their criticisms, but it doesn't hurt to look at your work from a new angle and see if there are places where you can improve it.

GOOD THINGS COME IN SMALL PACKAGES

There are literally thousands of traditional publishing companies out there. When considering the range of options, from international billion dollar conglomerates to local one-person shops, remember that bigger is not necessarily better. Many smaller publishers are known for publishing books for niche markets (e.g. religious, inspirational, or graphic) whose avid readers keep these companies and their authors successful. Authors choose to go with smaller publishers for a variety of reasons—from wanting to target a specific regional audience to wanting more personal attention and guidance. Even bestselling author, Tom Clancy, when he wrote *Red Storm Rising*, nearly opted for a smaller publisher who couldn't even come up with 20% of the offer he had from another larger publisher. He simply felt a sense of loyalty to them because they accepted his first book, *The Hunt for Red October*, which launched his career.

Beyond the specialization in certain genres and being able to market to select groups of people, there are a number of other reasons to work with one of the thousands of smaller publishers, including university presses. Not only will they give you more personal attention in working with your manuscript to get it ready for publication, but they are also likely to spend more time promoting you than a much larger house with hundreds of titles coming out that season, which could lead to you building a speaking and readership platform to open your literary career. Of course, the smaller publisher doesn't have the same resources as the larger one, but personal attention is worth more than a marketing budget to many an author. Despite not having the same cash flow, smaller publishers have unique opportunities open to them that can help you to launch your literary career or expand the reach of your hobby. An example would be offering you a chance to win the Pushcart Prize, an award given by an organization that chooses the best fiction that comes exclusively from small presses, which they feature in a yearly compilation. Many authors, including Edward P. Jones, who recently won the National Book Critics Circle Award and The Pulitzer Prize for his novel *The Known World*, got their first dose of publicity courtesy of the Pushcart Prize. Countless other opportunities for the author published by an independent press abound, and, of course, you are still eligible (just like the authors from the big houses) for many of the big national grants, fellowships, and literary awards given each year.

Editors Can Be "Good Guys" (or Gals)

If your manuscript is accepted by a publishing company (by the way, you always want to keep a copy when you send it out to publishers) an editor will help with broad-stroke editing, while a copy editor will check grammar and spelling. As a whole, the editorial team can guide you in making your book more reader-friendly and coherent or make suggestions to improve the development of the characters or the plot. These are crucial elements in creating a finished copy that looks sharp and professional. With another path to print, you would either have to edit it yourself, which is a tall order for most people, or hire a freelance editor, who may not have the experience, connections, or loyalty to your project.

Publishing company editors also may have innovative suggestions for ways to make your book unique because of their wealth of knowledge of the marketplace and what has been successful in the past. They also help in selecting a title, designing an appealing cover, coming up with a biography and summary of the book, and they can obtain quotations or blurbs from other recognized authorities, authors, and celebrities. Needless to say, editors are likely to mold the manuscript into its best possible form in ways that most people are unable to do for themselves. Access to their expertise is, therefore, a major reason to go the traditional publishing route.

The following three authors are featured in this chapter because they represent the range of publishing experiences within the traditional publishing industry. Many authors will choose to pursue the largest publishers with their manuscripts, while others will forego the potential for a bigger advance and opt for the personal attention and support from a smaller publisher.

OVERCOMING THE ODDS

Every successful writer was unknown at one time and faced the same seemingly insurmountable odds of having their work accepted by a traditional publisher, especially a major one. Catherine Cantrell, author of *Constance*, which was recently published by Random House, had her doubts and low moments while submitting manuscripts for publication. However, she stayed focused by concentrating on one agent or publisher at a time, thus avoiding the feeling of being overwhelmed—a feeling that we believe has caused many manuscripts to never end up leaving the home of the author. Her focus was very similar to the *1% Solution* which we mentioned in Chapter 4, as it related to planning the manuscript before working through it. In her case, she sketched out a well-organized plan of attack for pursuing publishers before ever sending out a manuscript or even a query letter. Thus, she was able to keep a handle on the process and be the most efficient with her time.

Despite her planning and positive attitude, Cantrell's manuscript was rejected by an agent early on, as she tried to land a representative to serve as an intermediary with a possible publisher. Instead of being discouraged; however, she let the rejection fuel her and spent six months rewriting her book—a decision that made all the difference. "When I look back on it now, I think I was fortunate that this earlier version of *Constance* wasn't accepted because it forced me to write a better book. Sometimes rejection turns out to be a blessing in disguise."

Her persistence eventually paid off when a friend introduced her to his editor at Random House and her newly-revised manuscript was accepted. Not only did Cantrell have the opportunity to receive the backing of such a large publisher, but she also fell under the tutelage of a key executive with the publisher and with Pulitzer Prize-winner William Styron, who both happened to be graduates of her alma mater. In fact, she recommends turning to the alumni network of your college or university first when looking for an "in," because you might be able to establish a genuine rapport with them, and any assistance that they can provide, in addition to their friendship, is a big plus in the traditional publishing industry.

Even though connections are important, and Cantrell believes you should do your best to cultivate them, she recommends two additional strategies in order to increase your chance of success. First, you should read the work of writers who speak to you because they will show you your passions and guide you to where you will make the greatest literary contribution. Second, instead of starting out spending a lot of your time and energy battling to gain acceptance—though sometimes tough to do with the feeling of the need to complete a lingering task hanging over your head—you should first devote yourself to your writing. It will lead to the best finished product and your greatest chance for success in breaking onto the literary scene if you focus fully on one task at a time. Following this advice will more than make up for the time that you could have spent selling an "unpolished" manuscript.

Cantrell's success in the traditional publishing industry comes because she "loves" writing enough to have made sacrifices and to face the possibility of rejection, recognizing the many benefits that the path has offered her. Her take on the importance of writing in her life mirrors our thoughts on why you should try your hand at your own book. Cantrell says, "Almost all the good things in my life have come to me through writing. It's brought wonderful people into my life; it's allowed me to connect with other human beings, and it's expanded my inner world immeasurably."

CORPORATE THRILLERS BACKED BY BUSINESS SAVVY

Don Corace is a former roughneck from the oilfields of West Texas and is now a real estate developer in Naples, FL. Writing came as a secondary activity in his life, as it often does for many new writers who have families to support and primary careers to maintain. Corace feels right at home writing in his genre—the corporate thriller, and his debut novel, *Offshore*, is a brilliant mixture of offshore well drilling, murder, greed, and romance. It has received significant attention, including rave reviews from nationally syndicated radio host, Neil Boortz and an appearance on *Hannity and Colmes* on Fox News, in which Sean Hannity compared him to John Grisham. Following his motto that "Character is plot," Corace focuses on each individual player in his novel as he unravels a behind-the-scenes look at the oil industry. Corporate greed, a recurring element in *Offshore*, is a theme that he wants to weave into future novels about other industries. After spending years reading the bestselling books of Tom Clancy, John Grisham, and Robert Ludlum, he had an epiphany one day, while visiting his wife's family farm in Sweden. It suddenly struck him: "I could really do this."

While Corace was certainly not lacking in his writing ability, he fine-tuned his talent and approach over the course of hundreds of pages. When looking ahead to the publication process, a smaller publisher in Texas made the most sense for him to work with because it was in line with his tastes and allowed him to keep more control of his book than a larger publisher would have. Not to mention that he was able to negotiate a favorable deal and obtain higher royalty percentages in his contract than what most authors receive from a larger publisher. Recognizing that going with a smaller publisher typically results in a smaller promotional budget, he used his own money and enlisted the help of Rick Frishman and his team at a leading book publicity firm, Planned Television Arts (both of which we featured in Chapter 20). Employing Planned Television Arts enabled him to do over 100 satellite radio interviews, including 25 in one morning alone, and led to other major media appearances. He also took advantage of the timeliness of his novel, which related to the oil industry and drilling in the Gulf of Mexico, in light of the rising price of oil at the time and the number of wells that needed repair in the wake of Hurricane Katrina. He made an appearance at the largest oil conference in the world in Houston, enabling him to start to spread the word among the 50,000 attendees.

Overall, beyond just his writing, which has often been compared to that of Michael Crichton, for his ability to take current issues and wrap them into great fiction, it's Corace's experience as a businessman and leader that's helped him to navigate the publishing industry successfully. He understands the mechanics and back-office operations of the industry, and, due to his success with *Offshore*, he will be able to land major publishers in New York for future fiction and nonfiction books, which are in development right now. Some of these works are so innovative and timely, that he will probably appear on national television and radio shows again and continue to build his name and his readership. His experience demonstrates the success that you can have in going through a smaller publisher and also the doors that it can open for you to the much larger publishers, if you've got a great writing style and the ability to help your publisher to market.

WEAVING THROUGH THE WILDERNESS

Connie Bransilver, a conservationist and photographer, has traveled all over the world for her work—from communing with lemurs in Madagascar to going on safari alone in rarely traversed regions of central and western Africa. She made her entrance into the traditional publishing industry almost by accident. Bransilver, a resident of Southwest Florida, had been taking photographs in the swamps of the Everglades with another conservationist/photographer, Larry Richardson, when the two came across a book of regional photographs by another author. They had already been successful selling their own individual photographs of the flora and fauna of the region to national and international magazines, but together they believed that they could put together a superior book—one with better photographs and more information.

Given the excessive land development in the area, Bransilver and Richardson wanted to educate the public on the natural habitat of the Everglades—unequalled anywhere on Earth—believing that educating the public could lead to a greater conservation effort. The angle that they decided on would be, in Bransilver's words, the "Disney spoon full of sugar" one, in which the beauty of the subject would be focused on, in contrast to the work of many photographers which highlights the darker, bleaker side of the state of the environment.

During the collaborative process, Bransilver started researching and seeking out the publishers which could combine good marketing and an interest in conservation with the ability to reproduce their images at a high quality. She made a top ten list and began to explore her options. Westcliffe

Publishing, an established publisher of regional photo/environmental books, seemed like a good choice, but there was just one problem: they weren't marketing in Florida at the time. Despite this complication, the two authors still pursued the opportunity, and after pitching the idea over the phone, they paid a personal visit to Westcliffe's offices. Eventually a contract was negotiated and *Florida's Unsung Wilderness: The Swamps* was born.

Bransilver had enough capital to self-publish her book, but instead chose to come in as a partner with Westcliffe because she believed, along with thousands of writers each year, that more people would be reached with a traditionally published book. Also, she and Richardson were less than eager to bear full responsibility for the business side of the endeavor. In the deal they agreed to, the publisher would pay to market, warehouse, and distribute the book, and each party would receive half of the income from sales. Bransilver and Richardson fortunately were able to retain artistic control so they could discuss and resolve any differences of opinion with the publisher, and they even had the opportunity to work directly with the designer. The authors and the publisher opted to shy away from a high-priced "coffee table" book and print the book in paperback, thinking that a couple of first-time authors would have a better chance of selling copies at paperback prices. To add more credibility to the project, Bransilver convinced close friend and fellow conservationist, Jane Goodall, to write the introduction to the book, and was also able to get the president/CEO of Audubon Florida to write the preface.

Bransilver and Richardson enjoyed their experience with Westcliffe Publishing. In her words, "It was not a contentious process. We got on just fine." Despite not having total control, the authors felt that the overall process went smoothly—with a strong sense of trust between both parties that the other would do the best job possible. As a result of the success of *Florida's Unsung Wilderness: The Swamps*, Bransilver agreed to publish her book *Wild Love Affair: Essence of Florida's Native Orchids* with Westcliffe. Given the range of publishers available, Bransilver sums up her reason for selecting a smaller publisher: "You can either be a little fish in a big pond, or a big fish in a little pond. The latter was the right choice for us. It made creating this book that much easier."

Clearly traditional publishing has its advantages, otherwise a few hundred thousand people wouldn't be knocking on their door each year. But, as many of these people quickly find out, every rose has its thorns, and there are downsides to this path to print that you should consider. We are simply aiming to supply you with all the necessary information to help you weigh your options versus the other paths to print and bring to light some of the issues of which most people are unaware. Though it may seem that we present many downsides relating to traditional publishing, it is not meant to discourage you from choosing this path.

Traditional publishers put up all the money to publish a book, but they also pay out less per book sold than the author makes if they self-publish, since in the risk-reward relationship, they are the ones bearing the financial risk. Royalties range from 6-15% of the retail price of the book when traditionally published, while royalty rates for on-demand printing range from 20-80% of the retail price (depending on the print on-demand provider), and, of course, the author keeps all the profits when they self-publish. However, bear in mind that traditional publishing may lead to greater sales, making the total income higher, even with a lower percentage of each individual sale paid to the author. For the non-math majors out there, if you received 10% of publishing sales totaling $100,000, for example, you would receive $10,000 in income, and it would be more than if you received 40% of $20,000 of sales with a print on-demand company, which would leave you with $8,000 at the end of the day.

Along the same lines, it should be noted that when you go with a traditional publisher, you give up certain rights related to the book to the publisher, but the company shares the proceeds of sale of these rights with you. When you self-publish you retain all of the rights, but you must find buyers for the rights yourself, which can be difficult if you don't have direct access to any of these potential buyers or experience in negotiating with them. On-demand publishers usually allow you to retain your rights and sometimes they even do a highly-effective job of publicizing your work on their site, in hopes of attracting possible buyers of ancillary rights to your book. We will delve into the subject of "rights" in greater detail in Chapter 21.

If you are interested in pursuing traditional publishing for the chance to hit it big, it will be difficult, but there are plenty of financially successful authors out there. Authors such as John Grisham, Michael Crichton, Nora Roberts, and Mary Higgins Clark reportedly routinely make over 30 million dollars a year, so the sky is certainly the limit. Granted these few are at the top of the pyramid, but there are many full-time authors who make more than enough to cover their living expenses, and if you already have a day job, you can make enough money to feel that your spare time was well spent. Writing books can be an occupation that pays you well, but if you are contemplating putting all of your eggs in the publishing basket and shelving your resume in favor of your keyboard, reflect on the words of

John Steinbeck: "The profession of book-writing makes horse-racing seem like a solid, stable business."

The number one downside to the traditional publishing industry, which practically every author in the world has experienced at some point, is *rejection*. Publishers usually have limited resources to dedicate to new books and are almost always overwhelmed with submissions. Publishers select a manuscript after determining if it fits into one of the categories they publish, if it is well-written and interesting, and most importantly if they think that they can sell it. It all comes down to a calculated risk from the company's perspective, with their burden of recouping the thousands of dollars that they front for a book to be published (editing, printing, marketing), as well as any advances on royalties paid to the author. Later in the book, we discuss how to prepare an impressive book proposal and how to cope with repeated rejections. Just be prepared to send out many submissions before getting even a nibble of interest.

As part of the large volume of manuscript submissions, it sometimes feels like you are just a faceless number attached to a nameless manuscript, unless you have enjoyed success in the industry in the past. There isn't time to give a large amount of time to each submission and first-time authors often get overlooked. It's unfortunate that this situation arises, but welcome to the corporate culture in which all publishers operate. This is not always the case though. Jonathan Safran Foer, who wrote his first novel *Everything is Illuminated* when he was 24, had it very quickly accepted by Houghton Mifflin and was paid a large advance, despite being a newcomer to the industry, and was similarly rewarded with his second novel, *Extremely Loud & Incredibly Close*. Many other first-time authors have capitalized on a hot topic or had writing that was so intriguing or well-composed that the doors to the traditional publishing industry opened immediately. It could certainly happen to you too!

Even if accepted by a large publisher, a new author will likely not receive as much attention as given to the big names or more established authors published by the house, and, therefore, you must use your own imagination and effort to drive sales, which you would need to do with the other publishing avenues to an even greater degree. Large publishers release 200 or more books a year and they simply do not have the manpower, time, or money to give each author equal attention. Again, if you have enjoyed success in the past, the publisher is often more willing to devote resources and personnel to you and your book, but this is not always the case. There are exceptions to the general rule of needing to have a "name" first—with a book from a first time novelist occasionally generating an incredible buzz within a large publisher. A smaller publisher, although not as connected, might give you the personal attention that you need, which is why many people like Connie Bransilver choose to be the big fish in the little pond— one that may eventually end up being successful in the bigger pond once a readership base is created.

Another downside to traditional publishing occurs in the form of time lags before the public can see your book, a major criticism from the go-getters ready to aggressively market or from those waiting to receive a percentage of the sales. First of all, you need to get your manuscript accepted. Even if the first publisher you approach wants it, they may take up to three months to respond to your query or proposal. If it takes you several tries to find one interested in it, then you are already looking at anywhere from a few months to a year of waiting. From there, it may take up to a year from the date of acceptance for them to print the book and distribute it to the appropriate bookstores, online retailers, and book distributors. When you self-publish, you must handle the business of the book, but you have the ability to create your own timeframe for when it will be completed and available. Similarly, when you use on-demand printing, your book can be available in as little as ten days, and usually within three months.

THE LIGHTER SIDE OF PUBLISHING

Many queries and manuscripts submitted to publishing companies are well composed and professional looking, since the authors sending them typically went through a great deal of time and effort on their manuscript and wouldn't want to waste the opportunity by making a poor submission. However some individuals don't quite "get" what the publisher will respond favorably to and sort of "miss the boat." Here are some stories provided by Danielle, a long-time friend of Eric, who has screened manuscripts at several large publishing houses in New York, and who asked that we not reveal her full name for fear that her current publisher would never see any submissions from new authors again. Basically, while the submissions which Danielle recounts below got a good laugh out of the staff at the water cooler, unfortunately they were not accepted. In other words: Don't try this at home!

Probably one of the funniest submissions we ever received was from a gentleman who hand-wrote his submission. This was unusual to begin with, but what really separated his submission was the odd way in which he composed his sentences. He kept putting choice words and phrases in quotes. It went something like: "This is going to be the next 'big thing.' I will be on all the 'major networks.' You guys will 'become famous' if you 'publish' my 'masterpiece.'" If you have ever seen the old Chris Farley Saturday Night Live skit where he makes quotation mark gestures with his fingers after almost every phrase—this was the literary equivalent—and it was just as funny, even without the visuals. I literally had tears coming down my face by the time I finished reading it!

Another submission that caught my eye was a three-page, hand-written (in pencil) letter from a prison inmate, which described his three book ideas. One was about a complex crime and another was about a poison or something along those lines. The publishing company that I was working for only accepted agented submissions, so unfortunately we had to reject him. I felt bad sending him the cold, formulaic rejection letter. I mean, how was he supposed to find an agent WHILE IN PRISON? How would he work out interviews? Would he have to hand-write all three books? (Authors' Note: Writing and publishing books while in prison is actually possible. You Got Nothing Coming: Notes from a Prison Fish, by Jimmy Lerner, a chronicle of the author's stint in a Nevada prison, was written while the author was incarcerated and has become quite successful.)

Perhaps the most bizarre submission came from a man who pasted unusual pictures and words from magazines all over some sheets of paper and the envelope, almost as if he were holding someone for ransom and didn't want his handwriting traced; however, instead of demanding money, his collage comprised some sort of crazy message. According to the man, this was meant to be his manuscript. While his "manuscript" was obviously not accepted, he at least scored some points in the originality category, so he had that going for him.

Attempting to operate within the traditional publishing industry can be just as intimidating as trying to file your own income taxes and there are certainly just as many places to make wrong turns. The plus side of the traditional publishing versus filling out any standard form that begins with "W" (think W2); however, is that there is *actually* a very definite positive side. Yes, there are disadvantages to this form of publishing, but taken as a whole, it is certainly a smart option for many writers, both newer and more experienced ones, which is why so many people try to find a place every year. There are thousands of publishers, operating in many different genres, ready for someone like you to submit your manuscript. Make use of *Writer's Market* and the resources that we recommend in this book, find out who published the books of authors similar to you, and be sure to ask people you know to help you locate any publishers or contacts they may have. You *will* find a publisher if you persist long enough. If things don't work out on this path, though, you can always retrace your steps and try one of the other publishing options in the following chapters!

- **Traditional publishing holds some major advantages over the other forms of publishing, which is why so many people are willing to face rejection and time lags in the quest for a publisher.**

- **While traditional publishing may increase your chances to distribute your book and ultimately sell more copies, it's not for everyone. Compare it to the options presented in the next four chapters before making a decision.**

CHAPTER 14

Create Demand with Printing On-Demand

Just over twenty years ago, the Reagan administration was beginning, the Cold War was in full swing, and bad hairdos were everywhere. The "personal computer" was a radical new concept—one that many people felt would never catch on. The number of people on the Internet was only a few hundred nationally, if that. The publishing industry was primitive and rather elitist; many people wanted to publish books, but the traditional publishing industry could only support a few. Now, presidential elections can hinge on a hanging chad, Russia is our ally (sometimes), and hairdos have improved for the most part. Most of us use a computer at least once a day, and there are hundreds of millions of people on the Internet. Finally, with the advent of printing on-demand—an innovative and more affordable form of vanity publishing—the publishing industry has also evolved, allowing *anyone* to achieve the dream of having their book published.

As with many cutting-edge innovations; however, printing on-demand, also called web-based or personal publishing, has been slow to capture the public's eye, even though it has been around for several years and has the potential to revolutionize the *entire* industry. Many insiders feel that it is just a matter of time before this segment of the publishing industry really takes off. Thus, millions of dollars in venture capital has been raised by many large publishing-related corporations and publishing houses to fund the operation of print on-demand providers.

Printing on-demand, as many publishing insiders have noted, is the publishing industry's contribution to the do-it-yourself (DIY) movement, which has become prevalent in a number of industries, particularly in the arts and entertainment businesses. Essentially, the goal, in the case of publishing, is to eliminate all of the people and parties in the middle that separate the writer from their potential readers. To simplify, these individuals and entities include agents, editors (at traditional publishers), book reviewers, and even book retailers. In the non-DIY world, these people serve as gatekeepers between you and your crop of readers. But now, in the rapidly evolving DIY world, you can control your own destiny. Although, as you will see in this chapter, your print on-demand company can become your ally in navigating the terrain and in working around or working with gatekeepers as necessary.

Getting back to the basic tenets of printing on-demand, while it is certainly a dramatic advancement, the premise behind it is fairly simple. Instead of printing a set number of copies of books, which occurs in traditional publishing, they are printed one at a time, as customers order them. This ensures that the number of books printed exactly fits the demand and that there is no capital lost on printing or warehousing unsold copies. There are quite a number of print on-demand companies currently in operation, with websites detailing all of their services, which we will discuss later in the chapter. For just a few hundred dollars, an author can send in their manuscript and have it made into a book available through major retailers such as Amazon.com and B&N.com in as quickly as a month in some cases. This is a truly amazing timetable compared to the usually slow-as-molasses traditional publishing routes.

But the mechanics of the process of printing on-demand are not nearly as mind-blowing as the impact that this option can have on you as a writer. The publishing industry is no longer for a select few, even though the top of the industry will likely continue to be dominated by just a handful of the top names in the business. Anyone can now get a book published, on any topic of interest and importance to them, without fear of rejection, and people all over the world can read it! The general public, through the efforts of targeted advertising and several recent articles, such as the one written by Sarah Glazer in the April 24, 2005 issue of the *New York Times*, is starting to become aware of printing on-demand. Hopefully after reading this chapter, you will also recognize the opportunities that this might provide for you.

While some people often use the terms "on-demand publishing" and "vanity publishing" interchangeably, there are a number of differences, and we have divided them into separate chapters in this book. In both options an individual pays someone to print their book, but traditional vanity publishing often involves different royalty rates, more up-front costs, and printing a sizable quantity of books at one time, rather than one at a time, as in on-demand publishing.

Printing on-demand has become an ideal option for a number of different types of people/writers. Anyone targeting a smaller or specialized audience should strongly consider this path, since many traditional publishers stick to mainstream topics, and it has often been extremely difficult to get smaller market material published. Those days are now over with this new option. So, if you truly are among the millions who just want to write a book for family and friends, but want the finished product to look professional, essentially no different from any book in Barnes & Noble, this is your answer.

However, it's even optimal for someone targeting a large audience, especially if they are a fiction writer, because the odds of a first-time author having a fictional work accepted by a publisher are somewhere in the neighborhood of 1 in 400. By printing on-demand, you can ensure that your novel at least makes it into the marketplace, thus getting your name out to potential readers, and perhaps making you a decent amount of money. In other words, this is your chance to break in to the industry, and perhaps become a traditionally-published author after you build a track record. Without printing on-demand, you wouldn't have that chance to document sales if you your manuscript stayed in your house and didn't make it into the marketplace.

Even further, if you are planning on writing a book that you will update with future editions, printing on-demand might be ideal, as it will eliminate the possibility of being stuck with unsold copies of out-of-date versions of your book when your new version is released. A corollary of this would be that if you are planning on "test marketing" some ideas, of which some you will want to keep and others you will want to scrap, this is a great publishing option. Nearly every provider allows you to make changes to the book (even after it is for sale) for a nominal fee before they switch out the older version for the newer, refined version 30-45 days later.

The benefits of this type of publishing go far beyond its affordability, its accessibility (with rejection being a non-issue for the most part), the ease and speed of the process, and the built-in mechanism for distribution worldwide. With printing on-demand you retain all of the rights to your book, meaning that you can sell the rights to anyone at a later date with no strings attached. You could win the lottery. Your book could be spotted by an executive at a major studio. A movie mogul might purchase the rights and make it into a feature film.

Even though the print on-demand company that you use is allowing you to keep your rights, they still handle the business related to the book, such as designing a cover, printing and binding, obtaining an ISBN number, and making it available to major retailers after it is listed through R.R. Bowker and posted on the accompanying site, www.booksinprint.com. They even keep track of the sales each month and send royalty checks in a timely fashion. Royalties are much higher than in traditional publishing, and can range from 20-80%, depending on the provider, the services which they offer, and the fees that they charge you to publish.

Another major benefit is *exposure*. In the real world it might land you in jail or stuck with a hefty fine, but in the publishing industry it will help you to increase sales and reach potential readers. Printing on-demand gives authors the opportunity to attract agents and publishers, who often search the on-demand sites looking for interesting ideas and stories. Had you sent them your manuscript, you may have gotten lost in the sheer numbers of their submission pile and had the publishing process stall, but with your finished product on display, you just might get a bite from the right publisher! And, since you retain all of the rights, you are in quite an enviable position because not only did you make money on the sales of the book from the print on-demand provider, but now you can "double-dip" by selling the rights and re-releasing it.

We should point out that the same marketing techniques mentioned in Chapter 10 and in Chapter 20 all apply to this form of publishing. You can still get blurbs from critics and celebrities and submit them with your manuscript to be printed on the back of your book. Reviews and news stories are possible as well—often beginning in smaller publications. Remember, promotion is cumulative and getting a little attention now can lead to big things later on.

A big part of marketing comes from how the actual book looks when it is printed and bound. If you doubt this part of human psychology, keep track of how eye-catching the covers of the books that you are suddenly drawn to in a bookstore are on your next trip. Traditional publishers spend big bucks and use talented artists to create covers that will hopefully get a potential reader to examine a book more closely and ultimately purchase it.

Even though you will receive a lot of advice from your print on-demand company, be sure to take an active role in the design of the book. Examine the books similar to your title to gather information on any number of factors including: how the covers look, how the inside of the book reads (is the font chosen the right one), if there are any graphics or artwork included in the book, does the book include blurbs or endorsements on the back cover (maybe even from people that you might be able to enlist), does the presentation of the author's biography make the book more attractive (e.g. are they marketing themselves as an expert). Keep in mind that your print on-demand company will help you along in the process, but at the end of the day, you are supposed to know your book, your market, and the books that are similar which have come before you better than anyone…so your input is crucial.

Even though this path to print is relatively new, some authors have already had major success using it. Amanda Brown used on-demand printing to publish her first novel *Legally Blonde*, and it became a Hollywood blockbuster starring Reese Witherspoon. Following the movie's release, Plume, a major publisher, bought the rights to both *Legally Blonde* and its sequel, which was also made into a movie starring Witherspoon. David Brody published his book *Unlawful Deeds* using on-demand printing, and after selling copies at bookstores in the New England area, he eventually made it onto the *Boston Globe* bestseller list. And, Amy Montgomery, a freelance writer who creates material for a number of clients across a range of industries in addition to supporting the Christopher Reeve Foundation with her writing, used AuthorHouse, one of the large print on-demand companies, to produce *Just an Accident*. The book has won ForeWord Magazine's Book of the Year (Gold Medal—family and relationships category), USA BookNews Best Books (finalist), and Writer's Marketing Association Fresh Voices Award (winner—creative nonfiction).

In addition to the thousands of authors reaping the benefits, traditional publishers have also benefited from printing on-demand. Some houses have used it to eliminate warehousing or inventory costs and to avoid money lost from unsold copies. As a self-publisher, these are costs that on-demand printing also erases for you. Furthermore, publishers are able to keep more titles in print, bring back out-of-print ones, and even test-market new ones before releasing them in the traditional fashion. Lightning Source (www.lightningsource.com), which also acts as a distributor for many of the largest print on-demand providers, is primarily in the business of printing for traditional publishing houses, rather than searching for authors and providing author services. They work with over 4,000 publishing company clients to provide a more cost-effective way for them to publish certain books. To date, the company has printed nearly 20 million books, and with backing from Ingram Book Group, one of the large publishing industry conglomerates, they are likely to remain at the forefront of the publishing industry.

Printing on-demand truly is the best option for many new writers, but there are some downsides. Books printed on-demand are much less likely to be found on bookshelves for consumers to purchase because actual bookstores, unlike virtual ones, are constrained by shelf space and they must limit what they sell in the store. As a result of not being published by a traditional publisher and therefore located in the publisher's seasonal catalogue of titles, a book printed on-demand doesn't have a publishing sales force knocking on the doors of bookstores and other retailers. There is a sizable segment of the book buying population which acts on impulse— they want to browse in a bookstore and leave with a new book in hand. Then there are some people who are so eager to read a new book that they don't want to wait the three days for delivery.

Although your book is listed on the websites of the largest Internet retailers, you still must lead readers to your book, which can be challenging, considering all of the titles to choose from on a site like Amazon.com. While leading readers to your book online is indeed a hurdle to overcome as an on-demand author, it is an achievable feat. Anyone can learn the tricks of internet marketing, and Chapter 20 is designed to help get you on the right track and get started.

Other disadvantages of printing on-demand include higher per-unit costs of production. On-demand technology is improving but remains less economical than printing a book the traditional way, since traditional publishers save by printing in bulk quantities of hundreds, thousands, and even millions at one time. While this may not affect your book sales online to strangers, if you are interested in purchasing a number of personal copies to distribute friends, family, or customers, each book will cost you more than if you hired a printer and printed a large quantity.

Now that we've covered the basic advantages and disadvantages of this path to print, let's discuss some of the on-demand companies offering you the chance to print, bind, and sell your foray into the literary world. We encourage you to listen to our advice, but to explore your options, since everyone has different objectives and experiences with particular companies.

AuthorHouse (www.authorhouse.com), formerly 1st Books Library, has recently become the print on-demand publisher with the most published titles and sports an impressive array of services for authors. The company highlights a good number of authors on the AuthorHouse website, including listing the local, regional, or national publications in which the author has appeared.

It should be noted that when we were completing the first edition of *Get Between the Covers*, after 5 years of hard work and research, we knew that we wanted to use one of the print on-demand providers, for a couple of reasons. The first was to prove that anyone, even authors with backgrounds in the traditional publishing industry, can make use of this option. Beyond that, we also wanted to get the material into the marketplace as quickly as possible, so that we could test-market some of our ideas, knowing full well that we could go back and change the book in under 30 days at any point based on the feedback we received.

After considering all of the options and speaking with representatives of the leading print on-demand companies, we chose AuthorHouse to publish the work. The process went incredibly smoothly and with their help the book became a bestseller shortly after its release. Since our publication date, we have begun to develop strategic initiatives with AuthorHouse because they share our vision of helping everyday people to write and publish books on a large scale, even though this edition of *Get Between the Covers* is now a Morgan James title.

While AuthorHouse was the right choice for us, we encourage you to consider not only them, but also some of the other companies that we present in this chapter.

CANADIAN COLUMNIST ENTERS THE DIGITAL AGE

Syndicated Canadian columnist, Gordon Kirkland, best known for his hilarious insights into life in his column, *Gordon Kirkland at Large*, recently published one of his books using AuthorHouse, and, in fact, was so satisfied with the process and the company, that he returned with his next book. Both books, *When My Mind Wanders It Brings Back Souvenirs* and *I Think I'm Having One of Those Decades*, have sold very well through AuthorHouse, and Kirkland is quick to point out the upside of getting a royalty rate that is 2-4 times as high as with a traditional publisher, not to mention that he gets paid the royalty checks in a much more timely fashion. While he was initially apprehensive about going with the print on-demand route, recognizing that it is more difficult to get physical copies in bookstores around North America, AuthorHouse's programs helped to assuage his fears. He also factored in that, even though he is well-known and has won numerous literary awards (he's even a faculty member for Erma Bombeck's Writer's Workshop, in addition to facilitating writing seminars all over the country), most major publishers wouldn't put a large promotional budget behind him and aggressively try to sell his book. So, either way, Kirkland knew that he would have to be the driving force behind his own sales, but, as he says, "Luckily, I enjoy it."

The service and attention to detail that he received from the team at AuthorHouse contributed greatly to his positive experience, even though traditional publishers had worked with him in the past. "One of the other important factors for me was the team that AuthorHouse was able to put together to work on my books. I have found them to be extremely helpful and supportive, from the sales people, to the design team, to the book marketing personnel, all the way through to the senior management. There have been more people involved in bringing my AuthorHouse titles to print than in either of the two traditional publishers I have used."

Another one of the largest print on-demand companies is iUniverse (www. iuniverse.com), which has printed over one million books to date and has received significant financial support from Barnes & Noble, enabling certain on-demand printed books to find shelf space in the book retailer's stores if they reach a certain level of sales. To learn more about their services, you should visit their website and also flip through *Get Published!* by Susan Driscoll (CEO of iUniverse) and Diane Gedymin, as the book is catered to the company's potential clientele. To summarize, for as little as $459 (at the time of publication), an author can submit their edited manuscript online, have the cover and format designed by the staff, approve the final product, and have their trade paperback book made available for order in under 90 days.

Through their partnerships, iUniverse can get your book to Baker and Taylor or Ingram Book Group, the two largest book distributors in the world. In many cases, the book can be made available to the public much quicker if the author formats everything correctly prior to submission. iUniverse is able to print books in word counts ranging from approximately 30,000 to books ten times that size.

Recently, the company has begun to market heavily to everyday people with stories to tell who need a user-friendly mechanism to reach potential readers. They have even instituted a program wherein schoolchildren in a class all write stories, which their teacher compiles into a book that is printed using iUniverse. iUniverse takes pride in seeing the success of authors using their service, and several have been highly successful, such as Ralph Fertig, whose book *Love and Liberation: When the Jews Tore Down the Ghetto Walls*, made it onto the *Los Angeles Times Best Seller List*. Others have sold several thousand copies and then had their books picked up by traditional publishers. iUniverse routinely documents these success stories with news releases on their website. They have even introduced a "Star" program, wherein qualifying books that have been approved by a team of internal editors and sold a minimum of 500 copies are placed on the shelves of bookstores—thus allowing the authors to sell in the same fashion as their traditionally published counterparts.

Laurie Notaro originally published her book *The Idiot Girls' Action Adventure Club* using iUniverse and her story appeared on their website. After seven years of hearing "no" from traditional publishers, she knew that she simply needed to find another option. Using iUniverse, Notaro got her book through the publishing process and into the distribution channels available through iUniverse's partnerships, such as Amazon.com, BarnesandNoble.com, and Booksamillion.com.

Once listed on the website, Notaro gave talks at libraries and just about anywhere else people would listen to her. She even gave a talk at a bridge club in Sun City, Arizona. Also critical was the professional looking website she created, with help from the person who designed her book cover. The website address, which was printed on the back of her book, enabled readers, including editors and agents, to find out more about her.

About ten months after her book appeared on iUniverse, Notaro was able to get an agent who landed her a deal with Random House for *The Idiot Girls' Action Adventure Club*. According to Notaro it was her persistence that ultimately paid off. "The number one thing is that you never take no for an answer. If you've got something that you believe in and really feel strongly about, you go after it no matter what. If someone blocks one road, find another." *The Idiot Girls' Action Adventure Club* became a *New York Times* Best Seller shortly after publication with Random House.

Trafford (www.trafford.com) was the first company to offer printing on-demand in the mid-1990's and they still offer the same great services that they did then, backed by the latest technology and by having an overseas operation. The company boasts having published authors from over 105 countries around the world.

WRITING BOOKS AND SHARING INFORMATION GLOBALLY

During a recent conversation with Josè Albis, Marketing & Communications Manager at Trafford, which Eric had at BookExpo America 2007, it became clear how Trafford sees the bigger picture for how writing influences the world. Albis told a story about an exciting initiative that the company is undertaking, which we had to include in this book because it represents the highest ideals of *Get Between the Covers*.

In August 2005, the Department of Canadian Heritage sponsored 42 Indigenous language activists from around the world to the International Symposium of the World's Indigenous Languages in Japan. At this gathering, a Khwedam speaker, Bothas Marinda, from Namibia in South West Africa expressed concern that poor villages like his were denied access to the information technology that was transforming literacy for Indigenous people.

In response to his concerns, Trafford Publishing donated a computer and peripheral tools to Bothas, and a private fundraising drive provided solar charging equipment. Subsequently Trafford Publishing announced a further donation of $1.6 Million Canadian dollars for the publication of 650 Indigenous language books over the next ten years.

This program is administered by the FirstVoices team and its coordinator, Peter Brand, in collaboration with Trafford. As of today, 27 new Indigenous language books are nearing release to communities from around the world.

In terms of Trafford's overall operation and particular style, Albis offers the following:

At Trafford we are driven by the success of our authors. FirstVoices is an excellent example of what can be accomplished by writing a book. *The pen is mightier than the sword.* We, at Trafford Publishing, are proud of our role as bookmakers—facilitators in the preservation of thought processes, languages, and other forms of culture in an increasingly consumer-based society.

Maintaining the human touch is a common challenge faced by many companies today. At Trafford Publishing, we are driven to incorporate human principles into our corporate culture, because we understand that no matter how much the society changes to reflect emerging trends and ideas, we are humans, and our core values and philosophies will always stem from this. We also maintain close relationships with our authors, who keep us informed of their triumphs and success. Their success is our success, and we rejoice and celebrate with them.

Defining success is never easy, particularly when we have so many examples. For some, success is financial—landing a movie or publishing contract. Others define success as the ability to publish the memoirs of a deceased relative. For Trafford, authors—their individualism and experiences—are the essence of our business. Our success lies in enabling them to leave a lasting legacy.

Booksurge (www.booksurge.com) is a pioneer in self-publishing and print-on-demand services, enabling both authors and publishers to make content available to a rapidly growing online market. Offering unique publishing opportunities and access for authors, BookSurge boasts an unprecedented number of authors whose work has resulted in book deals with traditional publishers as well as successful *authorpreneurs* who enhance or build a business from their professional expertise. BookSurge is a division of On-Demand Publishing LLC, a subsidiary of Amazon.com Inc.

BookSurge Success Story

Patricia Annino is a nationally recognized authority on estate planning and a partner in a well-known Boston law firm. Not only does Annino represent authors in estate planning, she is also the published author of three books. After publishing her first two professional titles traditionally, Annino decided self-publishing was the best route for her third book, *Women and Money: A Practical Guide to Estate Planning.*

"Because *Women and Money* deals heavily with the ever-changing tax laws, I knew that an on-demand environment where the book's content could be easily revised was a necessity. I was also pleased that BookSurge allowed me to maintain control over all aspects of the book's design."

Xlibris (www.xlibris.com), of which Random House Ventures owns a minority share, is another of the largest three print on-demand providers, which offers services comparable to iUniverse. The cost of using Xlibris is slightly higher, but they may do more for the author post publication, including setting up a website that links with the major search engines and encouraging traditional publishers to examine their titles. They also have partnerships with the major Internet retailers and can make your books available anywhere in the world.

John Feldcamp, CEO of Xlibris, has seen a significant growth in the popularity of on-demand printing, with a little over 20,000 authors estimated to have used this form of publishing in 2003. In a 2004 interview, Feldcamp explained that the numbers have grown rapidly because of an increased awareness of the ability for anyone to produce a professional, well-made product, and place it on the market in an easy, fast, and inexpensive manner. For Xlibris's rise specifically, he points to their successful track record, their ability to print on-demand books in color, and their highly customized service for each author, or "author-centricity," as Feldcamp terms it. There are also many authors, who after proving themselves as writers on Xlibris, have landed book deals with major publishing houses for subsequent projects.

Ultimately Feldcamp doesn't see on-demand publishing, in and of itself, as being what changes the publishing industry. "What these businesses do well is to think differently and use new processes and new technology, to make publishing less expensive, more efficient, and more powerful than ever before." For all of these reasons, Feldcamp concludes, "There is no question that the vast majority of books (which generally have small markets) will be published by on-demand businesses." He does concede; however, that the larger traditional publishers, which he views as investment entities that take ownership rights of the most valuable property, will probably always be strong within the publishing industry because of their resources.

Llumina Press (www.llumina.com), a print on-demand provider with a number of great services for writers that goes a step further, offering first-class editing services (if required) and experienced personal assistance in getting books into marketable condition. Though most publishing companies care what your book looks like, Llumina takes the editing of self published books seriously enough to make sure the content is ready for the market. They offer a free, no-obligation editing evaluation and provide a written report based on samples from the author's text. The packages are straightforward and all-inclusive, and the royalties are based on list price not net.

When asked for some success stories, Deborah Greenspan, Publisher of Llumina Press, offered the following:

We have several successful books, a few of which have been picked up by larger traditional publishers. One of my favorite POD books is *The Man from Autumn* by Mario Martinez, a novel that not only probes the inner recesses of the Vatican and the process of choosing a new Pope, but also explores the inner recesses of the mind, body, and human relationships. In real life, the author does investigations of stigmata for the Vatican, and this has helped to get him several appearances on television in Ireland. As a result, his books sell very well. The first time he appeared on the equivalent of *Oprah* over there, the distribution networks got into an uproar trying to get the books into stock, but they managed. The book is now featured in the largest bookstore chain in the UK and is listed on Eason's Bestseller List for Fiction.

LuLu (www.lulu.com) is a recent addition to the on-demand world, and it was founded by Robert Young, former Chairman & CEO of Red Hat (that offers the competing operating system, Linux, against the ever-popular Windows from Microsoft). LuLu sports very high royalty rates and their North Carolina operation offers many benefits for any level of author.

Wheatmark (www.wheatmark.com) is another one of the recent print on-demand publishers which has instituted numerous innovative programs to assist authors, including putting money into the promotion of books that sell well. As the company notes on its website, it is the only self-publishing company that doubles as a publishing house, since they are investing their own money into the top selling titles, recognizing that sales are the best indicator of a book's long-term success. In the same way that a traditional publisher in New York would place additional capital and personnel on a book that was selling and generating a buzz, through Wheatmark's program, which they've termed the Great Expectations Program, newer authors have chance to make a name for themselves.

Printing on-demand is truly one of the greatest innovations in the publishing industry and someday it may become the norm. It allows any person, with any level of writing experience, to fulfill their literary dreams and have a printed and bound version of their achievement, which they can share with their closest friends and family or with people they don't even know anywhere in the world. We have highlighted the prominent print on-demand providers in this chapter. You can locate the websites of additional companies by using any of the major search engines and also by going to the Xerox website (www.xerox.com), which maintains a list of all of the print on-demand providers which operate using Xerox machinery. Also visit Lightning Source's website (www.lightningsource.com), since it lists all of the print on-demand providers that are catered to an author's needs.

We encourage you to check out the sites listed in this chapter, read about their services and partnerships, and find the right fit for your project. Many websites also list toll-free numbers you can call to speak to a customer service representative. Make sure when you compare companies that you understand all of the services provided, since this affects the cost of one service provider versus another, and consider checking their credentials (log on to the Better Business Bureau at <u>www.bbb.org</u> to see the history of any company and view its rating based on its business practices). With a little legwork, you will find the print on-demand provider that is right for you and you will be on your way to publication!

·**On-demand publishing is the easiest and most affordable way for newer writers to publish their books.**

·**While it may not be the first option to consider for reaching the masses or generating a significant source of income, it is ideal for people targeting small niche markets.**

·**There are a great number of on-demand publishers and you should find the one that fits your budget and provides the services you need.**

CHAPTER 15

START THE PRESSES:
Printing Your Book Yourself

When you hear the words *printing press*, perhaps you think of an antiquated, cumbersome machine, operated by a man who looks old enough to be your great-grandfather, which painfully churns out pages of a book one by one. While this image may have been accurate two centuries ago, printers today use sophisticated machines, are run by people of all ages, and can print a large volume of books in a short amount of time. Self-publishing by taking a manuscript to a printer and then working with your own resources to market and sell your book is the most pro-active path to print and allows for the most autonomy on the part of the author, as you need answer to only one person…yourself. In this chapter, we will highlight the advantages and disadvantages of self-publishing, and outline the options, both from a printing and business standpoint, by presenting the stories of several self-published authors.

Before getting started on the intricacies of this path to print, perhaps we should first dispel a common misconception about self-publishing—that it leads to a life of anonymity for the writer and that you simply can't sell a significant number of copies or generate a buzz about a self-published book. While, in general, the highest selling authors every year are individuals who go through traditional publishers, you may be surprised to learn that some of the biggest names in the publishing world have self-published books that went on to become immensely successful and also launched them into a lucrative career in the traditional publishing industry.

Ken Blanchard and Spencer Johnson originally self-published *The One Minute Manager*. After selling an impressive number of copies in the early 1980's, the rights were purchased and it has since sold 12 million copies. Richard Bolles self-published *What Color is Your Parachute?*, which eventually went on to spend 288 weeks on the *New York Times* bestseller list. Going back a couple of centuries, Ben Franklin self-published *Poor Richard's Almanack* (spelling later changed) and continued to print it, meeting demand for more than 25 years. Bestselling author Pat Conroy self-published his first book, which cost him a fair amount of money to print and distribute. When his agent called him to tell him he had just sold the rights to Conroy's second book, saying, "It looks like $10,000." Conroy, unaware that someone was actually paying *him* an advance, replied, "I can't afford to keep spending money like that." [1]

---

1   For more self-publishing success stories check out marketing expert John Kremer's website at   http://www.bookmarket.com/selfpublish. html.

While it must be conceded that authors often continue to self-publish their books and make a great living doing it, many authors are simply looking to get their material into print because they believe that the public will respond positively, they will sell a significant number of copies, and then a major publisher will come knocking. For them, self-publishing provides a "back door" into the traditional publishing industry. This was the case for both Vince Flynn, who self-published his first novel *Term Limits* and for Robert Kiyosaki, author and creator of the *Rich Dad, Poor Dad* series of books, who both faced rejection in the traditional publishing industry and decided to go with the self-publishing route to prove their meddle. They are now both published by the largest publishing houses in New York and have sold millions of copies of all of their books, since going with the self-publishing option in the late 1990's.

Taking these success stories to heart, let's delve into the basics of self-publishing. First of all, this path to print could be the right option for you if you want to enjoy creative control of your book and you have somewhat of an entrepreneurial mindset. As a self-publisher you retain all of the rights to your work (be sure to read Chapter 21), meaning that you receive all of the profits from any sales, in addition to having final say in all matters related to your book. If you are a fairly self-motivated person this can mean much greater financial rewards because instead of getting a small percentage of each sale, you get the whole sum minus your expenses for printing, distributing, warehousing, and promoting. Since you are printing a quantity of books each run, instead of one at a time as in on-demand printing, the cost per book is kept relatively low, although you must then factor in warehousing costs. Your book will likely have more longevity because you can keep it in print, whereas a traditional publisher might cease printing runs after a few months, unless the book is really moving off of the shelves.

If your book is somehow related to your company or family business, you may be able to run the business end of self-publishing as an extension of your existing organization. Thus you can keep control, build a name as an author, and help to promote your business, all at the same time. Doctors, lawyers, financial planners…there is an endless list of business owners who have increased their patient, client, or customer base as an author and self-propelled expert. The increased revenue of the business often produces much more money than the sale of the book.

Marketing your book might be your biggest challenge, but with advances in the publishing industry you have a much better chance to be successful. Many, but not all, self-published books are listed on Amazon. com, BarnesandNoble.com, and other websites. With some perseverance your book can end up on the shelves of local bookstores or in rare cases distributed to a national chain, especially if you can document sales to other retailers and organizations or develop a relationship with the store owner, although it is a bit of an uphill battle. Having your book listed on BooksInPrint.com will open the door for a book distributor, such as Ingram Book Group, to place copies in additional locations and/or help with sales promotions, since they are linked to the largest retailers.

In order to increase legitimacy and attract attention as a self-publisher, you can get blurbs from celebrities, famous authors, and authorities in your field for the covers of your book, just like traditionally-published authors do. You can attempt to reach these notables through their websites and also by referencing *Who's Who in America* (2006 edition). The key for you to market successfully is to find your target audience, and as you will see in Chapter 20, it all starts on your home turf. Keep in mind that marketing is usually a "continuing endeavor" for all authors, even with the backing of a traditional publisher. So, as a self-publisher, you aren't necessarily at that much of a disadvantage, except that you likely won't have the media and press contacts of the PR department of a traditional publisher.

Admittedly, there are other downsides to self-publishing, which can include the cumbersome hassle of having to deal with printing specifications and needing capital to pay for the book to be printed and other ongoing expenses. This capital will be greater than the fee for any print on-demand provider to produce a finished product, and the ongoing expenses like warehousing and possibly web design and maintenance (if you have a website) can add up.

Without the backing of a traditional publisher or even a large print on-demand provider (that puts out 200-500 titles a month and thus has strong relationships with distributors), it will be harder for you to get in the distribution network. For this reason, it's quite common for self-published authors to be active in selling their books in other venues...at book signings or speaking events they arrange, through their own websites, and even sometimes as part of their business (as quasi-marketing materials).

Beyond the difficulties in distribution, there is also the whole business end of things which is left in the hands of the author: accounting, fulfilling orders, finding distribution channels, and keeping track of inventory. Luckily, delegating some of these tasks to others is always an option. If some of these activities don't appeal to you because you either do enough of them in your day job or because you are inexperienced or unsure of your abilities, you can always enlist the help of friends and business acquaintances to help you along the way. Perhaps you know art or graphic design students who could help you put together your book or its cover—often at a minimal cost. You may have a relative who is an accountant and can act as your bookkeeper in their spare time. Maybe someone you know works at a public relations agency and can help you publicize and promote your work, or you know a salesperson you can enlist to sell copies to potential purchasers of bulk orders. For example, someone might be able to sell 500 health-related books to the Human Resources department of a company as a push to improve company health and reduce the number of sick days taken by employees. Similarly, a friend with special contacts might sell 200 novels to the president of a company to give away to customers or employees during the holiday season.

Successful self-publishing includes good writing, as well as effective designing, printing, marketing, and distributing of the book.

THE PRINTER'S PERSPECTIVE

Shannon Scheel works on the sales team of a *Fortune 1000* printing company and deals with prospective customers interested in printing—clientele that can range from an individual wanting to self-publish a book to some of the larger publishing houses in New York. Scheel is typically contacted by individuals or companies looking to publish a quantity of books, who either researched major printing companies on the Internet or were referred by another customer who had a favorable experience.

Shannon sees his job more or less as a form of consulting, because he must find the best solution for the needs of the customer, in order to customize the specifications of the print job. The many specifications, which you will soon learn about if you select this path to print, include the quantity of books to be printed, the page count, the trim size, and also how the book is furnished pre-press, meaning which layout program is used for text/graphics. Most first-time self-published authors don't know their options and can use the consultation of a trained professional in deciding how their book will appear when it's ready for the bookstore.

Beyond these basic specifications, there are other considerations. Scheel recommends visiting your local bookstore and examining different kinds of books. In much the same way that reading the works of others can help you to generate creative ideas and define your own work, comparing the final physical copies of different books may help you select the type of paper you want to use, what color or colors you would like the text to be, what type of binding you prefer, and also what kind of cover coating you want. Varnish, UV coating, or laminate are all commonly used, but offer different levels of protection. Currently, there is even a company producing new types of books, termed DuraBooks, which use a different type of material for pages and have a protective seal that makes them waterproof—ensuring that you can bring a great book with you to read in the bath or at the beach without fear of damaging it. All of these technical specifications may sound confusing, but a sales representative for a printing company can sit down with you and explain the pros and cons of each option, as well as the difference in price.

When self-publishing, it's important to consider all of the elements that go into the visual design. Minor changes in appearance can have a major impact on sales. You may decide to mimic a format that has been successful for other books of your genre. Extreme examples of this strategy can be found in several recent books, whose authors, in an effort to capitalize on the success of the Harry Potter series and on The South Beach Diet, used designs and even titles which closely mirrored their well-known predecessors. Even though the subjects of these books were not necessarily related to boy wizards or dieting, their presentation caught readers' eyes in the bookstore, landed them some media attention, and has helped them to increase their sales. Choosing a cover design can be such a determining factor in sales that several publishing experts, such as John Kremer, who has worked with a number of the most successful self-publishers, offer cover evaluation services. For more information, visit Kremer's website at www.bookmarket.com. Also visit www.aiga.org and check out the award-winning covers that they feature.

Once the author decides on all of the specifications and the book is printed, the cartons of books can be warehoused by the printing company or shipped to the author, if he or she is eager to sell them to a crop of ready readers. Many printers provide fulfillment, meaning that they can print and ship any quantity of books as they are ordered—a variation of the print on-demand system described in the previous chapter. For example, a corporate client, perhaps a chain of home improvement stores that specializes in certain types of instructional books, may print them using Scheel's company and then sell them in their stores nationwide. If they run out in any store, they simply call the fulfillment center and more will be shipped instantly, ensuring that supply meets demand. An individual self-published author can get the same service; if the author receives an order from Amazon.com or Borders.com, the printing company is ready to ship the books immediately, ensuring that ready readers will not be kept waiting. These services are not offered at every printing company, so make sure to ask before you contract for a print job if you need this service.

For self-publishers, Scheel recommends "The Rule of Three." Once you figure out the specifications for your book, you should approach at least three printers to compare prices and services, because the more options you look at, the more likely you are to find an organization that suits your needs and budget. The website www.literarymarketplace.com offers an extensive list of printers, which will help you to narrow the list down either geographically or by the size of the organization. Whichever printers make your A-list of potential candidates, make sure to give each of them the exact same specifications to ensure that you are comparing "apples to apples" when they quote their prices. Printers are fairly easy to locate. In addition to Literary Marketplace, you can look up options on the Internet or in the yellow pages, or you might even be redirected from one printing company to another, which offers services more customized to your print job. With a little persistence, you will find the right printer, for the right price, and you will be on your way to having your own self-published book.

THE SOURCE FOR SELF-PUBLISHING

Earlier in this book we highlighted Dan Poynter and the many ways that he can assist an author of any level. In the self-publishing world, beyond just Dan, Marilyn Ross, President & CEO of Self-Publishing Resources and coauthor of *The Complete Guide to Self-Publishing*, is a one-stop expert for anyone seeking assistance. Ross enjoys working with well-organized self-starters, since they are the most likely to stay on top of all of the details and thus succeed in self-publishing. Through her website, www.SelfPublishingResources.com, she offers phone consulting, ongoing coaching, and even onsite visits to help authors. She even helped us immensely by providing the most updated information on eBooks as we worked on Chapter 18.

Ross believes that beyond being entrepreneurial minded, if an author has a niche market to cater to, self-publishing may just be the right option. In her words, "Niches equal riches." You may write a book on how to make college affordable for parents or you may come up with a book dealing with alternative medicines for pets. Basically, if you are willing to put in the sweat equity to promote your work and you've got a definite market targeted with your subject, you *can* control your own destiny.

In terms of passing on information to future generations in the form of a book—one of the main catalysts for our work on *Get Between the Covers*—Ross believes that writing a book is "an ideal way to capture important memories and pass along your philosophy about life." She is quick to point out that while neither you nor your family may be famous, it's not to say that you haven't led a fascinating life. Sharing family history, information, or insights from your perspective, in the form of a book, might be interesting, as well as highly useful, even for non-family readers.

When asked what excites her about writing, publishing, and working with other authors, Ross offers:

I have great passion for books and the people who write them. Books change lives, even save them! Every book is an individual creation; no two are alike. Writers are typically daring, driven, and bright souls. They put their opinions, experiences, and research out for all to see. And in the process not only are they stretched, but the whole world can be enriched by their message.

In fact, if you believe that you would like to self-publish several books and are confident in your business capabilities, it may make financial sense to incorporate and start your own publishing company. Thousands of individuals or small groups of individuals, including Neil, have done so, both because of the tax-advantages afforded the owner of the business and also because it allows a reader of one of your books to be directed to others that you offer, allowing for cross-selling opportunities. Even though Neil has been published with several of the largest publishing houses in New York, he has run his own publishing company, Rx Humor, for a number of years, and has used it to produce several successful novels, nonfiction books, and children's books, which have been distributed through large Internet retailers, on his website, and at his talks around the country. Who knows, once you get the company up and running, you may even discover other authors who share a similar vision or style and have an interest in partnering with you in the business.

The following authors had varying degrees of success in reaching their target audience, but more importantly, they were all successful in their own right because they didn't let their manuscript collect dust on a shelf in their study. They put in the time and effort necessary in order to get their book out there. Hopefully their stories will help you determine whether this might be your choice of a path to print.

Jacqueline Marcell, a former television executive, who gave up her job to care for her two elderly parents, both of whom had Alzheimer's Disease, has had great success with her self-published book, *Elder Rage, or Take My Father…Please!:How to Survive Caring for Aging Parents*. She has appeared on many of the major network shows, been featured prominently in *AARP Bulletin*, been named a Book-of-the-Month Selection, gotten rave reviews from both medical professionals and notable individuals like Hugh Downs and Regis Philbin, and is now even hosting her own radio show. There's even talk of a movie being developed from her guide about how to deal with aging parents. Her website, www.elderrage.com, is heavily trafficked and facilitates the interaction of Marcell with the many individuals and groups who book her for speaking events.

While Marcell has certainly faced challenges throughout her self-publishing career, her passion and personal connection to the subject have kept the fire fueled. "I don't even think of this as work--this is my mission, my life's most important and rewarding project. I have always had incredible persistence, determination, and a positive attitude, so I didn't even think I wouldn't succeed starting a totally new line of work in middle age!" Luckily for all of us, especially with so many Baby Boomers caring for aging parents, Marcell continues to use her book as a tool to assist healthcare professionals, families, and those suffering from Alzheimer's. She also uses it to raise funds for medical research, and to encourage long-term care insurance/planning.

Brian Egeston recently self-published his book, *Granddaddy's Dirt*, a novel about the relationship between a grandfather and grandson. For the print run for the first edition he had 500 hardback copies and 10,000 paperback copies printed, a sizable number, which was made possible with $15,000 in capital from investors. Even though raising the money was challenging, he decided to self-publish for several reasons. The first was the stack of 24 rejection letters that he had received from traditional publishers for the novel. He found that because he was a new novelist, it was difficult to get the attention of the large publishing houses. Several years earlier, he had vanity published (explained in Chapter 17) his first book, *Crossing Bridges*, and, even though it was easier to have his material accepted by a vanity publisher than by a traditional one, he had run into a slew of difficulties. According to Brian, "I knew I was in trouble when they told me to come to pick up my 1,000 printed copies at the local Greyhound station." It turns out that his fears were justified. A number of copies had words running off pages, smudges, and even pages printed backwards. After these setbacks, he vowed to self-publish, so that he would have more control over the quality of the finished product.

The biggest challenge that Brian faced as a self-publisher was not the printing, but rather the marketing. Despite his feeling that the publishing industry is not set up for a self-publisher to succeed unless they work incredibly hard, he was able to roll up his sleeves, generate some creative marketing strategies, and sell books. He took *Granddaddy's Dirt* to his fraternity's convention and was able to sell copies there. He promoted and sold his book on the Internet through his website, www.brianwrites.com, which listed upcoming dates for his book tour and had a downloadable version of the first chapter. He also sent out press kits and promotional items to the cities he intended to visit. Eventually, his determination paid off; for example, when the *Atlanta Journal-Constitution* published a favorable review of his book. Although his path to publishing has been difficult, he still feels that it was worth it. In the words of Brian, "It is a special feeling, when people have the book in front of them and see that you have accomplished something."

Dr. Bobbie Stevens wrote her book, *Unlimited Futures*, about her mind, body, and spirit approach to life, which has been the basis of her successful self-help workshops. She wrote the book because she believes wholeheartedly in the strategies she outlines, and would like to help people create the lives they long for.

She decided to print the book herself, finding it difficult to get attention from traditional publishers, since there are so many self-help books already in the marketplace. Believing that the marketing of the book would be far more crucial than printing specifications or other business-related activities and it would take more time than she had to do a good job of it, she hired a friend, Tara Tuck, to do all of the promotion and publicity. On the inside of the cover, they listed the name Tara Publishing as the publisher, giving the public the impression that a traditional publisher had published it. People would not then disregard it simply because it had been self-published.

After putting her strategies onto paper, getting the finished copy into the marketplace wasn't that complicated, as they used the distributor, Book World, and had the book listed on Amazon.com and BarnesandNoble.com. A number of the larger book distributors and the two Internet retailers above are always looking for new authors because they are not constrained by shelf space, and therefore increase their profits by offering the greatest number of book choices to consumers. Despite the ease of having the book available to the masses through these channels, there are inherent expenses within this system for Dr. Stevens and many other self-published authors. The first is that Amazon.com orders books as there is a demand for them, meaning that if they need five books, they will only order five—not wait until more orders arrive. Stevens must pay for the shipping each time, and the per-unit cost of shipping is much higher for these smaller orders. In addition to covering the sometimes inefficient shipping costs, the author must also pay to have the books warehoused with Book World until they are sold and generate revenue.

Having the books warehoused and listed on the Internet retailers' sites is one thing, but being able to sell them to people is quite another. Thus marketing, as Stevens had predicted, proved to be the biggest challenge on this project. Tuck had little prior experience with publicity and had to learn from the "school of hard knocks," as she received numerous rejections from news editors and book critics. As we mentioned earlier, these individuals have a limited amount of time, and it is challenging, though not impossible, to get their attention as a self-publisher. They were finally successful; however, in getting an advertisement about Stevens in the self-help section of an issue of *Radio Television Interview Report*, a publication which goes out to radio and television producers, as well as copy writers who write headlines for newspapers and magazines. Tuck used the database of this publication's parent company, Bradley Communications, to find the appropriate contacts at newspapers, magazines, and radio and television stations around the country and to send out still more press releases. More recently, Dr. Stevens has also appeared in *Natural Awakenings*, a publication specific to various metropolitan markets, which features health-related articles and advertisements. Their efforts were aided by testimonials from successful individuals, such as *Chicken Soup for the Soul* co-author, Jack Canfield, and from reader feedback on Dr. Stevens' website www.unlimitedfutures.org.

Despite some setbacks, Dr. Stevens is optimistic about her efforts and attends the meetings of many women's groups nationwide promoting her book and seminars. In Chapter 20, we mention the importance of giving any kind of talk related to your book, even to small groups. Tuck reinforces this point. "People love presentations, and once they meet Bobbie, they believe in the program she supports." While the presentations have proved to be an excellent way to sell books, it is expensive to travel around the country, and Stevens has not been able to appear in person at every desired locale. But, for all the hard work, the opportunity to share her vision for self-betterment in *Unlimited Futures* with whoever will listen is worth the sacrifices along the way, and it continues to drive her efforts.

Dr. Michael Norwood, author of the highly successful *Wealthy Soul* series, learned some interesting lessons in marketing with his first major book, *Taking Stock*, which centers on the wisdom—deeply meaningful ideas about life wrapped up in stock advice—that his father imparted upon him before he passed away from terminal cancer.

Earlier in his life, Norwood's sister had also passed away as a result of terminal cancer, and he had wanted to write something to shine a light on the experience, but was unable to express the words at the time because he was still very young. His father opened a new door of creativity for him and gave him an amusing and entertaining means to share his experience and ideas on a difficult subject. Unfortunately, because of the original title of the book he began to get publicity, but in the wrong way. While most authors relish the opportunity for any kind of publicity, Norwood was a little concerned because all of the attention was focused on the stock advice aspect of the book, rather than the far more important spiritual messages. Despite publicity from an article in *The Wall Street Journal* and an onslaught of fans contacting him for financial advice, he knew that an adjustment had to be made. He changed the title of the book to *The Wealthy Soul* just before Christmas one year and participated in a book signing over several days at a Waldenbooks store. To his amazement, Norwood found that his real message sparked a flame in many hearts. He signed over a thousand copies in just a couple of days.

Since then, Norwood's Wealthy Soul series has achieved great success, and his good fortune has given him insight into what it takes to write a book. He notes that "you should write about something that you are passionate about and also know a little bit about." Even though he acknowledges that marketing is the main force that has led him to success, as it typically is with a self-published author, he is quick to point out how unnatural it is for many people, and writers specifically, to push their creative products. He recommends sitting down and thinking about who your market is: their age group, their gender, their race, and even what their hobbies might be. This can help to gain the confidence to reach out to people who may be interested in you and your book. If you can combine this thought process with writing on something of importance to you, Norwood believes, "Your passion will get you through the bumps and grinds and help you to pursue marketing the book."

Authors who self-publish enjoy all levels of success, from capturing the attention of the world and residing on a number of bestseller lists, to simply reaching a small audience in their hometown. Many self-published authors also achieve other kinds of successes, in addition to a network of readers. As a result of their books; a new business may sprout (maybe even a publishing company), the author may be asked to speak in different parts of the country, a freelance job at a newspaper or magazine could open up, or perhaps a traditional publisher will come knocking for the follow-up book. No matter what the goals and ultimate accomplishments of these self-published authors, they all share a common bond; they had an idea for a book, put the idea in motion by writing it, packaged it for printing, marketed it to potential buyers, and have reached a group of readers. While marketing the book and handling the business of printing can be a burden, there is great satisfaction in knowing that you alone are responsible for the creative output and are the sole recipient of its rewards. It was worth the sacrifice.

·**Self-publishing can be labor intensive. However, it can produce big rewards, especially if the author can get the creative juices flowing and implement innovative marketing and distribution strategies.**

·**Many successful authors have used self-publishing with their first books to build a name for themselves before trying to attract the attention of traditional publishers, while others who want to retain more control of their publishing destiny continue to self-publish.**

·**If you believe that self-publishing is the best option for you, but you lack the skills or know-how in certain aspects of the business, enlist the help of an expert.**

CHAPTER 16

Customize Your Readership With Custom Publishing

E very year, millions of college students attend classes on campuses across the country—at community colleges, large state universities, and at highly-prestigious private universities. At least, theoretically, they regularly attend classes—when the other distractions of college life can be avoided for a few hours. While these students come from all walks of life and choose from among thousands of courses, they all have at least one thing in common. They spend lots of money on the scholarly texts required for their classes, which are usually written by distinguished professors in a particular field. Or, rather, the writing and publishing of these books contributes to endowing the professors with distinction. For this reason some academics are quite competitive in trying to get the traditional publishers to acquire and rigorously market their works—a difficult task—since their books are not catered to mainstream America. Luckily there is an easier way for *any* professor to have their books published, regardless of what they teach or where their school is located, and it is called custom publishing.

But it's not just students, professors, and universities in general that benefit from custom publishing. All sorts of businesses and non-profits are another huge market for this path to print. Depending on the size, financial position, and the nature of the business, custom publishing is often used, either to produce books to help train, enlighten, or entertain their employees or, perhaps more commonly, to produce a quantity of books to sell for profit or use promotionally as an extension of the business. Obviously there are other ways for a corporation to produce a quantity of books, including self-publishing by going to a printer directly or using a print on-demand company, but decision makers often prefer hiring a third party to handle much of the design and layout work. Thus custom publishing is an attractive option for many companies.

The central force behind custom publishing is *guaranteed sales*. In the publishing industry, those two words will turn just about anyone's head, since sales are rarely a sure thing. The highly coveted guarantee in custom publishing often comes from the authors, because, in the case of professors, not only are they writing the book or text, but they are also requiring students who take their classes to purchase their book from the campus bookstore, thereby assuring a crop of buyers each semester. Who knows, if the book is well-written, it may also find distribution at other schools or universities beyond its target market, thus increasing the visibility of the professor and increasing their income from the book.

So how does the custom publishing process actually work? Custom publishers are set up differently from traditional publishers, although many are subsidiaries of the large general publishers and textbook publishers, such as Harcourt-Brace and McGraw-Hill. Custom publishers don't have to spend lots of money on a nationwide sales force to market the book. They merely arrange to print enough books for an individual professor's classes based on the number of students. This is the form of custom publishing in which the authors don't put up any money, but they do receives royalties... exactly like in traditional publishing.

There's also another form of custom publishing—the one more commonly used by corporations—in which the company pays a certain fee to a custom publisher to design, edit, critique, and eventually print and ship a quantity of books. Individuals can also make use of this method of custom publishing, but sometimes it can be difficult to raise the necessary capital investment in the same manner that a corporation or a nonprofit organization can through its business operations.

CUTTING-EDGE CUSTOM PUBLISHING WITH JENKINS GROUP

While a number of the major publishers have subsidiaries which operate as custom publishers, Jenkins Group, Inc. (www.jenkinsgroupinc.com), based out of Michigan, is one of the leading unaffiliated players in this path to print. Jenkins Group, run by CEO, Jerrold Jenkins, works primarily with corporations—essentially companies that want to control all the aspects of the production of their book, including retaining all of the rights, but need a third party expert to handle the business details. Many of these corporations use the professional-looking books produced by Jenkins Group as calling cards in the course of their business, rather than send other sales and promotional materials that are more likely to get tossed by the wayside by potential customers.

In addition to all of the pre-publication steps, the Jenkins Group helps their clients to develop a complex marketing strategy (making use of some of their partners and a one-day strategy session), and to get listed with all of the major Internet retailers, distributors and wholesalers. They even show them how to connect with the top literary agents and PR firms, should they desire to take the project beyond the smaller group of guaranteed readers. If you represent a corporation or non-profit organization looking to self-publish using custom publishing or if you are an individual with a large enough group of guaranteed readers (which would quickly make you back the capital that you would have to invest), then you should definitely consider contacting Jenkins Group, Inc. and seeing if it is the right fit for you.

As CEO, Jerrold Jenkins puts it:

Separating from the crowd as a business professional or corporation is increasingly difficult. Having the right tools to compete is essential to a successful future. At the Jenkins Group, we work side by side with each client to deliver their vision as a custom-published book, a permanent and vital element of thought leadership and the overall branding of any winning business.

Custom publishing is appealing for many professors because they don't necessarily have to put up any money, which they would have to do if they used a vanity publisher. Even though professors will usually include the best texts in their field as required reading, they are still guaranteed that their book will be published and used as a supplement to the other reading materials—one which provides a more personalized spin on the course content. With traditional publishing, they would be competing to get accepted by a publisher and then to have their book placed in any schools nationwide. On the other hand, with custom publishing they can start to build the "buzz" on their own campus before approaching professors at other schools and universities about having them add it to their courses.

There is always the risk of the university perceiving a conflict of interest if a professor self-publishes, since they are requiring the book as course material and personally selling it to the bookstore, sometimes without having an intermediary handle the business negotiations (e.g. pricing). With custom printing, however, the publishers handle the editing and printing, and sales to the bookstore, thus at least minimizing any perceived conflict between the professor and their employer or their students. Of course, in reality, the extra income generated by writing an entire book for the class is usually minimal considering the extra hours needed to complete such a project.

Beyond the possible conflict of interest risk, for better or worse, there is stigma attached to a professor self-publishing. In some cases, their colleagues tend to disregard the published work as being sub par, simply because if it were "that good" a traditional publisher would have picked it up, as these professors "mentally anchor" on traditional publishing being the "best" or the "most scholarly" publication option. It's important to note that this stigma exists for the thousands of non-professor writers in the world who self-publish, which is why it's harder to get reviews or bookstore placement if you have a self-published title. But the psychological barriers to "thinking outside the box" in academia are much greater. On campus professors are rewarded for their research efforts, the material they publish in scholarly journals or in complete books (where the saying "Publish or perish" comes from), and in their ability to teach effectively in their specialty. Their track towards tenure and their livelihood is very dependent on these factors. For these reasons, they are sometimes very reluctant to try a new method of publishing. Hopefully, as the drive for thousands of new individuals to write books increases (possibly partially as a result of *Get Between the Covers*), professors and other school administrators will consider other publication options.

But getting back to the mechanism in place, let's simplify how the process works using Associate Professor Picasso: Pedro Picasso teaches Art History at X University, and he decides to write a book for his Art 101 class of 250 freshmen students. He merely hands the manuscript to Custom Publisher Y, who edits, prints, and distributes the book at $10 each. However, the Publisher puts a $60 price tag on it. Associate Professor Picasso requires his students to read the book for his course. The bookstore sells 250 X $60 ($15,000) worth of books each semester. The bookstore gets 20% ($3,000). The professor gets 5% ($750), plus an academic promotion to a full professorship because he can list the book on his resume. Perhaps he can even use it as leverage with a traditional publisher when he writes a second textbook. And the publisher profits the remainder ($8,750 after expenses). Everybody's happy!

Custom publishing might be your path to print if you are a professor or teacher with a small to medium repeat market of readers and the topic of your book is catered to a particular course, or if you represent a company which would like to incorporate an internally-generated book into its business plan. While you may end up sharing the profit with the publisher, you won't necessarily have to put up any capital to ensure publication and you won't have to deal with as many publishing and marketing logistics on your own. If you are considering this option, contact a number of custom publishers and compare their proposed services. Read the section in *Writer's Market* in the appendix for assistance with locating these types of publishers, in addition to contacting the Jenkins Group, Inc.

CHAPTER 17

CONVENTIONAL VANITY PUBLISHING: *Paying for Publication*

Traditional vanity publishing, also called author-subsidy publishing, is another way to publish your book. It does not require looking into a handheld mirror or believing that you make Brad Pitt look like an average guy. What it does involve, however, are companies who are delighted to publish your book, as long as you pay them to do it.

You may be wondering why a publisher, which on the surface resembles a traditional publisher, rather than a print on-demand provider, would ask you to pay them money to publish your book. The reason for this cost to the author derives from the two advantages this form of publishing provides you. First of all, a vanity publisher will almost automatically accept your manuscript, so therefore you have a much better chance of getting published versus the other paths to print. However, the trade-off is that they make money even if the publisher doesn't sell a single copy because of the built-in money that you must invest, which may not give them much incentive to help you drive sales. But, this path to print could be useful for a first-time author of a novel, since novels are usually hard to sell to traditional publishers. As we previously mentioned, on average, only one out of about 400 fiction manuscripts are accepted by traditional publishers. Similarly, with nonfiction manuscripts, a traditional publisher is looking for your track record in your specialty, in addition to the quality of the writing, and whether they can access the appropriate market. Of course, as you now know, ease of entrance is also an advantage of print on-demand publishing, and even though traditional vanity publishing and POD are very similar, the upfront cost is significantly less with POD, not to mention that you may have to give up the rights to your book when you vanity publish—quite a different story to the control that you maintain in the print on-demand world.

On the other hand, whether you are writing fiction or nonfiction, a big advantage of vanity publishing, besides a near guarantee of being published can be the very fact that you do give up control. Having the publisher handle all of the details that go into printing a book can be extremely helpful to those who don't have the time, experience, or patience to do this themselves. Also, if the vanity published book sells well, you have a greater chance of acceptance of a second book by a traditional publisher, which, of course, is also true of the other paths to print.

Many successful authors have tried their hand with vanity publishing. International bestselling author, Deepak Chopra, vanity published his first book, before selling the rights to a major publisher. Willa Cather vanity published her first novel and it went on to win the Pulitzer Prize. And Ernest Hemingway, one of the most famous novelists of all time, paid for the publication of his first novel, as did James Joyce with his critically acclaimed, Ulysses.

A major drawback of vanity publishing should be obvious—you need to have enough money to publish the book when you approach the publisher. Costs are determined by factors such as the length of the book, the number of copies printed, and how much profit the publisher wants to make from the percentage split with the author. Suffice it to say that it will cost at least several thousand or even tens of thousands of dollars. Sometimes an author can get the startup costs covered by a government or foundation grant, but apart from holding your breath in hopes of winning this kind of monetary award, or waiting until you've scrimped and saved the necessary amount, you would perhaps be better suited for some of the other more cost-effective paths to print, if you don't have enough capital to invest upfront.

Another disadvantage to the author stems from the setup of vanity publishing. Newly-established publishers often start out doing only vanity publishing, before converting into traditional methods of publishing. Once they have enough capital to take risks and pay for all of the costs of publishing themselves, they no longer have to demand payment up front from the author and can be more selective in what they accept. Until the publisher makes this transition, they do not have as much credibility with reviewers and other important publishing insiders. Critics tend to disregard vanity published material because it has not gone through the scrutiny of the traditional publishing route. Since you pay the publisher, essentially eliminating risk from the company's perspective, the publisher is much more willing to accept your submission, even if it's not well written or does not have an easily-accessible market of potential readers. In general, with the volume of book submissions that critics receive and with press releases coming from all directions in the news industry, it can be difficult to get attention unless you are with a traditional publisher. Using vanity publishing does not mean that every critic, TV/radio host, or newspaper reporter will turn their back on you, but it will be more difficult to convince them that your book is interesting enough and of high enough quality to be worth their time.

There is one last point we should make about vanity publishing. Because you are paying a large amount of money upfront and not typically retaining many of the rights, you should scrutinize where the money is going and exactly what you are getting in return for it. The vanity publisher may not put much effort into marketing your book and simply keep the profits derived from your upfront investment. Review your contract closely to determine what rights you keep and whether and how you can get the other rights back. Make sure that you examine the invoices detailing how the money is spent. Vantage Press, located in New York, is one of the most well-established vanity publishers, with over fifty years of experience and a solid track record, but you should also use Google or Yahoo to search for other vanity publishers and research the services that they provide. Overall, remember to proceed with caution and to shop around for the best deal to fit your needs, in addition to considering the other publishing options before making the plunge with traditional vanity publishing.

CHAPTER 18

E-PUBLISHING: *Expanding the Literary Horizon*

The Internet, that most intricate and intriguing web of communication ever created, has spawned a generation of "Es." First there was eMail; then came eCommerce. It was only a matter of time before the publishing industry caught on. The output of ePublishing (read eBooks) is an electronic computer file formatted to look and read like a book. It is either read on a screen — more about that later — or sometimes printed out on paper. Since it has the potential to open doors for first-time authors and to provide another distribution mechanism for experienced authors, we have included this chapter to discuss E-publishing, the "virtual" path to print.

Let's start with a brief history of this publishing option. Basically, this whole movement was introduced in the late 1990's. Some people said eBooks would replace paper books. There was lots of talk, not a lot of action. Publishers were not concerning themselves with what the consumer wanted and needed. Content was limited; formats restrictive. Additionally, the early reading devices were bulky, hard on the eyes, and expensive. Consequently, by the early part of this century, eBooks had already fallen out of favor.

Not so today. Electronic publishing is now the fastest growing area in publishing. *Publishers Weekly* ran a story in their 5/29/06 issue titled "The Digital Future is Now." *USA Today* and *Business Week* also sported articles in early '06. "What started as a fad, failed, then became a trend, is now becoming a revolution," says publishing guru Marilyn Ross. The American Booksellers Association reports that for the 2nd quarter of 2006, eBook sales rose 40.3 percent.

What does this mean to you? Plenty! Consider that consumers are suffering from sticker shock with mass market paperback books selling for as much as $9.95 and hardcovers inching toward $30.00. There is a growing demand for books people can afford. eBooks offer a comparable value for a lower price. Also, because we live in the age of instant gratification, folks like the aspect of immediate delivery of digital files. There is no wait. No shipping charges. And people can order 24/7 from anywhere in the world. This translates into a huge potential international buying audience for you, both for fiction and nonfiction.

Furthermore, there is a big difference between getting into print traditionally and cyber publishing: Submitting proposal packages and manuscripts to traditional publishers or agents can be tedious; you may spend months, even years, trying to get published. Getting your book posted on an eBookstore is as simple as providing a PDF file. You need very little personal technical knowledge. While most places charge you a fee, a few are free, such as DPPpress, which specializes in helping authors and self-publishers create a new revenue stream with eBooks. Believing in this new phenomenon of "Reinventing Reading," they also have the DPPstore. When your eBook is sold from their on-line store, you make anywhere from 30 to 60 percent of the selling price. It's "found" money.

Be sure when signing a contract, however, that you do not give up the right to place your book on various kinds of eEstablishments, such as your own website, Amazon.com, and other online bookstores. You don't want any one entity to have exclusivity. Wondering if this will interfere with an already-in-print paper book? Studies show that eBooks do not detract from the sale of paper books. In fact, one format supports the other.

Besides being free and generating new revenue (not to mention leaving you in control of your book), there are other advantages of using this format for getting into print. Sometimes big traditional publishers and agents hunt for promising new properties to acquire by stalking eBook sites. Should you want to establish yourself as an "expert," this is a great way to quickly attain the cachet of being a published author. E-books can provide leads for writing, speaking, or consulting business as well.

You don't even have to start with a complete book. We know of authors who put their books up serially as they write them: one chapter at a time. You can even slice and dice your non-fiction material in various ways: sell separate chapter excerpts, develop a Special Report or White Paper, create a booklet, provide timely updates, or produce a companion product.

Marilyn Ross, coauthor of *The Complete Guide to Self-Publishing*, took the latter approach. She and Matt Brown wrote *The Complete Guide to Self-Publishing Companion*, which delivers hotlinks to current contacts and bonus resources to complement the best-selling *Guide*. Cross-referenced page numbers for the paper book are included so the two formats support each other.

For those inclined to self-publish, eBooks are as attractive as cold lemonade on a hot summer day. Imagine not having any money tied up in print inventory, no freight charges, warehousing fees, fulfillment costs, or returns! And the irksome job of shipping books disappears. So does the "double-dipping" of two layers of middle-men discounts: to distributors/ wholesalers and bookstores. Furthermore, eBooks can be used for review copies, thus eliminating your complimentary paper review copies showing up for sale on Ebay or Amazon.

Many of the present reading devices — "smart phones," Blackberries, and Palms, to name a few — are now slim and lightweight. Students and travelers especially love these handy tools. Instead of schlepping tome after tome, they simply download any number of books onto the gadget. One of the reasons ePublishing has become more popular of late is the new generation of portable reading devices that have introduced a screen with a special, much more readable, ink technology. Sony even has one of the latest digital readers, which has been termed the "iPod of ink," and the company plans to offer titles for download in the same fashion that Apple has cashed in on selling millions of songs through its virtual store, iTunes.

Is this a total panacea? No. Many people, especially the older generation, will always hanker for the tactile feel and smell of paper books. What is a blessing to one, can be a curse to another. Some folks are just not computer savvy. They can't relate to the web and have no interest in anything digital.

Another disadvantage is the fear of piracy. There are two camps addressing this potential copyright infringement issue. One says "Don't sweat it. Most people are honest. And besides, the more people who hear my name and read my material, the better." The other side says, "We need protection. Period." For that reason, Digital Rights Management (DRM) can, and often is, built into an eBook so only the person who purchases it can use it. This is to prevent piracy similar to what we saw in the music world with the rise of Napster and Kazaa, in which users were sharing and downloading songs without ever having purchased them.

While eBooks may be relatively new to the average person, up-and-coming authors have had success getting their material into the marketplace through this path. Even established authors have begun to use them as an alternative, or at the very minimum, as an additional format in which to publish their books and attract readers. The late Leslie Waller, author of more than 50 novels, including best-sellers, such as *The Banker* and *The Swiss Account*, recently E-published his novel, *Target Diana*. Waller, who writes about conspiracy and cover up, has had several of his books made into movies, including *Dog Day Afternoon* and *Close Encounters of the Third Kind*, which he co-wrote with the movie's director, Steven Spielberg. *Target Diana*, a fictional look at the events surrounding the death of Princess Diana, was written about six months after the car accident that tragically ended her life.

Unfortunately, Waller and his agent were unable to find anyone to publish the novel initially, mostly because it suggested that MI-6, the British Secret Service, was involved in a plot to assassinate Princess Diana by staging the accident. He based the theory behind his novel on research and interviews conducted with his personal contacts within the British government, with whom he had established relationships over the years. Waller reported in an article in the *Naples Daily News* (February 8, 2002) that around 95-98 percent of the book is true, but he wrote it as a novel for legal reasons and to protect himself and those who had provided information. Still, traditional publishers were wary about taking a chance on such a controversial book in the wake of the outpouring of sympathy for Princess Diana. Facing this roadblock, publishing the novel as an eBook was a way to get his ideas out to the public. Transatlantic published it in April 2001 and it was eventually released in paperback format after circulating as an eBook.

For more information on E-publishing and how to market your eBooks, consult *How to Publish and Promote Online*, by M.J. Rose and Angela Adair-Hoy, two of the most knowledgeable authors on the subject. Literary agent and successful author, Richard Curtis, coauthor (along with W.T. Quick) of *How to Get Your E-Book Published: An Insider's Guide to the World of Electronic Publishing*, was one of the pioneers in helping E-publishing and eBooks to become more mainstream in the late 1990's, and his book is a great read for anyone who thinks that their book might fit well as an eBook. A title just released in 2006 is *eBook Secrets Exposed* by Jim Edwards and David Garfinkel. Beyond these sources, be sure to examine the websites of the major print on-demand providers that we listed in Chapter 14 to see if they offer the eBook option, and, if all else fails, visit your handy Yahoo or Google search engine and locate the websites of E-publishers. With some persistence, you can join this fascinating and potentially lucrative publishing revolution!

WHICH PATH IS RIGHT FOR YOU?

Type of Publishing	Cost	Barriers to Entry
Traditional Publishing	None. Publisher pays all expenses.	Manuscript must first be accepted by an editor at publishing house, may require an agent for submission as well.
Self-Publishing	Varies depending on who prints it, how many copies you print, how much you spend on advertising and marketing, warehousing expenses, etc. Several hundred to several thousand dollars on average for under 1000 books.	None from a publication standpoint. More difficult to get media attention and publicity than with traditional publishing.
On-Demand Publishing	You pay on average between $400-700 to have the manuscript published and sold through Internet retailers.	In general, none from a publication standpoint, though some screening for sensitive content occurs.
Vanity Publishing	Usually costs several thousand dollars or more to publish the book, depending on the print run.	Very few barriers to entry, since you are paying to have them publish the book. The manuscript goes through little scrutiny.
Custom Publishing	Varies: Sometimes publisher pays upfront expenses—like traditional publishing. Other times you pay the upfront free and get to keep a large part of the profits rather than royalties.	They either have an approval process for your manuscript or automatically your work is accepted if you pay the upfront fee.
E-book Publishing	Varies from free to several hundred dollars.	Some eBook publishers operate like traditional publishers and are selective, while others operate like print on-demand providers and accept almost all manuscripts.

WHICH PATH IS RIGHT FOR YOU (CONT.)?

Type of Publishing	Business Details	Marketing Potential
Traditional Publishing	Publisher coordinates/ manages business and tracks sales. They handle the editing of the book and help to publicize it.	Varies depending on the size and type of the publisher and the resources they want to commit. Most best-selling authors use traditional publishers.
Self-Publishing	You must handle the business details from choosing a printer and the size of the print run, to doing the accounting, to coordinating marketing, storage, and distribution or else you need to hire someone to do these tasks for you.	Varies depending on your level of commitment and subject. In general, authors sell fewer copies than traditionally published ones. Since 100% of profits are yours, you may make more money, especially if you can land large bulk purchases.
On-Demand Publishing	On-demand provider handles many of the business/printing details. You must run any marketing and promoting campaigns or hire someone to do it. Some of the providers will do it for you for a fee.	Comparable to self-publishing in terms of marketing potential. Through promotion on websites and listing with Internet retailers you can potentially reach readers all over the world.

Vanity Publishing	Vanity publisher handles editing, layout, and printing details, but may not effectively promote the book for you.	Tougher to get reviews and media attention. Varies depending on your commitment.
Custom Publishing	Publisher handles all of the business details; you just need to provide a ready crop of readers.	Marketing potential typically limited to predetermined group of readers, but some custom
E-book Publishing	eBook publishers handle the details and pay you a royalty. Often you can put your eBook up on your	As of now, not great marketing potential because of limited exposure of eBooks in the marketplace.

WHICH PATH IS RIGHT FOR YOU (CONT.)?

Type of Publishing	Income from Book	Might be suited for you if...
Traditional Publishing	You may receive an advance on royalties. You get 6-15% of profits and it can be determined from the wholesale price or the retail price. Publisher absorbs any losses.	You are willing to face rejection as you go through the submission channels because you want someone else to handle all the business related to the book. You don't mind working with others and giving up some control. You have aspirations to have a highly successful book.

Self-Publishing	You receive 100% of the profits from the book and absorb any losses. You also can sell the rights to the book to third parties and keep all proceeds.	You want to manage your own affairs and want minimal barriers to entry. You have the capital to pay the upfront costs. You have ways to market and distribute the book.
On-Demand Publishing	You don't receive an advance, but do receive a 20-80% royalty rate. You also retain the rights to the book, which you can sell to a third party.	You want to take advantage of the easiest, most flexible publishing option and don't want to invest a lot of capital upfront.
Vanity Publishing	You split the proceeds from the book with the traditional vanity publisher at a predetermined percentage.	You don't want to deal with the barriers to entry of traditional publishing, but aren't interested in on-demand publishing or self-publishing.
Custom Publishing	You receive royalties from the publishing company or a percentage of the profits, depending on the type of custom publisher.	You are a professor or specialist with a guaranteed group of buyers or a corporation looking to produce a bulk quantity of books and you don't want to go through a traditional publisher.
E-book Publishing	If you self-publish you keep the proceeds, but otherwise you receive 40-70% of the selling price as a royalty from the publisher.	You want to experience no barriers to entry and get your book out quickly. Also, if you have an Internet savvy group of readers.

PART 4

ANECDOTES, ADVICE, AND ACTIVITIES LEADING YOU TO SUCCESS

At this point, you have the core knowledge necessary to write a book and you are now aware of the numerous publication options. The following chapters will reinforce the information and advice in the first three parts of the book, and include examples of ways that other authors have found success, which will hopefully boost your confidence and help you to conceptualize strategies of your own. Some of the advice may not apply directly to you, depending on your goals for your book and your choice of publication. If this is the case, it could still be valuable to store it in your "mental toolbox," because you never know when it might come in handy in your publishing future...our literary journeys frequently take us down some unexpected avenues in our lifetimes. Plus, as you become more interested in writing, it's always valuable to learn more about the publishing industry, even if you plan on operating in just a small area of it.

CHAPTER 19

Impress an Editor for Under $10

When either you or your agent sends in a query letter, book proposal, or completed manuscript to a publisher, it will first be reviewed by an editor, or at least a reader who will pass it on to an editor. As you've learned in earlier chapters, this initial editor will have the power to move your manuscript on to the next step, or to send it back to you with a rejection letter, so it is very important for your submission to leave a favorable impression. In life and in publishing, you rarely get a second chance to make a good first impression, and editors are usually too busy to reread material. So what's the best way to catch an editor's eye and move towards a contract? We certainly don't have all the answers for how to impress an editor, and sometimes it is just a matter of chance and putting enough lines in the water until you get a bite. However, we can tell you that it doesn't involve showering the editor with gifts or having your manuscript gold plated.

251

In this chapter, we outline some of the basic elements that will increase your odds of success. For further information on submitting queries and proposals in correct and eye-catching formats, consult *Writer's Market, How to Write a Book Proposal* by Michael Larsen, *Author 101: Bestselling Book Proposals* by Rick Frishman and Robyn Freedman Spizman, and *Write the Perfect Book Proposal: 10 That Sold and Why, 2ⁿᵈ Edition*, by Jeff Herman.

Depending on the type of book that you are writing and whether you have already had contact with a particular editor or are using a literary agent, the order of events can vary, but there is a general structure to how the process typically evolves. Initially, you or your agent usually sends a one page query letter to an appropriate editor for your book, unless the agent has a strong enough relationship and rapport with an editor to just make a phone call. The query is to solicit an indication of interest—the editor will ask for the book proposal, sample chapters or the completed manuscript if there is an interest. If the editor isn't interested or doesn't feel like "there is a fit" with the books they publish, he or she will most likely send a letter letting you know that they are going to pass, although sometimes the editor may not respond at all if they are swamped and you get lost in the shuffle.

With nonfiction, the book proposal is usually the second step in the process, after you've received a positive response to your query. When publishers accept a project, they are committing to putting up capital for a book which may or may not pan out financially. As we mentioned earlier, the situation is analogous to a venture capital firm, which reviews business plans before deciding whether to provide funding for a startup company. There is an inherent risk and reward, and the VC firm must determine the viability of your proposed company. In the publishing world, *you* are the startup company and the book proposal is like the business plan that you present to get a "yes" and the funding to move ahead. In fact, most nonfiction is sold with a book proposal and sample chapters—not the actual completed book.

Fiction is sometimes also sold using a book proposal, but the manuscript or sample chapters become much more important, since fiction is less about who you are or your topic of expertise, and more about your writing style, your ability to produce an entertaining plot, and your capacity to keep a reader captivated for thousands of words. The only way for a publisher to get a clear picture of these elements is to see the actual writing. But, as we've mentioned, many of the best fiction writers and most notable fictional works were rejected numerous times before eventual publication. Because the determining factors are a "matter of taste," it is enormously challenging for the editor to predict how the population will respond to a book.

Susan Driscoll, CEO of iUniverse, who we've cited in this book several times because she is one of the leading experts in the publishing industry, discusses in her book *Get Published!* (with Diane Gedymin) how sometimes timing can influence decisions for an editor. You can write a great manuscript, but fail to have it get picked up by a particular publisher because they happen to be looking at a completely different kind of book for the next season. Or, they may have just acquired a book on the same subject and thus would rather diversify, rather than load up in one area. Similarly, it's possible that some competing publishers just picked up similar titles and the target publisher doesn't want to try to compete in a saturated market. For all of these reasons, as we have emphasized with many aspects of publishing throughout this book, you need to be persistent and try several options in anything that you do. Sometimes hearing "no" has nothing to do with the quality of your product. The more you put yourself out there, the less that randomness will work against you and your publishing future.

While there are entire books written about how to successfully approach an editor, some of which we've strongly recommended you look at, here are some basic keys to success:

1.   **Only send well-edited material; the fastest way to get a rejection letter is to submit a poorly constructed proposal or query, or a manuscript full of grammatical and typographical errors, not to mention choppy writing or a weak plot.** For basic grammatical and spelling errors, put the spell checker on your computer to good use and read *The Elements of Style* or *The Chicago Manual of Style*. Also, check facts to ensure accuracy. A good proofread is always invaluable. If you want to be sure that you've caught everything, have a professional edit the material for you. At the very least ask someone knowledgeable in the subject matter who has had editing experience to make suggestions. In terms of fixing the structure of the manuscript, you can start by rereading Chapters 6 and 7 for suggestions on editing and getting peer reviews prior to submission.

2.   **Once you have your polished manuscript in hand, make sure your material fits within the guidelines of the publishing house.** No matter how good your writing is, if your manuscript is in a genre that

a publisher does not represent, then it won't be accepted. Even Harry Potter and his current reign atop the publishing world would be passed on by a publisher which only publishes biographies (though in this case any publisher might make an exception).

Determining *exactly* what editors want has always been a mystery, but by following the guidelines of each house, you at least increase your chances. To find publishers and the genres they publish look for the listings in *Writer's Market*, as it will help you to narrow your focus. When you send a query letter or book proposal, it helps if you can reference something about the publisher you're submitting to, since this will help to convince whoever is reading your query or proposal that you have done your homework and feel that your manuscript is in line with what they typically accept.

As authors, and thus entrepreneurs of a sort, we tend to be risk takers and to try to present our material in a different way. When writing your book that's a fantastic trait to possess, as it leads to unique, fresh outlooks on the world...and publishers love fresh new material. What they don't like, however, is trying to evaluate a project that gets submitted in a non-traditional format. Editors are already severely constrained by time, so having to search for the essential information in order to properly judge the potential for your project will hurt your chances. Editors, while obviously very connected with the creative world, also work in the corporate world, where there is supposed to be order and a certain degree of uniformity of style to business proposals. Follow the format for submissions and within those boundaries show the editor that you and your work stand out from the crowd.

COMPROMISES AND PREPARATION

Diligent preparation, researching a number of potential publishers, and submitting well-polished manuscripts has led Evelyn Coleman to positive experiences with editors. She has gone on to win several awards, including *The Smithsonian Most Outstanding Children's Book Title* and *The Parents' Choice Honor Book* for her children's book *White Socks Only*.

To explore one of the winning formulas for impressing editors, look no further than Coleman. Even though she initially received rejection letters from editors, she didn't allow them to discourage her, but used them as fuel to take better aim with her next submission. Often the editors provided constructive criticism and recommended other publishers who might have a special interest in her manuscript. She also read as many books as she could find that were similar in content and style to her own. She then tracked down the editors who had worked on those books and sent query letters and book proposals to them, eventually putting her material in front of the right people. Her initial mistake is one that she feels many new writers commit. "People don't do their homework before they send their material out, and it greatly reduces their chances of gaining acceptance. They finish a story and immediately try to send out their manuscript before doing the necessary research on publishers."

After Coleman had identified a number of publishers who put out material similar to hers, she targeted the largest ones because they have a broader reach *and* they pay more. Fortunately she was accepted by some of the larger publishers, but she was prepared to work her way down to regional and even local publishers if necessary. There have even been cases where she considered going straight to a regional publisher, when the topic of the book was narrower in scope, and approaching a larger publisher would have been more of an uphill battle.

Every time one of her books has been accepted, she has kept an open mind when receiving advice from her editors. She tries to find solutions when her editor identifies a problem, rather than acting defensive, because, in her words, "I'm very willing to lose words. The manuscript is not written *in blood*." The editors appreciate her openness and have praised her positive attitude, not to mention expressing their gratitude because she makes their jobs easier. This has opened doors for her and kept the editors eager and willing to look at her new material.

While Coleman admits that working with editors is sometimes challenging, she has never considered self-publishing. As an African-American author, she is proud to be published by the "big boys." In the past these doors were shut to African-Americans, and there is a sense of satisfaction in being able to share her message with a larger audience—through the increased exposure a traditional publisher can offer. Coleman's credo is that "Writing influences the world because words have incredible power," and she has carried this belief throughout her literary career. This is the reason she believes that others should keep writing and publishing.

---

3.   **Prepare a good sales pitch and explain why your book is the perfect fit for a particular publishing house, yet is still different from other works they've seen before.** In order to develop your pitch and distinguish yourself from the herd, you need to know the competition. The easiest way to accomplish this is to run a search on Internet retailer sites such as Amazon.com or Barnes&Noble.com. Alternatively, check out the selection at a large bookstore or ask a sales person to run a search for you. Or you can ask a librarian what is popular that might be similar to your book—they usually will have a fairly good idea of what people are currently reading. Studying the competition can help you to succinctly describe your work by comparison in your query or proposal and can also help you identify your target audience, perhaps giving you a competitive advantage for gaining readers.

While it is advisable to stay within guidelines of each publishing house, both in terms of which types of books they publish and the formats of the queries and proposals they would like to see, it is in your best interest to get creative in your submissions—within the overall structure. Rick Frishman and Robyn Freedman Spizman, authors of *Author 101: Bestselling Book Proposals,* recommend a number of great strategies to help you separate yourself from the pack, which is why we advise you to pick up a copy of their book. One of the more compelling techniques is to ask provocative questions at the start of a query letter or proposal. The questions can be anything related to your topic or background and if constructed properly, they could really spark the interest of the editor—thus getting them to carefully read over your material, rather than just giving it a cursory scan. With all of the advertisements that we see every day, how many commercials ask thought-provoking, rhetorical questions that instantly cause us to "tune in?" (Note: By the way, the previous question would be a prime example, if we were writing a query letter for a book about creative advertising).

We hope to continually remind you that everyone has unique ideas and experiences, as well as a distinct imagination, which deserve to find a voice in a published book. Your book WILL be different from the other titles on the shelf. Focus first on telling your story in the best way possible, and allow your writing to bring out your individuality. Later you can spotlight this uniqueness to a potential editor with your sales pitch, especially if you have a humorous style, a viewpoint which challenges the traditional mindset, or a fictional tale which is so vivid that you take readers on a captivating journey.

4.   **If you have specific ideas on how your book might be marketed, it is important to communicate this to the editor in the book proposal.** For example, you would want to let the editor know if you have a specific buyer who is interested in purchasing a bulk quantity of books. A pharmaceutical company might place a large order for a book on a medical condition for which the company made a particular device or medication. Or a national chain of flower shops might want to give out a brochure with each delivery, based on a chapter from a book about flower arranging, and may be willing to include an order form for the book in the packaging.

In general, publishers love writers who operate like entrepreneurs when it comes to promoting their work and building a platform. These are the kinds of authors who don't just turn in a manuscript and wait for royalty checks—they pound the pavement either on their own volition or at the publisher's request and bring readers to their book.

To that end, any endorsements you provide from successful authors, celebrities, or experts in your field that add to the credibility of the book will also be music to your editor's ears. Tying your book to a national event or holiday could be a great marketing concept. Publishers often develop special relationships with specific groups, such as schools or libraries. If you can pitch your book to the editor as the ideal fit for an organization that the publishing house often sells to, it will be another enticement to the editor to accept your manuscript.

5.   **Editors representing a particular genre of book may have special criteria for selecting a manuscript.** For example, Laurie Rosatone, representing the textbook division of John Wiley, looks at the content of the book as well as the accolades of the author. Someone with a Ph.D. in their field from a prestigious university has an obvious advantage, but Rosatone's division also investigates whether the author is a good teacher, either by interviewing colleagues or by sitting in on classes. She feels that in academic publishing, the best teachers also make the best authors because they care about educating the students. If an editor or publishing house does have particular criteria they use for judging a manuscript or author, it is important to know about this ahead of time. Use *Writer's Market* to research specific criteria of the publishers you are investigating.

6. The virtue of patience is an often overlooked key to success. One of the biggest mistakes authors can make is to call or email editors excessively because they haven't heard back about their manuscript. Be patient; it sometimes takes several months for them to sift through their pile of manuscripts or proposals before getting to your submission. Remember, even the best editors can only edit about ten pages a day for their current authors, with whom they must work, while also juggling their schedules to allow time to search for new manuscripts. Plus, as part of working within a corporation, they have regular meetings to attend, deadlines for projects to meet, various activities of numerous individuals to coordinate, and a sanity to maintain.

7. Learning from experience never hurts (well at least not permanently). Even if you aren't successful at first in gaining acceptance or even getting beyond the query stage with editors at publishing houses, don't be dismayed. Nearly every famous author has faced rejection numerous times before they went on to great success. With so many submissions, it often becomes simply a numbers game—with the editors struggling to find the time to evaluate incoming projects. This is why so many people submit through literary agents, on whom the editors often rely heavily in order to save time in the evaluation process. In any case, try to make the most of the feedback that you get from those who don't give you the "go ahead;" many times it can be valuable insight into minor changes that you can make to your query, proposal, or manuscript, which will open the door for you at another publishing house.

Overall, no matter what the topic or style of writing, editors are looking for books they feel confident will sell at least enough copies to improve the company's bottom line. The magic number might be as few as 1,000 copies or less, depending on the size of the publisher and the numerous other cost factors they calculate. There are about 6 billion people in the world and 280 million in the United States alone. Even though not everyone regularly reads books, there is a real possibility that your book could reach that magic number of readers. If an editor likes your ideas and writing style, and feels that the company can reach your market and sell a fraction of that magic number of books, then you've likely got a deal!

CHAPTER 20

AUTHOR-GENERATED HYPE:
The Key to Heightened Sales

Whether you self-publish or go through a traditional publisher, and whether you want to sell your book to the masses in hopes of creating a significant source of income or simply cater to a small group of readers in a niche market, possibly as a hobby, the best promoter and advocate for your book is *you*. Don't worry; you don't need an M.B.A. in Marketing to succeed. Most of the avenues for connecting with potential readers are easy to access, and with a little bit of elbow grease and some tenacity you can become an effective self-promoter in no time. Recognizing the importance of this chapter, we've included perspectives from a number of the leading authorities on marketing and book publicity, as well as examples of innovative strategies employed by successful authors from all backgrounds.

For starters, as you probably knew before ever picking up this book, the book selling business is very competitive. A reader browsing at a Barnes

& Noble or on Amazon.com has anywhere from 100,000, to over eight million books to choose from, and it would take a lifetime to sift through all of them, especially considering the hundreds of new titles added daily. While it's been said that a reader doesn't choose a book, it chooses them; the reality is that most of the time someone reads a book because they've heard or seen something about it. Think of the newer authors who have risen to immediate success, such as Dan Brown, Cecelia Ahearn, and Andre Dubois. All relied on the positive feedback and word-of-mouth buzz from their readers in order to capture the attention of the masses and sell a huge number of copies.

The most cost-effective way to stand out in the literary crowd and help lead readers to *your* book is self-promotion. Ironically, this has generally been tagged as a "negative, egocentric activity" for an individual to engage in, and yet it is totally acceptable for corporations when pushing their products. Whatever your feelings are on self-promotion, you need to understand that in the literary world, talking about yourself, your achievements, and your book for the benefit of readers or potential readers is not narcissistic; it's a positive way to share your creativity. Inquiring minds want to learn more about the person whose name is on the cover. More specifically, they want to know what experiences or motivation went into the creative work in front of them. If you can position yourself as an expert, which we believe anyone can who has written a book, then it will only add to your appeal.

And really, no matter what business you are in, it's good marketing in today's culture to self-promote; some of the most successful people—Donald Trump, Mel Gibson, and Oprah Winfrey—are experts at marketing themselves, their projects, and their products. Daphne du Maurier's quotation, "Writers should be read, but neither seen nor heard," couldn't be farther from the truth in the modern publishing world, if you want readers to find out about your book, take an interest in it and in you, and ultimately purchase copies.

So how do people get the inside scoop on your book? Is it as simple as telling people on the street about it? **Yes.** In fact, there are a number of authors who pass out their books to potential readers as quasi-business cards instead of or in addition to actual business cards or handouts. While it may seem crazy to give away something that you are trying to sell, you'd be amazed at how fast certain ambitious individuals have generated a buzz about their projects and catapulted themselves to seemingly impossible sales levels. Even some of the most famous authors, such as John Grisham and James Redfield (author of *The Celestine Prophesy*), started by handing out their first books or selling them out of the trunks of their cars.

What you need to realize when marketing your book is that anything (and by that we mean anything *legal*) that you can do to reach potential readers and convince them to buy your book is considered good marketing. Bestselling author, Po Bronson, even sold shares of his book *Bombardiers* in a New York bar, as if it were a an IPO on NASDAQ. The ploy landed him on *Entertainment Tonight* and *CNN*. The book eventually became an international bestseller. Teenage author, Christopher Paolini, dressed up in costumes depicting characters in his self-published fantasy novel, *Eragon*, and traveled to schools and bookstores all around the country giving talks to groups of children, young readers, and even their parents—a ploy that skyrocketed sales and eventually landed him a large deal with a major publisher, Alfred A. Knopf. More recently, Michael Stadher authored *A*

Treasure's Trove, a children's book that he boosted to the top of Amazon. com's bestseller list (and many others) in 2005. For his follow-up book, *Secrets of the Alchemist Dar*, he will help spark interest by using clues in the book to create a worldwide treasure hunt for 100 jeweled rings valued at over $2 million. Clearly, the opportunities for creative marketing are endless, but unless you are really skilled, you may want to avoid the Philippe Petit approach. He walked a tightrope almost fifty feet off the ground without a net, to promote his book, *To Reach the Clouds: My High Wire Walk Between the Twin Towers*.

Of course, we would all like to believe that the market for our book or the ideal reader is "everyone," but this is a rookie mistake. Even the top authors in the world know that millions will never have an interest in reading their work. So, the first rule that you need to follow is to figure out who your target reader is and then find a way to direct your efforts towards that type of person.

This leads into the second crucial part of marketing, which is finding "hooks" that mesh with you and the theme/message of your book and either get the attention of your prototypical target reader or of other critical individuals like members of the media. You can use "hooks" in virtually anything marketing related…from landing speaking gigs, to convincing bookstores to hold a signing for you, to getting featured articles written about your book. You can emphasize how your book will spark dialogue on a current media-worthy subject, how you are a local resident with a great new book (local newspapers love articles like this), or even how you plan to use the proceeds of the book (if you are charitably inclined).

In this chapter we will tell the stories of traditionally published and self-published authors whose creativity boosted book sales and helped them to connect with readers all over the country. They didn't start out with a big budget or an advanced knowledge of how to market. They simply sought to inform readers of their books, and, whenever possible, to do it face-to-face. We hope that these examples help you customize a plan to fit your book, considering your audience, schedule, and budget. Once you formulate any plan, all you need to do is follow through with the necessary legwork and determine what's effective and what's not, making adjustments as needed. Later in this chapter, we will also discuss outside publicists and what they can do for you if your book has the potential for a large readership or if you just feel more comfortable turning the reins of your marketing campaign over to a professional.

Bear in mind that no source can possibly list all of the ways to market a book because there are so many types of books and so many desired audiences for such a diverse range of authors. And again, employ your imagination when conjuring up marketing plans…the sky is the limit if you do! For guidance and ideas, any writer hoping to reach as many readers as possible and generate income from their book should read *1001 Ways to Market Your Books* and *Guerilla Marketing for Writers*. Both books offer a "one-stop" approach for marketing—giving you more creative ideas than you can imagine, while detailing how you can actually implement them. In fact, since reading both sources, we have begun to utilize a number of their strategies to promote this book and others that we have in development.

BOOK MARKETING'S MAIN MAN

John Kremer "eats and sleeps" book marketing. In addition to reading his book, *1001 Ways to Market Your Books,* it would be well worth your time to visit the website (www.bookmarket.com). Kremer has mentored many of the most profitable self-publishers and he even has his own publishing consulting practice that can assist you with the marketing strategy for your book. He regularly speaks all over the country at publishing conventions and offers a variety of publishing seminars throughout the year.

The importance of marketing almost can't be put into words, if you truly are seeking to increase the number of readers of your book. According to Kremer, "Marketing is a high priority for only one reason. That's how you reach potential readers of your book—and why would you want to write if you didn't want readers?" For this reason, Kremer's ideal clients are those with an entrepreneurial sense about them. He recognizes, like most successful authors, that you have to be willing to do a lot of marketing yourself. You can't just rely on having someone do it all for you, if you really hope to reach readers beyond your circle of friends and family.

Looking back on his work in the publishing industry over the course of many years, he cites several reasons for his continued enjoyment in helping authors, especially those who write for the love of writing—not because they feel compelled to. "I love great book ideas, great book execution, and great book reading experiences. When an author is passionate about his or her work, then I'm interested. Then I get excited."

For an author of any level, giving talks and participating in book signings are two of the simplest and most effective ways to sell books and attract attention, even if you are only able to do them in your hometown. You will make contacts, get new ideas, earn a profit either through book sales or from an honorarium, and, most importantly, you will be able to connect with your readers on a grassroots level. Many authors who go through traditional publishers and every author who self-publishes can set up their own signings and talks. It can be a very quick way to reach readers and to gain credibility. In fact, George Bernard Shaw, winner of the Nobel Prize for Literature and one of the most famous playwrights of all time, began to speak everywhere that he could arrange it after his first six novels and eight plays were rejected. He did it to make himself appear to be an expert and to try to increase his chances of acceptance for future works. In all, he gave around 1000 speeches to anyone who would listen…the results speak for themselves.

In terms of speaking at bookstores, as we discussed in Chapter 12, you can try starting with smaller bookstores on your home turf or go directly to the person who books authors at individual stores of the national chains. The stores will then promote your appearance to their customers through emails, newsletters, signage in the store, flyers, and sometimes even by posting information about you in the calendar of events section in local newspapers. Try to visit as many stores as possible, especially the independent ones, as they may be more likely to carry your books. Just be sure that wherever you give a talk they have copies available for sale in the store or that you at least bring some with you to sell. The worst thing that could happen is that you spend the time putting together an event and succeed in getting people excited about purchasing your book, only to have them not be able to get copies right away. It's never a bad idea to keep a few spare copies boxed in your trunk just in case.

Libraries are another site for speaking opportunities. In addition to meeting and greeting readers, you may be able to convince the library to purchase copies of your book, if they haven't already done so. Becoming a member of the Friends of the Library in your neighborhood might open up the possibility of speaking to the group's members and being promoted in the monthly newsletter (Visit www.folusa.com to find a chapter near you).

You can also arrange to speak at local or national clubs, schools, associations, or churches in your area. Additionally, many local groups— press clubs, women's clubs, Rotary clubs, writers groups, etc.—often host seminars and workshops and invite local authors and freelance writers to speak on various publishing-related topics. You may be able to convince the organizers to let you appear, or, at the very least, you could attend, meet others who share your passion, and perhaps develop valuable contacts, which could open doors that take your literary project to the next level. Basically, in any community anywhere in the world, you should be able to find opportunities to speak about your book.

If you are apprehensive about meeting new people in this context or being able to capture their interest, remember that it often gets easier the more you do it. The best way for you to communicate is not to put yourself on a pedestal, but rather connect with people as though you were talking to a friend—reminiscing about your thoughts and experiences and seeking their feedback and insights. Don't worry about people laughing at you, even if you goof up. Whether they are laughing with you or at you, you're still making them happy! And there's nothing wrong with people challenging or correcting you; it's healthy for you to take pride in being self-critical and self-reflective. An audience is frequently more sympathetic to one who doesn't stand on a pedestal, but considers themselves a student as well as a teacher. However, you have every right to be the featured speaker. You've devoted a big chunk of your time to researching, thinking about, and agonizing over a certain topic, which gives you somewhat of an authority status in the field.

This is a great learning experience for you, because the response from the audience will give you new perspectives on and understanding of your subject matter, or, in the case of fiction can help you to pinpoint your greatest storytelling strengths. You don't even really know what you've written until you get the spectrum of responses from the many vantage points of your readers.

Apart from you benefiting from feedback, your talks often create a buzz in the community resulting in a ripple effect of: more invitations to speak (possibly even in other parts of the country), more reviews, news stories on television, radio, and in print, free advertising opportunities (for example, a free book when you buy a certain kind of car, join a health club, purchase a time share, etc.), and most importantly building the word-of-mouth hype.

If you are really serious about making your speaking appearances an extension of your book and its marketing campaign, you should keep records of all of the places where you've spoken and consider collecting comment cards from attendees or giving yourself a grade on each appearance. It will help you to fine-tune your approach and allow you to be even more captivating the next time. For more exposure, join either a speaker's bureau (a booking agency for speakers) or one of the national associations like Toastmasters or the National Speakers Association, which help you to network and improve your public speaking abilities. And, no matter what level you are at—whether you are speaking for free and selling a few copies here and there or getting paid a fee of $10,000 and are the headliner at a dinner—always be sure to send thank-you notes to the organizers and sponsors of events. You just never know where the sense of goodwill that you leave behind will take you in the future.

THE DOORS E-MARKETING CAN OPEN ARE ENDLESS

These days, authors create their own websites to promote their books and stay in touch with readers. If you don't have the technical know-how to design your own site, you might want to hire an independent web designer. Or you might consider hiring *AuthorsontheWeb.com*. They specialize in creating professional looking websites for authors. One of the authors who used this service, Neil Gaiman, was able to get over a hundred thousand hits on his site, and his book, *American Gods* became a bestseller. You can also create an email list of your fans and keep them posted on your activities. To that end, you may even follow in the footsteps of many independent musicians and artists: Myspace.com has a become a popular venue for posting your own website/profile, which can easily be done with limited computer skills, and can allow you to share information about you and your project, including the ability to send out electronic bulletins to interested individuals.

The value of E-Marketing can't be overstated. Even authors with big budgets do it. But for you, the main advantage is the cost effectiveness of this method of reaching readers. By having your own website, perhaps maintaining a blog, and staying connected with links to your products listed on online retailers, you can effectively drive people to purchase your book and to tell all of their friends to as well.

Using the Internet, in addition to saving you money, might ideal if you are intimidated about promoting in person, but are still driven to succeed. It's also great if your audience is spread around the world. Finally, with so many books sold on the Internet (Amazon.com is the 3rd biggest retailer behind Barnes & Noble and Borders…Borders even uses Amazon system online to sell books) this has become a great option for many people. Heck, there are even "virtual" book tours now, wherein the author appears on select websites to promote books and answer questions for a certain amount of time. So instead of logging the miles on your book tour, you could do it all in your bathrobe over the course of a few hours in front of the computer.

We will talk about reviews later in the chapter, but for now, it should be pointed out that having online reviews, either on general sites or even on retailer sites, is a tremendous advancement for everyone in the publishing industry. First of all, you don't have to wait months for a review to come out…everything happens in real time. Secondly, anyone can leave a review, not just a handful of reviewers around the country who are tied to finite number of publications that review books. Finally, you can respond to the reviews online if you agree or disagree, which creates a form of scholarly discourse between you and readers that can lead to more attention and thus more sales. No longer must you simply "accept" a bad review…make a logical counter-argument for why you wrote your book the way you did.

If you are more of a "low-tech" person, you can always write letters to people you meet at talks who might be interested in your books, in addition to any thank-you notes to organizers. In fact, Barbara Cartland, who has written hundreds of novels, and has some of the highest sales totals in modern history (with over 650 million copies sold worldwide), personally answers letters from her fans. With the number of books she has sold, she obviously receives droves of fan mail, but just think about how special each person feels when they get a letter back from her. They are certainly likely to purchase her books again.

In addition to major publications, which only review or write articles about a select number of books, there are thousands of other, smaller publications which carry book reviews. You can send press releases out to your college's alumni magazine, your local alternative newspaper, or to regional newsletters. Often these smaller publications are more accessible to newer writers because they are not as barraged with requests and they like to publish stories with a local slant. Plus, you never know who might catch wind of your local buzz and spread the word to a larger audience. Reviews in local, regional, or national publications may lead to interviews on television and radio shows, which often cater to particular groups, such as women, Baby Boomers, or people sharing a certain political affiliation.

Who knows, maybe you will even create a new trend like Julia Child, who, when asked to come on a public television station to promote her first cookbook, brought along cooking utensils and some eggs to demonstrate how to make omelets, only to spark the idea for cooking shows on television. Without Julia's spontaneity, we might not have cooking shows such as *Emeril*, and there may not be a Rachael Ray showing us how to eat well in interesting locations for $40 a day, while also topping the bestseller lists with her cookbooks.

Clearly word-of-mouth is one of the best ways to sell books; the more people who read a book, the more people who can recommend it to others to buy, borrow, or steal. You can add to this hype by continuing to contact target groups of people who share something in common with you or may be able to relate to the subject matter of your book. Some of these individuals may include: family members, friends, neighbors, co-workers or colleagues, book reviewers, book clubs, appropriate special interest groups (e.g. students, via teachers/ professors in a related field of study), and freelance writers (who may want to pitch a story relating to your book to a local/national magazine, newspaper, or trade publication).

One of the most fruitful ways to market a book, which is often overlooked by authors, is to sell it in bulk quantities. An article in a local newspaper might result in a hundred books being sold at the local bookstores. However, a visit to the human resource department of a company to pitch a health book to keep employees healthy, a cookbook to give to each employee for their birthday, or a fantasy novel to give out during the Christmas/Chanukah/Quanza season could result in a single sale of a thousand copies.

Books typically retail at eight times what it costs to print because the process of selling one book at a time is very costly. Therefore, publishers or self-published authors can afford to offer steep discounts for large quantity purchases and still make a nice profit (with a share going to the author in royalties if sold through the publisher). If you're lucky enough to land a large sale to a corporation, non-profit organization, or a government agency off of the manuscript alone, then you don't have to risk any money upfront and you can still make a profit as a self-publisher, by selling the book at a deep discount, but still allowing yourself a tidy sum above the costs of printing.

Just as you're creative when you write your book, think creatively about entities to approach where you can sell large quantities. A nursing home chain might have an appetite for a humorous novel about nursing homes; a gym might be enticed by a book on diet and exercise; and a stock brokerage firm may have a need for a bulk quantity of books that deal with secure financial practices for their clients. Additional bait could be to offer the option of adding the logo of the company on all copies printed for them.

Another innovative way to market is to partner with a non-profit organization, whereby the non-profit gets a percentage of the profits from the sale of all books. This can be noted on the back cover or on a separate page of the book. For instance, the Humane Society might get 20% of the royalties from book sales of a children's story about pets. The non-profit might help push sales; a pet lover might be more motivated to buy the book; and the author can feel good about their book sales helping a worthy cause.

The Purpose-Driven Life, by Rick Warren, which has sold over 30 million copies in the past several years, is a perfect example of the potential when connecting with a non-profit organization. In order to spread his message, Rick offered the book to the pastors in his area at a significant discount. The pastors ordered over 500,000 copies of the book for the members of their congregations and it was only a matter of time before the word-of-mouth spread like wildfire and he had a crop of readers all over the world.

Another marketing tactic commonly used is to seek testimonials from other authors, from authorities in your field, or from reviewers. While some marketing experts believe that testimonials are less important in publishing than in other lines of business, it certainly doesn't hurt sales to add them to the cover of your book. Not to mention that they may help you to network with colleagues, inspire stories or reviews written in various publications, and add credibility to your book. In some cases, notable individuals will even agree to write a foreword or an introduction, which serves to not only explain the writing to come in the rest of the book, but also to bolster the "eye-catching" appeal of your book.

HOW TO DOUBLE OR TRIPLE YOUR INCOME AS AN AUTHOR OR PUBLISHER

The section below contains information provided directly by Fred Gleeck (www.fredgleeck.com), who's been described as the "king of content," as well as being a product guru and a marketing expert. He also happens to run a number of highly-successful marketing seminars with John Kremer. We've included this section for those readers who want to focus on generating a significant amount of revenue from their books.

Less than 1% of all authors make more than $50,000 a year. Sad but true. Want to be in the 1% group? Then keep reading.

The reality of publishing is that the "real" money isn't made from books. It's made from all of the other products and services that you sell people AFTER they buy your book. I'm the author of more than 10 books myself, so I speak from experience.

To make the "big bucks" as a publisher you need to create a LINE of products related to your book AND an automated system to sell them. This may sound like a daunting task but compared to writing your book it will be relatively easy.

Since people learn using different modalities, you'll need to eventually create products that can be read (books, ebooks), watched (videos and DVDs), listened to (audios of all kinds) and experienced (seminars, teleseminars, etc.). The products you create should range in price from $10 to $1000.

Don't worry. You don't have to create them all at once. BUT, if you don't have a skeletal line of products lined up before your book comes out, you'll be losing money right from the start. If your book is already done and printed you can always insert a postcard into the book to "bounce them back" to you.

Think of your book as a way to get people into your "funnel" to then upsell them all of the other materials that you offer. I recommend a program called WebMarketingMagic (www.WebMarketingMagic. com) to help you manage your online efforts.

To get people into your funnel you'll need to create bounce-back offers in your book. I suggest including various kinds of offers imbedded in the text of the book itself. One of mine (on page 43 of one of my books) says: "to collect your free gift worth $47, send an email to tips@ SeminarExpert.com. I also put that same bounce-back offer at the bottom of each of the pages in my book. I suggest you consider doing the same.

Do NOT send people to a website. You are not certain of capturing their email address if you do it that way. Instead, ask them to email you. That way you'll be certain to get THEIR email address.

When people don't buy from you directly, you don't know who they are. The only way to get them to identify themselves is to offer them a bribe, preferably a digital bribe (like an ebook or an ecourse) that has high perceived value. Offering people this bribe in your book will give them a strong incentive to get them into your funnel at NO cost to you.

After you get peoples' email addresses you'll want to send them some great content to make them comfortable buying other products and services from you. You can do this all automatically with autoresponders, another feature of WebMarketingMagic.

Each product you produce (whether audio or video) should have its own website. Take a look at www.PinkGoat.com to get some ideas.

To create your audios, videos and events, you'll need to learn the process before jumping in. I highly recommend that you check www.TheProductGuru.com to get a better idea of how to do those things the RIGHT way. I've coached many authors just like you, so feel free to give me a call and I'll make sure to help you get it done right.

(Author's Note: You can find the most updated contact information for Fred on any of his websites.)

NOMAD NABS NEW READERS

Author Rita Golden Gelman's story of her cross-country book selling voyage will give you insight into creative marketing. Her book, *Tales of a Female Nomad*, was published by Crown, a Random House subsidiary, and is a travelogue, covering fifteen years of her adventures after having traded in a comfortable lifestyle in California in favor of "economy traveling" the world. *Tales of a Female Nomad* chronicles her time spent in countries all over the globe, including Mexico, Nicaragua, New Zealand, Bali, and Thailand.

After finishing the book and having it accepted, Rita requested that Crown underwrite a national book tour, but the publisher was only willing to commit to booking a few National Public Radio interviews. She decided to take charge, realizing that otherwise the book would likely die off after the slight 2-3 month push the publisher would give her. The book is a tale of how she became a confident, self-reliant woman, after having unbelievable experiences with fascinating people in exotic places, and she wanted it to reach as many people as possible. She channeled this self-confidence into a self-propelled cross-country book tour, by tapping into her extensive email list of people she had befriended on her past travels—people who would be willing to invite her into their homes as she toured, thus helping her to keep the cost of the trip within her budget. Once the initial plan was concocted, Gelman bought a car, sat down with a map of the United States, and prepared for an adventure. She also hired a publicity firm and read the book *Jump Start Your Book Sales*, by Marilyn and Tom Ross, which she feels is a particularly useful read for writers interested in increasing their sales.

With the tour just beginning, Gelman and the publisher faced two major hurdles. One was that the media was focused on the issues of national security and readjustment after the tragic events of September 11th, and most of the books or articles NOT dealing with that subject were put on the backburner. The other was that Rita had a fondness for the small, locally-owned bookstores, so she requested that every book signing take place in an independent bookstore. This complicated matters because each one had to be called individually, rather than just making one phone call to a national chain such as Barnes & Noble or Borders. In addition to the initial phone calls to arrange the signings, Gelman also had to deal with the detail work of the book tour. Questions loomed every week. Did the bookstore have copies of the book in stock? Were promotional fliers available in the store? Was the media publicizing the event?

Her book tour, which started at the end of May 2001 and continued until the end of March 2002, took her to 2-3 bookstores a week. It was easy to convince the independent bookstores to host signings because her book was unique and appealed to women. Also, they appreciated the opportunity to host an author on a national tour, since the larger chains sometimes hold a monopoly on these types of local events. The challenge of organizing over 100 book-signing events, while on the road driving thousands of miles, did pay off. She sold lots of books. The book tour was an extension of her nomadic lifestyle, and she broadened her network in each city, keeping in touch with new and old contacts.

According to *Guerilla Marketing for Writers*, Gelman's approach is called "viral marketing," which is not marketing involving anything likely to make you ill, but rather marketing that reproduces itself, much like a virus does in your body. Through emailing and maintaining her website, Gelman was able to notify her readers of her whereabouts. In many cases, these initial readers forwarded her emails and directed others to her website, thereby reaching people with whom she had never had any direct contact. As a result of this word-of-mouth buzz, people from the next degree of separation attended her talks and purchased books. Essentially "viral marketing" is what we commonly refer to as word-of-mouth, and it is a huge reason, perhaps the biggest one, that goods and services become popular in our culture.

CLIMBING THE STAIRS OF SELF-PROMOTION

Sometimes an author can begin marketing long before the writing of the book is even completed. Stefana Williams, a former liaison between corporate clients and the media, is an author who actually ended up developing marketing material before she wrote her book, *Portland's Little Red Book of Stairs*, a guide to more than 150 curious and colorful outdoor stairways. In her mind, it would never have seen the light of day had it not been for this preemptive marketing effort.

The event that cemented Stefana's place in the literary world was the OHS (Oregon Historical Society) "Holiday Cheer and Author's Party," which is an annual gathering attended by about 25 selected Oregonian writers. When Williams requested to be included in the event as the author of a new book, the response was one that many self-publishers hear: "We get many submissions every year, so don't be discouraged if you don't make it." Even though OHS had told her that the odds were not great, they suggested she send in a brochure about her book, from which they would make their determination. She hadn't even yet assembled the material for her book; however, she had experience creating professional looking brochures as part of her job. At the time, she thought they were trying to encourage her by asking for the brochure and didn't realize that OHS was trying to "let her down easy." In their minds, rejecting her brochure instead of the actual book might not be as tough a pill to swallow.

She spent a grueling three days developing a winning brochure about her book; however, the brochure ended up being an ancillary product of those 72 hours. The real gem was the vision for the entire book that the act of creating the brochure had solidified for her. Whether she was accepted or not, she now had a very good idea of how the book would evolve over the next several months. But fate being what it is, OHS was thoroughly impressed with her brochure and did end up inviting her to be included in the select company of the other authors at the event. In order to complete the book in time for the event, Williams took a crash course in desktop publishing from some friends, wrote the manuscript, compiled all the pictures, and published the book on schedule.

The lessons Williams learned along the way were invaluable, and her advice to new writers is simple: Enlist the help of whoever (family, friends, coworkers, etc.) will offer assistance. Also, tell everybody about your project because they all have skills, expertise, and connections to tap into. Williams, who had to get over the hurdle of aversion to self-promotion, also stresses the necessity of being able to "package yourself" and to "check your humility at the door so you can engage readers."

Even with all of the books already published, there remains vast uncharted territory to explore in the world of literature. There are always new topics to explore or existing ones that can be presented from a different angle. When you write a book that fills a literary void, marketing can be easier because you at least have novelty on your side. A fresh concept can capture the public's attention, and, once that attention is yours, sales can spread like wildfire.

INEXPERIENCED YET UNMISTAKABLY SUCCESSFUL

Suzette Tyler has been highly successful in marketing her self-published book, *Been There, (Should've) Done That*, a book of helpful tips for college students. She was able to sell 8,000 copies in the first month with no marketing background, little knowledge of the publishing industry, and no previous books to her name. Amazing for someone who still doesn't even consider herself a writer. How did she get the idea for this book? In her words, "I followed my nose." Tyler, a Baby Boomer who had two children in college when she wrote the book, believes that the best inventions come from inventors who need something. She realized that putting kids through college and having them get the most out of the experience was a top priority not just for her, but also for many other Boomers. When she searched her local bookstore one day and found no books on the subject, she knew that she had discovered a hole in the market—one that she was going to fill.

Before learning much about the publishing industry, Tyler dove right in and wrote her book. However, after finishing it, she was disappointed to learn that traditional publishers usually only pay a 6-15% royalty rate (depending on the publisher) on the sale of each paperback book. Believing that she had worked way too hard to give up the bulk of the profits, she took the manuscript to a printer and published the book herself. After press releases garnered a decent amount of attention from smaller publications, a major St. Louis newspaper ran a feature story about the book, and it wasn't long before bookstores were calling to order copies.

After several months, she was encouraged to attend BookExpo America, which is one of the largest national publishers' exhibitions. She had never attended such an event before, and, due to her inexperience, she only brought 12 copies of the book with her to display. Executives from Dell, Hyperion, and Warner Books, all leading publishing houses, requested copies of her book early on at the expo. Unaware of the marketing potential of these publishing giants and their ability to write big checks, she asked if they could come back at the end of the event, and she would do her best to give them a copy, if she hadn't sold out. "Other authors were shocked that I had written a popular book and was not aware of the publishing powers-that-be, especially when they came knocking at *my* door." Fortunately, this story had a happy ending, as the major publishers did make offers on her book, despite nearly failing to receive a copy. However, because of the interest her book had drummed up at the convention and a renewed desire to run the show herself, Tyler refused their offers and remained the sole owner of her popular work.

Ultimately, a good idea for a book, a lot of hard work, and promoting the book to anybody and everybody paid off for Tyler. She likes to call her book a "hybrid" because it fits into a lot of markets, and she has placed the book in gift shops, sold it to colleges as give-aways to incoming freshmen, and gotten it into traditional bookstores. "I don't know anything about marketing; I just realized that I had a good idea, and that there would be high school seniors graduating every year, who would be potential new readers." At times she regrets not having a major publisher who could do much of the work; however, her entrepreneurial instincts paved the path to a successful sales record—one which would certainly impress the "Big Boys" in New York.

PR: ROLLING WITH THE PUNCHES

Doing PR for your book may do more than help you sell copies and connect with readers; it may also leave you with some hilarious stories to tell.

After finding a publisher for one of my first novels, *Finally...I'm a Doctor*, I hit the road to publicize the book. I found myself on AM San Francisco, being interviewed on the same set as a dog trainer. Well, as it turned out, the host got mixed up with his next guest and started asking me questions about Collies. We were live, so I whispered to the host "I'm the Doctor, not the dog trainer," but he didn't hear me. I knew a little about Collies and Cocker Spaniels, but I missed every question about Dachshunds. Then the dog trainer came on and did such a good job answering questions about my book, that I was worried that my publisher, Scribner, might ask him to replace me on my book tour.

-Neil Shulman

IN THE PUBLIC'S EYE THROUGH A PUBLICIST

When it comes to book publicity, Rick Frishman, President of Planned Television Arts (a subsidiary of Ruder Finn—the largest PR firm in New York), is the best in the business. With several specialty divisions which cater to a variety of markets, and decades of experience working with all types of books—everything from novels to cookbooks, Planned Television Arts (www.plannedtvarts.com) has built an impressive number of successful marketing campaigns for its authors.

Frishman, as we've mentioned, is also a successful author of several books to help writers, including *Guerilla Marketing for Writers* (along with Michael Larsen and Jay Conrad Levinson), and the *Author 101* series with coauthor, Robyn Freedman Spizman. He notes the value of writing a book, particularly a nonfiction one, when he says, "The book is your business card and makes you the leading authority—if you are in business you NEED to have a book." There are certainly millions of business owners who would love to have their own book which they could tie into their operations, but the persistent fear of not being good enough is widespread among "non-writers" and hard to overcome. Frishman is quick to put their fear in perspective and also to take a humble view of himself, despite his significant success. "You don't have to be a great writer. I am a crappy writer and I have 8 books out there and have sold 100,000 copies." And he has more on the way.

Although there is no limit to the innovative ways that you alone can promote your book, sometimes having a professional publicist behind you can help you to attract a greater number of readers by gaining media access. Many a publicist or PR person has been heard uttering the famous P.T. Barnum quotation, "Without publicity a terrible thing happens—NOTHING." Frishman backs up this assertion when he describes the necessity for authors to take control and also to seek some outside PR help. Because the publisher's in-house PR person is swamped with responsibilities or may not have the necessary contacts, you may either get lost in the shuffle or not be able to reach the publications and media outlets that you desire for your material.

Jacqueline Deval, author of *Publicize Your Book!*, a useful guide that we recommend, is also the former director of publicity for several publishing houses, which ran the publicity and marketing campaigns of many notable authors, including John Feinstein, Isaac Asimov, and Sidney Sheldon. In her book, Deval points out that it might be valuable for you to hire an outside publicist for a number of reasons. Examples include: sensing a general lack of enthusiasm for your project from your publisher's marketing department or having a publisher that may be newer to the industry and lacks the media experience or contacts to gain you exposure.

Recognizing the importance of the media and the need to contribute to the publisher's marketing efforts, many authors may be willing to work hard to publicize themselves and their books, but they lack time, experience, and the contact list of producers and/or reviewers in print, radio, and television. There are certainly many mistakes authors can make when publicizing a book themselves for the first time: believing that they are going to start out on major network shows, not planning far enough in advance, being uncooperative with reporters/editors who work on tight deadlines, failing to familiarize themselves with the publications they are trying to contact, and overlooking secondary niche markets where further interest can be cultivated, to name a few.

An outside publicist can help an author avoid the pitfalls. Each one is different, but because of the track record it has built up since 1962, Planned Television Arts is able to deliver the leading television and radio shows for many of its authors. Also, they operate on a pay-as-you-go basis, meaning that the author only pays a fee if the firm reaches specific agreed upon goals. However, every company operates in its own fashion, and this strategy stands in sharp contrast to the bulk of PR firms or publicists, who generally charge a retainer upfront, regardless of whether or not they eventually have success. While it should be conceded that many of these companies and individuals are also quite successful at getting media attention for their clients, thus making their retainers worthwhile, some authors prefer the sense of security built into the Planned Television Arts's system.

Independent publicists, like those employed by publishing companies, are familiar with the right publications and mass media outlets to target, have the right contacts at those targets, and know how to customize press releases and press packages to achieve the maximum results. Also, they can provide personalized service, whereas a publishers' publicity department has many authors to publicize and promote simultaneously. However, while the publicist may have the industry know-how, your creativity and knowledge of who might be interested in your book will still be instrumental to its success. Publicists are experts at navigating the media, but not necessarily on the subject of your book. Keeping them informed of events, functions, or news stories which could have an impact on sales will enable them to make the most informed decisions.

Results can vary, but what authors should expect from a publicist are professionally composed materials which are sent out in a timely fashion to the correct contacts on a comprehensive media list. You should also expect that your publicist will keep you updated on a weekly basis. We recommend finding out what types of clients a publicist represents before querying them, since some specialize in other industries, such as business or medicine, and may not have anything to do with publishing at all. Also, it is important to ask very specifically about the publicist's recent successes and to find out which television shows, radio shows, and print publications they have gotten their clients coverage in.

If your book has a large potential market of readers, having a knowledgeable and well-connected representative willing to go to bat for you and your book can mean a major boost in sales. However, hiring a publicist is not the right move for every author. A major downside of having a professional publicize your book is the cost for their services. Fees vary depending on the publicist and the length of the publicity campaign. There can also be additional fees for phone calls or press packets—so be sure to ask before hiring them. If you are considering hiring a publicist, we recommend asking for referrals and finding out how effective their campaigns were for authors who have had projects or a background similar to yours. You should also ask for the publicist's candid opinion on what they think they can generate, as there is no point in hiring a publicist who does not believe in your book. In this situation, you, the author, would not get what you paid for and the publicist would be forced to spend hours on a book that they feel has no media potential.

The list of ways to market your book is endless, and hopefully after reading this chapter, you will sit down and begin to brainstorm ideas for your marketing campaign. The standard publicity generated by publishers covered in Chapter 10 can be highly effective; however, most publishers do not invest big bucks for promotion, except for a select group of authors who already earn significant revenue for the company. And, of course, if you self-publish, you are a one-person sales force and must be your own promoter. So, regardless of your "path to print," if you hope to sell copies beyond your circle of family and friends, it's time for you to explore the marketing options in your community and implement your creative sales ideas.

·Whether you have a traditional publisher behind you or not, you, as the author, can be instrumental in marketing your book and reaching potential readers.

·To increase sales of your book, find the most efficient ways to attract book reviewers and be persistent with your techniques to keep the buzz going.

·Build a fan club that can spread the word-of-mouth hype, and keep in touch with groups/individuals who have expressed interest in your book.

·Consider hiring an outside publicist if you have the resources and want to increase your odds of publicity access.

·For creative ideas and marketing or publicity services, be sure to peruse *1001 Ways to Market Your Books* and *Guerilla Marketing for Writers*. Also visit John Kremer's website (www. bookmarket.com), Fred Gleeck's website (www.pinkgoat.com), and Rick Frishman's Planned Television Arts website (www. plannedtvarts.com).

CHAPTER 21

Exercise Your Rights in Contracts

O ver two hundred years ago the Declaration of Independence granted every resident of the United States the fundamental rights to life, liberty, and the pursuit of happiness. While the Founding Fathers were brilliant in the drafting of this monumental document, they unfortunately forgot to include a section devoted to rights for the author in publishing contracts. One can only assume that copyrighting played second fiddle to more important issues at the time, such as England and its desire for "taxation without representation." And so, authors have been left to fend for themselves.

From the perspective of many modern writers, contracts are created on an entirely different planet, where lawyers speak in their own language and there is a financial pitfall lurking around every legal clause. Although contracts, as you well know from other aspects of your life, sometimes appear complicated, by taking the time to learn the basics you can protect your work of art and any profits derived from it.

First, let's discuss copyrighting, since it is relatively easy to understand and is the first thing that you should do once you have finished your manuscript if you aren't already hooked up with a publisher. According to copyright law, you are the owner of your completed manuscript and are entitled to all of the rights and privileges that go along with being the owner. If you self-publish by going to a printing press, you will continue to retain all of the rights related to your book, as you would if you self-published through a print on-demand provider. But, before proceeding with any form of publication, you should immediately copyright your work by writing your name, the date, and "Copyright" on the page after the title page. This legally protects your work from being copied by others. If you are planning on self-publishing, you can register it and create a public record of your copyright with the Library of Congress (www.loc.gov). The library will give you a catalog number that will be used by libraries to reference your book. You can create an identifier of your book in the publishing community by going to www.ISBN.com and purchasing an ISBN number for it. If you aren't self-publishing, these matters are usually handled by your publisher or on-demand publisher. If you'd like to document the date you completed the manuscript, you can mail a copy of it to yourself. Keep the unopened postmarked envelope as proof of the date of completion, in case there is ever a dispute in the future. For example, if someone plagiarizes your work, you will have evidence that your work was written before theirs.

Now, let's focus on the actual publishing contract. If you choose to go through a traditional publisher, the various rights associated with the book will be dealt with in a contract. Don't be frightened by the word *contract*; we will break it down in plain language, so you can understand the basics. If you are interested in learning more about E-rights, specifically related to eBooks, please refer to the Chapter 18, where we discuss them in greater detail.

In a nutshell, a publishing contract licenses certain rights to the publisher so the publisher's team can produce, market, and sell a book. Typically the book will be printed in hardcover or paperback, though it may also be in eBook format. As the copyright holder, the author is the one who transfers the right to publish the book. Usually there is a limit to the region where the sales can occur (United States for example), to help distinguish from the sales that will occur as part of any foreign rights sold. The contract should specify the royalty rate that the author will receive from the sales of the book, along with the payment schedule for royalties, the percentage the author will receive from sales of ancillary rights, and any advances or upfront cash that will be paid to the author. It may also specify a deadline for submission of the final manuscript or the "delivery date" as it's commonly called, if the author has not yet completed the book.

The publisher typically keeps the reprint rights, which usually take the form of a trade paperback or mass-market paperback reprint of a hardcover book. Reprints typically come out one to two years after the original publication, but this varies depending on the author and the topic. Usually publishers will also retain the first serial and second serial rights, authorizing them to sell excerpts to magazines or newspapers both before and after publication of the book. Keep in mind that although the publisher retains these rights, the author typically receives at least half (50%) of the proceeds from the sales of these rights. All rights usually revert back to the author if the book goes out of print and the publisher is no longer offering it for sale. However, often this doesn't happen automatically, and you or your agent will need to request this option from your publisher within a certain window of time.

Many ultra-successful authors, such as Robert Ludlum and Michael Crichton, first published books which didn't attain a high level of success until many years later when they were reprinted. For both authors, Hollywood, in addition to their increased publishing success with more recent works, helped to generate a large market for reprint sales—with *The 13th Warrior* for Crichton and *The Bourne Identity* for Ludlum. As a result of the increased exposure of these earlier works and their big screen adaptations, many of their other lesser-known books have also recently been reprinted.

Before we get into the other types of rights and the royalty rates typically found in contracts, perhaps a quick explanation of how the process comes about is warranted. So far you understand most of what goes into the acceptance part of the publication process, starting with a query and ending with an editor either giving you the green light or telling you to look for another publisher. What you may not be familiar with yet is what happens in the deal-making part of the process. Basically, once a publishing house or several publishing houses agree to move forward, several possible scenarios could ensue. To simplify, a publisher will make an individual offer to you (or your agent on behalf of you), make a preemptive offer, or enter into an auction (of which there are two types) with other publishers who want it. The advantage of the preemptive offer over the auction is the surety of having a deal now—kind of like applying Early Decision to your top choice for college and finding out whether you are accepted in January, rather than in April like the rest of the high schools students who apply during the regular application period. The downside is also similar to the college application analogy…if you apply Early Decision and get accepted (i.e. accept the publishing offer), you may miss out on the chance to drum up interest and end up with a higher offer from another publisher. Also, the publisher will usually place a time limit on the preemptive offer—anywhere from 24-48 hours—just to be sure that you don't have time to shop the manuscript to other publishers.

As for the auction option, essentially several publishers offer competing bids (usually in a predetermined format) until one publisher ends up winning the prize of publishing your book—a possible advantage if the hype of the auction and the sense of competition drives the price of your book up. Agents are experts at the bidding process, understanding what to expect from it, and how to use it to the author's advantage, which is why we highly recommend enlisting the services of one, especially if you have a "hot" manuscript. Also, it's important to reiterate that many publishers will only accept manuscript submissions from agents who are representing the author and their work.

It may seem counterintuitive, but the best offer from a publishing company is not always the one that pays you the most money upfront. As Arielle Eckstut and David Henry Sterry note in their successful book *Putting Your Passion Into Print*, there are other factors to consider. These could include:

the amount of personal attention the publisher is going to give to you, the size of the book's promotional budget, the editor that you get to work with to fine-tune your book, and the publisher's enthusiasm for your book. The authors are quick to note that if the publishing company is very excited about your project and makes a big push to get it out there, you may end up selling significantly more copies, which in the long run can actually result in more money than you would have received from the publisher willing to put up more cash upfront, but had less initial enthusiasm.

Now that you understand a little more about the process, what kind of numbers should you expect to see in a contract from a standard publisher? Royalties are generally given as a percentage of the retail sales, based on the "sticker price" (the price the consumer pays for your book). So, if John or Jane Smith walks into a Barnes & Noble and buys your book for $20 and in your contract it states that you will receive 10% of retail sales, you will receive $2 for each book sold. On the other hand, if you receive 10% of the wholesale price of the book (the discounted price that bookstores pay for your book), you may end up with less. If your $20 book was sold at a wholesale price of $12 to a bookstore, then your 10% would equal $1.20, instead of the $2.00 from above.

A best-case scenario for hardcover retail sales royalties, before you really establish a name in the publishing industry, might look like this:

-10% of retail sales on 1-5,000 copies.

-12.5% of retail sales on 5,000-10,000 copies.

-15% of retail sales on 10,000+ copies.

For trade paperback books (large paperbacks), a normal scenario is 7.5% of retail sales regardless of the number of copies, and for mass market paperbacks (compact paperbacks), the rate can be anywhere from 8%-10%. Again, these rates will vary from publisher to publisher, depending on your level of experience in the publishing industry and track record of success.

In some cases, an author may get an advance upon signing a book deal, meaning that the publisher will give the author a certain amount of money before the book is actually completed. This money is an early payment applied against future royalties. Once the book is published, the author won't get any additional money from the book sales until his royalties and/or the money generated from the sale of ancillary rights exceed the amount that the publisher has already given as an advance. But, if a book doesn't do as well as expected the author does not have to give back any of the advance, even if the royalties received never equal the amount of the upfront money given to the author. Usually, the only time an author would be required to return an advance would be if they failed to deliver the book to the publisher by the agreed date. Advances can range from a few hundred dollars for a new author working with a smaller publisher to millions for world-famous authors published by the largest houses. Considering how common it is for publishers to give out advances, it may surprise you that only about 10% of books actually earn out their advances—meaning that the authors' royalties don't end up exceeding the amount of the upfront money that a publisher pays them. This investment, in light of all of the production and operational expenses, is why publishing a book is so risky for a traditional publisher.

The majority of the rights dealt with in a contract, and also the most negotiable ones, are called subsidiary or ancillary rights. In addition to the paperback reprint rights and the serial rights (for publication in magazines, newspapers, etc.), these include movie and television rights, theatrical rights, electronic rights (which can refer to anything from eBooks to online magazines), audio rights (remember that over 20 million people in the United States alone listen to audio books on cassettes, CD's, iPods, and other MP3 players), foreign language rights (printing the book in a foreign language), as well as foreign English language rights (publishing the book in English in countries other than the United States or Canada, where English is the native language, such as in England or Australia). Sometimes the author gets certain rights and other times the publisher does, depending on the individual circumstances. In general, an author should try to retain subsidiary rights if he or she believes that they (or their agent) may be able to sell them more effectively than the publishing company. Regardless of the terms of agreement, the author should contact the subsidiary department of the publishing house to make sure that it's pursuing the subsidiary rights which it has been granted.

As for the actual numbers, the primary publishing company and the author split the revenue that comes from a third party for subsidiary rights. The actual percentages vary depending on the type of right. Movie rights are usually 90/10 in the author's favor, while book club rights might be 50/50. Here is an example. An author writes a book about the history of beef in the Americas and contracts to have it published in the United States with publishing house A. They agree to split the Spanish language rights 50/50. Publishing house A then contacts publishing house B in Argentina and publishing house B decides to print it. The author and publishing house A would then split the advance and the royalties that publishing house B would pay them for the right to print the book in Spanish. A single book can be published by multiple companies, in multiple languages, and in multiple countries. In this way, some books become popular all over the world. For example, *The Alchemist*, by Paulo Coehlo, has sold tens of millions of copies, is printed in many languages by several publishers, and has been on bestseller lists in over 150 countries.

FROM THE COMPUTER SCREEN TO THE SILVER SCREEN

The world of Hollywood is as foreign to many authors as it is to everyone else. We have included this humorous section because the literary community, as you probably know, is integral in the dynamics of the flashy, big-budget movie industry. Many of the biggest blockbusters of the past 20 years were originally successful novels and nonfiction books before their rights were sold and they ended up on a reel in a theater. Neil relates the following stories of movie rights, negotiation, and the results of a hit movie:

HOBNOBBING WITH HOLLYWOOD

When my humorous novel, *What? Dead...Again?* was published and received good reviews, my publisher was bombarded with phone calls from all types of Hollywood insiders who were interested in optioning movie or TV rights. They all had essentially the same approach; something like, "Hey baby, wanna become rich and famous? Then come out to LA and we'll do lunch." This was just the tip of the iceberg, and when it came to negotiating the deal, the terrain was no less slippery. I had a lawyer who was charging an exorbitant sum per hour, and a five minute phone call with him was like going out for a nice dinner.

The actual negotiations were unlike anything I had ever experienced. You call someone, eventually get into an argument over the terms, and one party hangs up. In the real world this typically wouldn't be a good sign and would probably indicate an end to all negotiation. Not in Hollywood. In Hollywood, the party which hung up promptly calls you back and you're on to the next round of negotiations. This is nothing more than a commonly-used technique to move things along, though it probably wouldn't work in many of your other personal or business relationships.

Finally, after literally years of negotiations, the movie rights were sold to Warner Brothers. My book ultimately became the basis for the major motion picture *Doc Hollywood*, released in the summer of 1991 and starring Michael J. Fox. It went on to become one of the number one movies that year; however the whole process of getting the movie made, beginning with the publication of the book and ending with it appearing in theaters, took 13 years!

The screenplay went through many rewrites by several different screenwriters. One of the screenwriting teams had written a script for *Who Framed Roger Rabbit* and *The Grinch Who Stole Christmas*. They called me up, wanting to visit Georgia to get a feel for the culture of the rural South, since the book takes place in the South. Because they were sort of caught up in the closed sphere of Hollywood, they asked me, "By the way, do you wear shoes in Georgia?" Since I'm a medical doctor, I arrived to greet them at the airport in my white coat, with a stethoscope hanging out of my pocket, and barefoot!

The movie had quite an impact on people. For example, in one scene of the movie, the actress, Julie Warner, pees on a tree to keep deer away. An elderly woman got in touch with me after the movie was released and described how she had a problem with deer eating her garden. After seeing the scene, she tried the remedy herself and it proved to be highly effective. And here I was thinking the movie would educate people on the dire need for doctors in rural America! It did some unexpected educating!

Speaking of animals, the pig in the movie became quite famous. After the movie's release, I heard rumors that the pig gave hoof prints all over the country and enjoyed celebrity status (as much as can be said for a pig). You might even say that thanks to my book and the movie, his career really took off; certainly I wasn't imagining I would ever be responsible for putting a pig in the limelight when I first set pen to paper!

In addition to looking into the rights mentioned in this chapter, it's also a good idea to inquire about how the publishing company expects to distribute your book and how much of a priority it will be in relation to the other books the company is putting out in the calendar year. A bigger advance does not necessarily mean a better deal, so be sure to examine the contract from a variety of angles. For example, are you going to be sent around the country on an author's tour? Will a press release be sent out to the media highlighting a new research finding in your book? Overall, you are trying to gain a sense of the publisher's marketing game-plan.

Read the contract language carefully even if you are represented by an agent. Express any concerns that you may have to your agent and/or the editors at the publishing houses…it's better to resolve the issues now. It may be worth consulting an attorney who is an expert in the field if you are unsure of your options. Just don't forget to find out what the lawyer's fees are upfront. You might also want to read *From Pen to Print*, by Ellen Kozak, *The Writer's Legal Companion* by Brad Bunnin and Peter Beren, or *Negotiating a Book Contract: A Guide for Authors, Agents, and Lawyers* by Mark Levine. These all offer advice on the business side of publishing, especially focusing on contracts, and will help you to better understand the elements being discussed.

It's also helpful to keep good notes, either on a tape recorder or in writing, as you go through the negotiation and contract generation process. If you have an agent or attorney, they may be doing this already, but it's valuable to have extra records. Make sure any sources are cited correctly in your book and that you didn't "borrow" any writing without permission. The publisher's contract will often include a warrant (not like the police kind) attesting that the writing is solely yours. With the various major lawsuits that have occurred in the publishing industry regarding the originality of the work of some of the biggest-name authors, this is especially important for both you and your publisher. Both of your reputations could be at stake should you cross the line, even if it is just accidentally.

Finally, since you may actually be generating an income from this endeavor, you may want to consult your accountant or attorney about the types of business expenses that you can deduct. It may also make sense to incorporate, particularly if you want to write-off business expenses related to creating your book...travel, research materials, editing or marketing fees, etc. It frequently does make things easier in self-publishing, since you are really running your own small company, but it's up to you if you plan on publishing through a publisher.

Remember, a proposed contract is not set in stone. You can and should negotiate with publishers, although as a first-time author you likely won't have as much leverage as an established author. Also, bear in mind that contract writing is one of the final stages of the publishing process and there's no need to get hung up on contract-related details while writing your book. When you do ultimately have a contract in front of you, don't be intimidated. It's time to celebrate! It may not be New Year's, but you have succeeded in having your manuscript accepted by a publisher, and in a few months your book will hit the market. Who knows, if everything goes well, you may even end up with a handful of publishers fighting for an option on your future works, if you haven't already included these works as part of your original deal with your publisher!

·Publishing contracts, like other types of contracts, should be read carefully. Consider having a lawyer or an agent look over them before signing your name on the dotted line.

PART 5

FINALE…THE ULTIMATE PEP TALK BEFORE TURNING THE PEN OVER

Throughout this book, we have attempted to shed light on the writing process, the publishing industry, your options for publication, and ultimately how to find a readership for your book once it is available to the public. With this core knowledge base, you now have the tools to get started, but you will likely need to consult other writing-specific sources to answer particular questions or to help format submissions. Similarly you will probably need to hone your skills as a writer, but that will come with time spent researching, writing, and editing as you proceed in your literary endeavor. After all, the best way to learn is by doing.

Even if you now possess the essential know-how to start the process of writing a book, have reveled in the excitement of learning about the successes of other authors, and you are armed with your own strategies for success, you may still need a final jump start to get you off of the fence and seated at your computer.

The next two chapters are meant to help you leap over any lingering psychological hurdles you may face. Chapter 22 deals with the fear of rejection or failure, an unfortunate reality of the publishing process, but one which thousands of authors before you have successfully overcome on their path to publication. Chapter 23 sums up a number of common obstacles which often prevent people from getting started and sticking to it. The chapter also reaffirms the value that you are adding to your own life and to those in the present and future by completing your book, as well as reminding you of your own abilities.

CHAPTER 22

REJECTION: *Paving the Road to Success*

After years of hearing "no" the women's suffrage movement finally gains momentum, results in a change to the Constitution allowing women to vote, and becomes the first big step on the path to equality between the sexes. Martin Luther King and Gandhi, after years of experiencing extreme displays of bias and oppression, individually use their non-violent approaches to pursue their ideals and win the support of the masses. Bill Gates, after dropping out of college, challenges the corporate system that rejected his ideas and builds Microsoft, the titan of technology, changing the face of how businesses and individuals use computers and how we, as a society, access knowledge.

Writing a book, while perhaps seemingly less notable than these achievements, also takes you on a path lined with resistance before getting published. Even if you follow the advice that you have read in previous chapters or learned from publishing resources and literary experts, rejection and temporary failure are usually an inherent part of the process. Whether it is not having a manuscript picked up by a publisher, not being able to convince an agent to represent you, receiving a negative review from a critic, or having your book not sell right away once it is released, nearly every writer faces rejection at some point or another. Although this chapter focuses on rejection in the world of traditional publishing, there can be setbacks in every publishing avenue. Our intent is to help any writer from becoming discouraged when obstacles present themselves. We want you to become inspired by successful authors who have overcome their obstacles. They represent just a handful of the many writers who have refused to let rejection get in the way of personal success.

Gene Landrum, Ph.D., founder of the Chuck E. Cheese concept of family restaurants, successful entrepreneur, author, and lecturer is one of the foremost experts on genius, creativity, and channeling innovative behavior to achieve significant results. His book, *Literary Genius: A Cathartic Inspiration*, is a must read for anyone who wants to learn what goes into the psyche of modern-day marvels like Danielle Steel, Stephen King, and Anne Rice, as well as the "greats" from previous generations…Hemingway, Christie, Dostoevsky. While writing in a range of genres and coming from a diverse set of backgrounds, all of the individuals he features in his book faced considerable rejection, were panned at the beginning of their writing careers, and were basically told that they "shouldn't quit their day job." Rather than let this stop them, these extraordinary authors became even more resilient, didn't let the negativity in their environments slow them down, and went on to prove their literary value, which they knew that they possessed all along. Their stories demonstrate their resolve—mentally, emotionally, and physically. Perhaps they will inspire you to develop the same strength and unwavering determination. Landrum's recently-published book *Empowerment*, which highlights different sports figures throughout history to illustrate the inward traits that lead to external success, often after overcoming great obstacles, is another great motivational read.

Gaining entrance into the traditional publishing world takes a lot of persistence for first-time authors, especially if you write fiction. Rejection is frequently part of the process, sometimes even after your first or second book is published. Many people assume that best-selling or award-winning authors have had a mass of fan club members from the very start and never had to struggle like the thousands of writers of lesser acclaim. What we don't often hear about is the years of blood, sweat, and tears that usually precede an "overnight success." While they are well-known now, most of these authors have worked their way up from humble beginnings. Success was not so much a result of luck or a gift from a "publishing philanthropist." These authors tried as many publishing houses as necessary until they found the one which believed in them and their work. You must do the same. After all, it took Thomas Edison 2,000 attempts to create and perfect the light bulb, though he never once claimed that he had encountered any failures; rather, that he had invented the light bulb, and it had merely been a 2,000 step process. Remember that if you can't get your foot in the door of a traditional publisher with your polished manuscript after numerous attempts, use the feedback that you receive from editors and consider reformatting your book proposal, re-editing your book, or exploring the other publishing routes. Do what it takes to make sure that your manuscript finds its way from your home or office into the hands of readers for years to come.

Eric Jerome Dickey, best-selling author of such books as *Liar's Game* and *Thieves' Paradise*, reportedly received over 300 rejection letters for his early novels—a staggering number to say the least. Most of us would have probably given up in the face of this much negative feedback, but this one time middle school teacher, stand up comic, actor, and computer programmer refused to let temporary failure slow him down. Dickey truly believed in his books and simply brushed aside the rejection. His goal was to publish using a traditional publisher, and with persistence he was eventually successful, enabling his urban love stories to reach the masses.

John Creasey, the celebrated British mystery writer, accumulated a whooping 743 rejection letters before his first novel was ever published! However, Creasey was undeterred; under a variety of pen names, he began churning out 10,000 words *per day* and a novel nearly every week. Over his lifetime, he managed to write over 600 novels and to sell approximately 100 million copies of his books worldwide.

Jari Holland Buck is the author of the book *24/7 or Dead: A Handbook for Families with Loved Ones in the Hospital* (www.24-7ordead.com), which has won the "Parent to Parent Adding Wisdom Award" and was a finalist for the "Fresh Voices of 2006" award. The success of her book has also resulted in the opportunity for Buck to host a radio show, as well as an invitation to teach the first ever patient advocacy certificate program. This all has happened because she was determined and fueled with a personal mission after experiencing her husband's lengthy stay in the hospital.

After sending out 225 packages to traditional publishers and getting a range of responses: from outright rejections, to constructive suggestions that she add a coauthor who was either an R.N. or an M.D. (otherwise the book wouldn't sell), to initial excitement from a smaller publisher, which then pulled the plug when they went over budget with another book, Buck decided that she'd had enough.

Her four years of relentlessly pounding the pavement taught her the "in's and out's" out of the publishing industry and gave her the confidence to move on to a different option—self-publishing by using a print on-demand provider. She decided she wanted to channel her energy into producing and promoting her own work, rather than trying to convince someone else to become her publisher. But, again, it was the bigger more personal connection to the project that fueled her desire to find a way— any way—to get the book into the marketplace. "Four years of seeing people die unnecessarily in hospitals because they lacked an advocate or the knowledge to prevent mistakes was simply more than I could bear." Buck believes that an author who continuously receives rejections should strongly consider self-publishing, thereby spending the time moving the project along, rather than burning out trying to find a home for it. Her advice for a writer of any level is simple: "If you feel strongly about your message, get your words in print at whatever cost. This is a mission for me and I simply would not 'go away' just because others could not see the value in my work." And most importantly, Buck sums up her reason for persevering and publishing, when she comments, "I only hope they remember my book when they need the information it provides, because they all eventually will... And, it will be in print, waiting for their need."

Rejection is certainly to be expected by individuals trying to get their first book published by a traditional publisher, but contrary to common misconceptions, authors with track records are also subject to rejection from major publishing houses. The strength of character and determination of almost every published author is called upon at one time or another. The experienced author remembers that rejection is a temporary state, and uses it to reedit and/or refocus their publishing strategy.

Robert James Waller, bestselling author of *The Bridges of Madison County*, which sold over twelve million copies in hardcover alone (a record for several years until a little book named *The Da Vinci Code* came along), was rejected by Warner Books for his sequel novel, *A Thousand Country Roads*, because editors disliked some of the elements of the plot and a compromise couldn't be reached. Instead of letting a moment of rejection defeat him, he surveyed his options and decided to publish with the small publishing company owned by his neighbor in Texas. Although he didn't have a major publisher behind him, he found another way to ensure that anxious readers would be enjoying his work once again. Because he persisted until finding the right backing, *A Thousand Country Roads* has become Waller's second bestseller.

Sometimes acceptance or rejection hinges on timeliness. An author's work may contain themes or styles of writing that are ahead of their time and meet rejection simply because society is not yet ready. Conversely, an author may capitalize on a hot media topic or present a new spin on an age-old subject of discussion to gain immediate acceptance and praise from the masses (e.g. *The Da Vinci Code*). But more often than not, when a radically innovative idea is presented, in publishing and in life, there's usually a time lag before the general population warms up to it.

Jack Canfield and Mark Victor Hansen's *Chicken Soup for the Soul*, was rejected 33 times because editors didn't think inspirational books were trendy at the time. Not only did they persist and ultimately sell millions of copies of this first book, but they have built a "Chicken Soup" literary empire based on it in just a few years. Sylvia Plath's widely-acclaimed novel *The Bell Jar*, has been a rite of passage for many women since the time that the feminist movement gained momentum, but the book didn't find a major audience until after her death, mostly because it explored mental illness, a topic which was not "in vogue" at the time she wrote it. And Dr. Atkins, whose book about the danger of carbohydrates challenged longstanding beliefs about diet and health, initially met great skepticism and doubt from readers, critics, and medical professionals. He kept pushing and eventually sold millions of copies of his books, built a successful brand name, and ended up with such a devoted group of followers that his name is now invoked during mealtimes all over the world.

What the success of these authors illustrates is the maxim lived by business mogul, Summer Redstone, Chairman and CEO of Viacom (which owns CBS and MTV), which is to follow your instincts, rather than acquiesce to the views of critics and nay-sayers who see the world differently.[1] In the case of publishing, there's no telling what kinds of doors may open for

1   "The Best Advice I Ever Got," *Fortune* 21 Mar. 2005: Vol. 151, No. 6.

your creative efforts and how many copies you may sell if you follow this sage advice. In fact, it's even been said that some of the things that you will be criticized for as a writer are the ones that you should actually keep doing…they're what make you unique and may be the compelling hook for readers. After all, if every book was homogenous and just like every other, readers would probably lose interest in books very quickly and no one would ever become someone's favorite author.

Following your instincts is a great way to function, but if it fails to net you the results that you want, studying the successful books in your field to see what has sold may help you to refine your efforts. Again, remember that it can be helpful to even read works outside of your field or genre which have been successful, for inspiration and to learn about innovative approaches that you can apply to your own work.

Robin Cook wrote his first novel, *The Year of the Intern*, in 1972, shortly after he finished his medical internship. When it proved more difficult than expected for him to get his book out there, Cook went back to the drawing board. He read every bestseller he could get his hands on in hopes of figuring out a formula for success, a strategy that many successful authors have employed. While these books may have been very different in theme and content, he knew that there must be similarities in the style and structure that made them successful. Once he started to see patterns, he worked at incorporating those same elements into his own writing. His next novel, *Coma*, was published in 1977. It became a best seller, and eventually the basis for a hit movie directed by Michael Crichton and starring Michael

Douglas. As a result of his early studies of the formula for a successful book, he has written many other bestsellers in the years since then.

Despite Neil's track record of success in so many facets of the publishing industry and Eric's track record of success in business and reaching out to top executives, we faced a great amount of skepticism with *Get Between the Covers*. Many individuals (whether they were agents, editors, or businesspeople) believed that this type of book had already been done. This was by far our favorite criticism, since "it's been done" has been said to the authors of hundreds of books that have gone on to sell millions of copies and sit on bestseller lists for years. Not only that, but, we argued, if it truly had *been done* before, how come there weren't hundreds of thousands or millions of authors around the world trying their hand at writing books each year?

Clearly there is still a gaping hole in this market, and it has fueled us every day to know that if we work hard enough to find the right approach, we might be able to connect with the millions of potential new writers around the world, even if they only pick up writing as a hobby and publish one book in their lifetime. We continuously reminded ourselves that in business and in publishing, there are always going to be people who believe in your product and those who don't...all that matters is that *you* believe in it. If you do, you will eventually meet with success, and your passion and confidence will be the wings that carry you there.

Neil often recounts with a chuckle the slew of rejection letters he received from New York publishers when he first submitted the novel *What? Dead Again?*, which later became the basis for the highly-successful Michael J. Fox movie *Doc Hollywood.* He also remembers the two major companies bidding for the paperback rights when the movie was about to come out. One of the companies was the very same one which had concluded that his book was "puerile" when Neil first submitted it. However, when the movie came out, it was identified as "a great novel." Publishing can be a funny business sometimes. Not only has Neil gone on to have success in the publishing industry, but the subsequent novels of his co-author, Carl Hiaasen, have become a permanent fixture on the *New York Times Best Seller List.*

At the end of the day, rejection and critical commentary must be taken lightly since all critiquing is simply a matter of taste. Even truly great literary works have been deemed meaningless drivel at one time or another. It doesn't matter if your book is virtually "perfect" and becomes a literary masterpiece; nothing you create will be everyone's cup of tea. You have not failed if certain people aren't interested in or have a negative opinion of your book; rather you have succeeded by informing, entertaining, or enthralling others. Author Sir Kingsley Amis once said, "A bad review may spoil your breakfast, but you shouldn't allow it to spoil your lunch."

Take a look at these quotations from actual rejections, which illustrate Christopher Hampton's observation, "Asking a working writer what he thinks about critics is like asking a lamppost how it feels about dogs."

The Diary of Anne Frank by Anne Frank

"The girl doesn't, it seems to me, have a special perception or feeling which would lift that book above the 'curiosity' level."

Animal Farm by George Orwell

"It's impossible to sell animal stories in the USA."[2]

Instead of letting rejection and criticism get you down, you can instead use it to your advantage. Perhaps the reason that your work was criticized or failed to find a publishing house is that it needs improvement in certain areas, and you may have even received feedback as to which elements to work on. Instead of being defensive, try to evaluate your work with an objective, critical eye and see if there are places where changes can be made—ones that will enable you to achieve the result desired for your book. And if you feel that the criticism was unwarranted, use it as a stimulus to motivate you to prove the naysayers wrong. Business leaders, activists, athletes, and just about anyone else who has arrived at great success in a particular field have been capitalizing on this source of motivation for years.

Bestselling author, Joel Saltzman (www.shakethatbrain.com), has written about subjects ranging from relationships to writing (his book, *If You Can Talk, You Can Write*, is a great read). He believes that success in the publishing industry comes down to three simple things, "Persistence, persistence, persistence." Having been through the ups and downs of writing and publishing, including a five year stretch of writer's block, which he terms his "personal Dark Ages," he recognizes that the entire process can be difficult and fraught with rejection and psychological hurdles, but his

---

2 From *Rotten Rejections: A Literary Companion*, by Andre Bernard.

advice for any new writer considering writing a book and trying to publish it is simple, "Face it. Fear it. Do it anyway."

―――――◡―――――

Having a book published is the result of luck, talent, perseverance, and often overcoming rejection. The more challenging the road you travel, the more you will appreciate and value the arrival at your destination. Rejection lets you know that you are reaching high enough in your attempt to share your creative output; you will usually hit your mark fairly quickly if you set your sights too low.

You have set your sights high by attempting to write and publish a book, and with a positive attitude, hard work, and refusal to give up in the face of rejection, you will go far in achieving your literary goals. Keep at it! Remember that if you can visualize your final outcome, you will likely reach your destination. Imagine the "satisfaction of completion" and let it spur you on through every step of the process. In this way, you will be able to see beyond any disappointments, including rejection.

CHAPTER 23

Pat Yourself on the Back

Thousands of people, residing in every corner of the globe, spend time researching, writing, editing, and ultimately publishing their own books every year, and are therefore able to share their creativity, knowledge, life experiences, and insight with others. While their contributions to the literary world are significant, they represent just a handful of all of those individuals who have the inspiration to write a book. But, so few of those who have an initial idea actually sit down and get the process started. Some may lack the discipline to set aside time to write and then actually fill the allotted time sitting at their computer, and give up after a few days or a few weeks. Others don't believe they have the talent to write a book and never really get to the point of having an initial brainstorming session or even sketching out a rough outline. Even those who are talented writers and have time in their schedule to write may not be aware of the many new options to publish once they finish, and the fear of rejection and the challenge of taking on an uphill battle force them to shelf their ideas. For all these basic reasons and perhaps many more personal ones, our society's output of books isn't close to the level of its potential, considering the millions who think longingly of writing their first book.

But who can really blame the people who, up to now, haven't followed through on their literary curiosity and inspiration? Everyday people—those who don't have extensive knowledge of the publishing industry or who need help because they aren't naturally talented writers—receive a tremendous amount of discouragement from the environment, both directly, when a friend, relative, or publishing insider openly doubts their ability to craft a completed book, and indirectly, when the would-be writer is confronted with an overwhelming barrage of information and advice that relates to publishing. Even books about the craft of writing or the publishing process, which are meant to alleviate these problems, can be difficult to navigate and a touch intimidating. This only further bewilders and deters potential writers. It seems like a major chore just to figure out how it all works, instead of being seen as an enjoyable activity with a fruitful conclusion.

Successful writers are often reluctant to offer encouragement because they don't believe that everyone *can* or *should* write their own books, and are sometimes even openly discouraging. Perhaps this hesitation to welcome "neo-authors" stems from a fear of competition in the marketplace. Maybe they just don't want so many people writing books because it makes what they do seem more human if a greater percentage of society is doing it. However, the bottom line is that the publishing industry, with all of its advances, is now open to anyone and everyone. There are numerous pathways for you to get your book out there and enjoy your own market of readers, large or small.

To some degree, one must agree with the critics and concede that not everyone can write a truly great book, especially not on his or her first try. This is hardly a reason to keep you from attempting this endeavor. Saying that you should only try to write a book if you are a highly skilled craftsman of words, a masterful storyteller, or an erudite scholar is like saying you should only step on a golf course if you strike the ball with the power and precision of Tiger Woods or play a musical instrument only if your talent can land you a soloist position with the likes of the Boston Pops. Hundreds of thousands of people play music and hit the links without letting their initial lack of skill or inexperience stop them. Not everyone plays well—in fact most would probably be classified as amateurs compared to the best in their field—but there is inherent value and pleasure derived for each person who steps on the tee or strums a few chords. They know that allowing themselves the time to practice will lead to improvement and a greater sense of self-worth.

Writing a book is no different. Even if you can't compose something that rivals Hemingway, Keruac, or Oates, you will at least enjoy the journey and revel in the sense of accomplishment in completion and in getting to share your wisdom, creativity, and experiences with others. Trying to become the best and win Pulitzer Prizes or National Book Awards may be the goal of some new writers, but if that is not the final result of your efforts, it doesn't mean that you are wasting your time. People write books for a variety of reasons, which can be as simple as wanting to pass something on to the next generation before the information and the time to write the book are lost. If you want to think of writing books as a hobby, like any other casual leisure activity that you would spend time on each week, it may help you to get started; it will make the project seem less like an intimidating chore and more like a pleasurable and rewarding activity that you want to fit into your schedule.

Along the same lines, a common misconception—one that frequently deters potential new writers—is that only those who write in other forums for a living or who write books full-time should be publishing books because they are the only ones with enough experience and talent to write for pay. While working in a writing-based occupation might help you to hone your skills, many great writers come from a range of occupations. Harper Lee, author of *To Kill a Mockingbird*, was a reservation clerk for an airline. Ayn Rand, well-known for *Atlas Shrugged*, worked in the wardrobe department at a Hollywood studio. Nobel Prize winner William Faulkner was postmaster at the University of Mississippi before writing classics like *The Sound and the Fury*. J.K. Rowling, author of the *Harry Potter* series, catapulted herself from the status of single mother to mega-author superstar in just a few years. Even William Shakespeare, arguably the best writer *ever*, had little formal writing training and never attended college. And, of course, numerous bestselling nonfiction authors have other primary jobs, including medical doctors, business leaders, and motivational speakers.

What we have tried to do with *Get Between the Covers* is to get you interested, excited, and motivated about writing your own book, as well as to help you overcome any discouragement about you attempting this literary foray. We have reinforced this message with useful information, by essentially giving you the few basics that you will need to begin the quest of writing your own book, but not to the point where your interest level is swamped by information overload. Hopefully we've convinced you that the road to authorship will be a rewarding experience for you and for others who ultimately read your book; the commitment to taking the journey is up to you.

There are a number of well-written books in the marketplace that go into greater detail on specific subjects, which you may want to reference if they apply to your writing or publishing situation, and we have referred you to them throughout this book. If you were reading a general book about how to start a business, the approach would be the same; depending on your business, its growth potential, your future client base, and your long-term goals, you would eventually need to find more books to address specific needs that a general business source couldn't tackle. *Get Between the Covers* gives you an overview or introduction to what you will generally need to know to write and publish your book.

Though we don't tout ourselves as publishing insiders or self-publishing gurus, we have had experience with different types of publishing, from self-publishing to having books published by the largest houses in New York. The range of genres between us encompasses novels, children's books, and non-fiction self-help books. Beyond that, we have done enough research to feel confident in our ability to keep you abreast of the latest trends and how they may open doors for you on your literary journeys. We believe that our ability to step back from the industry and look critically at the different options helps us to understand and be more connected with everyday people who may have a desire to write books. We have drawn on our backgrounds of communicating messages to different types of individuals to help to motivate you in this task, and, because of our own entrepreneurial experiences, to try to impress upon you the value of approaching writing, publishing, and marketing by taking an "outside the box" approach and following your own vision. Individuals who already write on a regular basis as part of their job or have done a significant amount of creative writing may already be more inclined to write a book, and as a result, need less of a push. But it is with the vast majority of the population in mind that we constructed this book, hoping that it will spawn a revolution of new writers.

Now for the best part. What do you really receive for writing a book other than money or attention from the media or your family, friends, or business associates? First of all, you have accomplished something that only a small percentage of the population successfully achieves. You have conquered a challenge and have become self-actualized. And just because everyone *can* write their own book, it doesn't make it any less of an achievement; you were one of the exceptional few who traveled to the end of the path and *did* write a book. But finishing your book is about more than just an abstract achievement of which you should feel proud. You are likely to experience tangible and positive growth as a person, as a result of the process of writing a book.

Even if you didn't think that you were a creative person because you always ended up pegged as "accountant" on those vocation tests in high school or because your job doesn't allow for self-expression, you are no less capable of creation than any artist. Stringing together words, sentences, and paragraphs with a direction that leads to a final point is every bit as artistic as spinning clay on a pottery wheel or brushing watercolors across a canvas. Once you have learned how to harness your creativity, there's no telling how far you may go in the literary world or even where you might find other artistic interests.

Along with the creativity that you develop and fine-tune over the course of writing a book, there are other positive changes which can occur. In general, such an achievement is bound to give you a more optimistic outlook on life, now knowing you are capable of accomplishing anything you set your mind to. You will likely improve your vocabulary, become more articulate, and thus be able to communicate much more effectively...whether at your day-job or during special moments in your personal relationships. Your knowledge base will increase as you research and complete your literary work, which could be useful as fodder at a cocktail party or if you have aspirations of becoming the next Ken Jennings and winning episode after episode of *Jeopardy*. You may also become more affable and self-confident as you discuss your book and get feedback at book signings, speaking events, or conventions. Ultimately, the book connects you with more people who may help you reach your future publishing goals. Who knows? They might help you with other goals in life or, even more simply, add to your circle of friends.

On a much larger scale, you have improved society; you have helped to expand the pool of ideas in the public sphere. This is incredibly powerful, though you may not be conscious of it today, tomorrow, or even a year from now. Who really knows how much your book may affect people? Someone may walk around for the rest of their life with a useful tidbit of information that they picked up from reading your book. Or maybe they will read how your protagonist overcame a scenario similar to something in their own life and they will apply the lesson to themselves. The possibilities are endless. You may even end up writing a novel like Michael Crichton's *State of Fear* or Dan Brown's *The Da Vinci Code*, which provokes controversy and scholarly debate, forcing people to question longstanding beliefs about the world around them.

You have also increased literacy because people are likely to be inspired to read more if material on whatever interests them is more readily available. With more people writing books, odds are that somebody is working on a book in their particular area of interest, whether it's the mating rituals of iguanas or a certain strain of ancient Chinese puppetry arts. Any change in the direction of increasing literacy is a positive one, especially given all of the less productive things that we often get caught up in on a regular basis. You will also personally contribute to increasing literacy rates before ever finishing your book, because reading books is a key component in writing books, whether to research a topic, study what's already popular in the marketplace, or improve the craft of writing. As Steven Spielberg notes, "Only a generation of readers will spawn a generation of writers."

Books can also act as magnets, attracting large clusters of persons with similar interests. Publishing, critiquing, and dialogue have long been the staple of academics and scholars around the world, but there is no reason why a book of more general interest, written by an everyday person, can't generate discourse at gatherings, in a newsletter, or over the Internet. It may even create discourse fifty or a hundred years from now, as future readers attempt to learn more about the era in which you wrote, or about you as an individual, and your psychological make-up when you wrote your book.

Even if your book doesn't spark public discourse; even if you write the most boring book in the world, you could be providing insomniacs out there with a cost-effective and potentially safer alternative to sleeping pills. No matter which way you look at it, there is always some positive potential for any and every book. No journey to publication is ever a total waste.

While you are a unique person in every way—from your fingerprints to your sense of creativity to your life experiences—there is at least one thing that you share with everyone else. *You have the ability to write a book.* In fact, you have always had this ability, even before you ever read this book or thought to write your own. All we have attempted to do is to help you to realize your potential and give you the motivational push that you need to go from an idea to a finished copy. By this point, some of you may be close to completing your book, but even if you haven't yet, we know that you will be soon if you keep focused and keep the process fun.

You are about to become one of the first drops in a wave of new authors all over the world. Ideally, in the near future it will become commonplace for everyday people to publish their own books—from cookbooks based on family recipes, to poetry written during high school math class, to novels created by full-time parents while their kids are sleeping, to scholarly texts written by professors or specialists from all over the world—you will be able to look back and reflect on your contribution as one of the pioneers who spearheaded this shift to a more literate and creative society. Steven Pressfield sums up the importance of sharing one's creativity in his book, *The War of Art*, when he says, "Creative work is not a selfish act or a bid for attention on the part of the actor. It's a gift to the world and every being in it. Don't cheat us of your contribution. Give us what you got."

On that note, there is just one final thing for us to say to you. Welcome to the world of authorship! Enjoy it because you are helping to shape it.

APPENDICES:
USEFUL RESOURCES

THE FOLLOWING THREE SECTIONS CONTAIN RESOURCES, both books and Internet sites, which will assist you before and during the writing and publication process. While all of these resources are valuable, some of them are specific to certain elements of writing and publishing, such as marketing or editing, and you should be selective as to which ones to consult, in order to make the most efficient use of your time and keep you moving on your book.

We have referenced many of these books and websites throughout the chapters of this book; however, they represent just a small selection of all of those available to you, and we encourage you to explore others that are not on our list as you proceed in this endeavor. Many of these sources are updated every year or every few years, so be on the look out for new editions. You should also run Internet searches on Yahoo, Google, or

Amazon about once every couple of months, as new websites are created all the time and a number of new books come out every year on the subject of writing and publishing.

APPENDIX A:
MAKING SENSE OF
WRITER'S MARKET

WHAT WORDS COME TO MIND WHEN YOU THINK OF books that are over 1000 pages long? *Intimidating, Dense, Difficult*? In general, if these are the words you use to describe books of this length, then you probably shy away from them, unless you absolutely need to reference them. Some of the books in this category may contain religious material, others may summarize court cases for the past 200 years, and still others may categorize every disease known to man. Depending on your chosen genre and subject, you may need to reference some of these types of books, but whatever you choose to write about, one weighty reference tool that you should take full advantage of is *Writer's Market*. This useful manual is a comprehensive catalog of sources related to writing and publishing, and it is important enough to merit its own chapter, particularly one in which we help you to navigate this resource.

The first thing that you need to know when reading through *Writer's Market* is that it contains details about many forms of writing, such as script writing, newspaper and magazine writing, public relations writing, and, of course, book writing. You may find these sections interesting, but being able to locate the information that pertains to writing a book will save you time and keep you focused.

Perhaps the most useful section for new writers is "Getting Published," which is found in the beginning of the book. It is the easiest to follow and explains the ideas and concepts in fairly simple terms. What might be most helpful in this section are the specifics, such as how to format your manuscript, how to submit to publishers or magazines, and how to write effective query letters. The tutorial on how to query is detailed and even contains sample query letters and editors' comments on them.

For any writer seeking publication, the most useful aspects of this resource are the detailed listing of publishers and magazines, and the section on literary agents, which we discussed in Chapter 11.

The 1,100+ publishing companies included in *Writer's Market* are sorted alphabetically, and clearly if you are trying to find a publisher who accepts your genre, reading through all of them in order would be a time consuming task. Luckily, *Writer's Market* includes a book publisher subject index, in which you can look up the subject of your book from a choice of categories where you'll find a listing all of the publishers both in United States and Canada who publish that type of material. You'll want to reference as many subjects that your book could possibly fit under to make sure your search is complete.

Once you have located the list of publishers you'd like to target, you can reference the alphabetical listing and view a brief summary of each one. This includes their contact information, how many titles a year they publish, what percentage of those titles come from first-time authors, what royalties they offer, how long a response time is expected for query letters and manuscripts, and even helpful tips to writers from the publisher. Each description should be self-explanatory, but if you have any questions for an individual publisher, their phone number, email address, or website address is listed. By following the guidelines of the individual publisher you will appear more professional, your manuscript will be handled expeditiously (keep in mind that things move slowly in publishing), and you will ultimately increase your chances of acceptance.

The listing of nearly 2,000 magazines, of which you see just a few at the newsstand, might also be useful for you as an author of a book, particularly if it is your first one. You can pitch a story about your upcoming book to gain public attention and even publish excerpts from your book and generate some hype before it is released. Having a published magazine article under your belt can also give you credibility when you approach a traditional publisher. In fact, many successful authors today started out by contributing to magazines, whether they had ideas for nonfiction works and submitted newsworthy articles to *Newsweek* or wanted to be the next successful novelist and began sending short stories to *Reader's Digest*.

The magazines are listed in the same manner as publishers so that you can easily locate the ones which might be interested in your work. The details listed for each magazine are essentially the same as for the publishing companies, with the addition of information on lead times, how to submit seasonal material, and what percentage of the magazine's articles come from freelance writers (people not on the paid staff of the magazine).

The contest and awards section and the resource section can also be useful to new writers. In addition to receiving prize money, adding a new trophy to your mantel, or just boosting your ego in general, winning a contest or an award can catch the attention of a publisher or a literary agent, and ultimately open doors for you. The awards and contests are arranged by genre, and a detailed description of each is listed. The resource section offers the titles of other helpful books for writers and lists Internet websites with pertinent information.

You will not necessarily need to reference *Writer's Market* if you are planning on self-publishing, but if you have time, you may want to give it a glance through because it contains plenty of useful knowledge and insider tips, and it will add to your overall understanding of the publishing world. If you need further explanation or clarification about how to reference the material, *Writer's Market FAQ's* and *Writer's Market Companion* are excellent supplements to *Writer's Market*, in addition to *Literary Marketplace*, which you can peruse in print or on their website (www.literarymarketplace. com). One final note to remember is that there is more than one way to get published, and the recommendations in *Writer's Market*, for the most part, direct you towards the traditional means.

•*Writer's Market* is perhaps the best resource for writers of all levels and genres.

• *Writer's Market* offers extensive information about literary agents and publishers, as well as tutorials on submitting written material to them.

Appendix B:
The Web of Resources

and while a little over three quarters of them are of the X-rated variety, there remain countless sites that can be useful for any type of writer. The list is endless: everything from sites that provide forums for constructive criticism of your work, to ones which provide you with a listing of publishers and agents nationwide, to ones which coach you on writing. In this chapter, we will highlight a few of the most useful sites. Keep in mind that many of these sites have links to other sites, which are also worth checking out. For a more complete listing of potentially helpful sites, you can also consult the "Resources" section in *Writer's Market* or go to the *Writer's Digest* website (www.writersdigest.com) and look through their list of the top sites for writers to visit.

Remember, also, that you can always search for the newest sites on Google or Yahoo, since they can spring up rapidly. And, of course, be sure to visit our website frequently at www.GetBetweentheCovers.com, as we will do our best to keep you abreast of the latest websites and feature a number of them which you might find particularly useful.

Getting helpful feedback on your manuscript, and getting publishers and agents to take notice of it, are certainly goals for many new writers. We've already mentioned some easy ways for anyone to obtain peer reviews or to receive help editing, but if one wanted to go the traditional publishing route, it also helps to have some extra exposure to garner attention prior to publication. Fortunately, there are two great sites that can allow you to obtain reviews *and* generate a buzz about your work. Authorlink (www.authorlink.com), which charges a fee, allows an author to post a manuscript for other members of the site to review and critique. Self-published authors are prominently featured and awards are given out to emerging authors. This site is the largest of its kind and has an impressive number of members, including readers, authors, publishers, and agents. RoseDog (www.RoseDog.com), a free critique site, allows authors to post excerpts from their manuscripts, and, it, too, is frequented by agents and publishers who can help a new author to attract attention from the publishing world. While these types of sites are set up to facilitate entry into the traditional publishing world, they may also be quite useful even if you plan to self-publish. Apart from valuable critiques, you can network with authors whose projects and ambitions are similar to yours, become more skillful at editing your own material by critiquing the manuscripts of others, and even meet people who may help publicize and promote your self-published work.

Larger Internet resources employ more of a "one-stop" approach to making general publishing information and advice available to the public.

BookWire (www.bookwire.com) and Books AtoZ (www.booksatoz. com) are two of the best link sites on the Internet, allowing you to find information about any element of the publishing industry in just seconds. Literary Marketplace (www.literarymarketplace.com) allows members to search through lists of publishers and agents over a number of fields, such as geographic location or genres that they represent. Book Marketing & Book Sales (www.bookmarket.com), a site run by publishing and marketing expert John Kremer, has a wealth of material available. Other helpful sites to visit are www.writers.net and www.writermag.com.

Sometimes what new writers need the most is instruction on how to develop the craft of writing, but since many of them do not have a lot of free time in their schedules, they are unable to attend adult education classes, creative writing classes at a local community college, or workshops with successful authors. Luckily, there are Internet sites that can help you from the convenience of your own home. The sites, www.noveladvice. com, www.thewritersmentor.com, and www.writingclasses.com, all give personalized instruction and advice for a fee, and along with providing general feedback, they can also direct you to other resources that cater to specific needs.

Perhaps you already have honed your writing skills and what you are really lacking is some background for your book. Instead of trudging over to your local library, you can bring the biggest library in the world to you. You can visit the Library of Congress at www.loc.gov to see titles in print and, for a fee, their librarians can even do research for you using the hundreds of databases at their disposal. Similar information can also be obtained at www.booksinprint.com, a site run by R.R. Bowker, well-known for their publishing databases and as the official agency for issuing ISBNs. R.R. Bowker's main site, www.bowker.com, also has many other helpful links. Another great site for general information is www.infoplease.com, an electronic almanac referencing just about every subject you can imagine. Wikipedia (www.wikipedia.org), which has replaced Britannica.com as the premier online encyclopedia, and is one of the most heavily-trafficked websites on the Internet, is a great starting point as well. Additionally, many ideas for books come straight out of the headlines, and www.enews.com and Mediafinder (www.oxbridge.com) can help you to locate numerous publications and catch up on the latest news. Finally and obviously, any search engine (Yahoo, Google) can provide you with useful links and articles for your topic of choice.

Clearly, there are *many* Internet sites that can provide information and advice, and potentially even open doors for writers. We have listed a few of these and we certainly encourage you to locate others—just be wary because not every site on the Internet is credible or offers good advice. Make sure whichever site you are viewing is reputable before following their advice or signing up for any services offered. Knowledge of the publishing industry is one of the keys to a successful literary journey, and with a little Internet researching in front of your trusty computer you can be well on your way to accomplishing your goals.

APPENDIX C:
SUGGESTED READING

and desire to write your own book. We've tried to make *Get Between the Covers* as user-friendly as possible, so that you won't be intimidated by the writing and publishing process, and so that you can easily access essential information. Along the way, we've referred you to certain websites and books which can give you further insight and advice on various aspects of the writing and publishing world. To make it easier for you to reference, we have included the chapter in which each source first appeared, even though we may refer to the same books, websites, and individuals throughout the book.

Be sure to visit us at our website, www.GetBetweentheCovers.com, for a listing of additional resources and individuals to assist you. Also remember to check some of the major writing blogs, as they contain information about the latest websites that have sprung up.

CHAPTER 2: ANYONE CAN FIND THE TIME

Get Organized, Get Published!: 225 Times to Make Time for Success, by Don Aslett and Carol Cartaino

On Writing, by Stephen King

CHAPTER 3: GENERATING A GENRE

Putting Your Passion Into Print: Get Your Book Published Successfully!, by Arielle Eckstut and David Sterry

Reading Like a Writer: A Guide for People Who Love Books and for Those Who Want to Write Them, by Francine Prose

CHAPTER 4: FROM CONCEPT TO COMPLETED MANUSCRIPT

The First Five Pages: A Writer's Guide to Staying out of the Rejection Pile, by Noah Lukeman

How to Get Happily Published, Fifth Edition by Judith Appelbaum

How to Write a Damn Good Novel, by James Frey

The Marshall Plan for Novel Writing, by Evan Marshall

The Marshall Plan for Getting Your Novel Published, by Evan Marshall

The Plot Thickens: 8 Ways to Bring Fiction to Life, by Noah Lukeman

What if?: Writing Exercises for Fiction Writers, by Anne Bernays

Write in Style: Using Your Word Processor and Other Techniques to Improve Your Writing, by Bobbie Christmas

www.parapublishing.com (Dan Poynter's website)

CHAPTER 5: UNBLOCKING WRITER'S BLOCK

The Shortest Distance Between You and a Published Book, by Susan Page

Writing Down the Bones, by Natalie Goldberg

CHAPTER 6: EDITED-DOWN ADVICE ON EDITING

Bryson's Dictionary of Troublesome Words, by Bill Bryson

Eats, Shoots & Leaves, by Lynne Truss

The Elements of Style, Fourth Edition, by William Strunk Jr., et al

Self-Editing for Fiction Writers, by Renni Browne and Dave King

Write Up the Corporate Ladder, by Kevin Ryan

www.freelanceonline.com

CHAPTER 7: IMPROVE YOUR MANUSCRIPT THROUGH PEER REVIEW

www.asja.org (American Society of Journalists and Authors)

www.wnba-books.org (Women's National Book Association)

CHAPTER 10: THE MULTI-faceted GRAPEVINE: HOW PUBLISHERS LET READERS KNOW ABOUT BOOKS

www.bookexpoamerica.com

www.bookweb.org

www.frankfurt-book-fair.com

www.mauiwriters.com

CHAPTER 11: LITERARY AGENTS: THE MATCHMAKERS OF PUBLISHING

Author 101: Bestselling Secrets from Top Agents, by Rick Frishman
    and Robyn Freedman Spizman

How to Write a Book Proposal, by Michael Larsen

Guide to Book Publishers, Editors, & Literary Agents, by Jeff Herman

2006 Guide to Literary Agents, by Kathryn Brogan, Robert Lee Brewer,
    and Joanna Masterson

*Literary Agents: What They Do, How They Do It, and How to Find
    and Work With the Right One for You*, by Michael Larsen

Literary Marketplace 2005, by Information Today

2005 Writer's Market, by Kathryn Brogan, et al

http://agentresearch.co.uk

www.everyonewhosanyone.com

www.literarymarketplace.com

www.publishersmarketplace.com/lunch/free

CHAPTER 12: BOOKSELLERS AND THE RETAIL MARKET UNDER THE MICROSCOPE

www.alibris.com

www.amazon.com

www.barnesandnoble.com

www.bookmarket.com

www.bookscan.com

www.btol.com

www.ingrambook.com

Chapter 14: Create Demand with Printing On-Demand

Get Published!, by Susan Driscoll and Diane Gedymin

www.authorhouse.com

www.bbb.org

www.booksinprint.com

www.booksurge.com

www.iuniverse.com

www.lightningsource.com

www.lluminapress.com

www.lulu.com

www.trafford.com

www.wheatmark.com

www.xerox.com

www.xlibris.com

Chapter 15: Start the Presses: Printing Your Own Book

The Complete Guide to Self-Publishing, Fourth Edition by Marilyn and Tom Ross

The Self-Publishing Manual, Fourteenth Edition, by Dan Poynter

www.aiga.org

www.selfpublishingresources.com

CHAPTER 16: CUSTOMIZE YOUR READERSHIP WITH CUSTOM PUBLISHING

www.jenkinsgroupinc.com

CHAPTER 18: E-PUBLISHING: EXPANDING THE LITERARY HORIZON

The Complete Guide to Self-Publishing Companion, by Marilyn Ross and Matt Brown

eBook Secrets Exposed, by Jim Edwards and David Garfinkel

How to Get Your E-Book Published: An Insider's Guide to the World of Electronic Publishing, by Richard Curtis and W.T. Quick

How to Publish and Promote Online, by M.J. Rose and Angela Adair-Hoy

CHAPTER 19: IMPRESS AN EDITOR FOR UNDER $10

Author 101: Bestselling Book Proposals by Rick Frishman and Robyn Freedman Spizman

The Chicago Manual of Style, Fifteenth Edition, by University of Chicago Press Staff

How to Write a Book Proposal, by Michael Larsen

Write the Perfect Book Proposal: 10 That Sold and Why, 2nd Edition, by Jeff Herman

CHAPTER 20: AUTHOR-GENERATED HYPE: THE KEY TO HEIGHTENED SALES

1001 Ways to Market Your Books, Fifth Edition, by John Kremer

Guerilla Marketing for Writers, by Jay Conrad Levinson, et al

Jump Start Your Book Sales, by Marilyn and Tom Ross

Publicize Your Book!: An Insider's Guide to Getting Your Book the Attention it Deserves, by Jacqueline Deval

www.authorsontheweb.com

www.bookmarket.com

www.folusa.com

www.fredgleeck.com

www.plannedtvarts.com

CHAPTER 21: EXERCISE YOUR RIGHTS IN CONTRACTS

From Pen to Print, by Ellen Kozak

Negotiating a Book Contract: A Guide for Authors, Agents, and Lawyers, by Mark Levine

The Writer's Legal Companion, by Brad Bunnin and Peter Beren

www.ISBN.com

www.loc.gov

www.writersdigest.com

Free Audio Recording
on Empowerment
Your Ability to Write a Book

Hosted by:

Gene Landrum, Ph.D.

Neil Shulman, M.D.

Eric Spencer

Listen as Gene Landrum, the founder of the Chuck E. **Cheese** concept of family restaurants and an experienced author/motivator, and Neil Shulman and Eric Spencer, International Bestselling authors, reveal how to change your life and the lives of others by writing your own book. It's the perfect 20 minute motivational pep talk to accompany *Get Between the Covers: Leave a Legacy by Writing a Book.*

DOWNLOAD YOUR FREE SPECIAL
BONUS RECORDING (VALUED AT $99) AT
WWW.GETBETWEENTHECOVERS.COM

Also, please visit us on our website, www.GetBetweentheCovers.com, for further motivation, success stories of authors just like you, information on the public appearances of Neil and Eric, links to our many publishing partners and to the best websites for those interested in writing, details of the other projects to which Neil and Eric devote a large portion of their time, and a blog written by the authors for the benefit of potential writers.

And BE SURE to tell a friend about *Get Between the Covers*. Everyone has a book in them, and people will always remember who turned them onto the idea of writing and showed them the best resource to motivate them and guide them through the process.

ABOUT THE AUTHORS

 **NEIL SHULMAN, M.D.** is the co-author (along with Carl Hiaasen) of the bestseller *Doc Hollywood*, which became a major motion picture starring Michael J. Fox. Neil was also an associate producer of the film.

In addition to his work on **Get Between the Covers**, Neil has had success in several different genres, using a variety of publication options, over the past 25+ years. He has demonstrated his ability to build a "brand" on several different projects. He has written or co-written over 20 books, and some of his works can be read in as many as 8 languages. He has sold hundreds of thousands of copies, invented a new type of children's book, designed innovative and life-saving websites from his books, and is one of the leading public speakers in America.

He has appeared on numerous news programs and syndicated talk shows in the past several years, in addition to the major print publications.

He resides in Atlanta, GA.

ERIC SPENCER is the 28-year-old co-author of the International Bestselling book, *Get Between the Covers: Leave a Legacy by Writing a Book*, which is now going into its 2nd edition. He has 7 more books in development, including an innovative self-help book, a 5 book series directed at his Generation Y peers, and a corporate thriller.

Eric is the CFO/Head of Investor Relations a leading hedge fund based out of Santa Monica, CA.

Eric is a former sub-deacon in the Episcopal Church, a member of MENSA, and is heavily involved in a number of charitable organizations.

He is a graduate of Duke University and currently splits time between New York City and Los Angeles.

Printed in the USA
CPSIA information can be obtained
at www.ICGtesting.com
JSHW082149140824
68134JS00014B/149